✓ OO4·62 BEN

THIS ITEM MAY BE RENEWED
TWICE EXCEPT WHEN
REQUESTED BY ANOTHER USER
PHONE (01633) 432310
FINE 10P PER DAY IF OVERDUE

D0511025

Practical WAP

UNIVERSITY OF WALES COLLEGE NEWPORT
LIBRARY AND LEARNING RESOURCES
ALLT-YR-YN

Breakthroughs in Application Development Series

Series Editor:

David Orchard
Solutions Architect, IBM
Burnaby, British Columbia

The Breakthroughs in Application Development series is dedicated to providing hard knowledge in the form of detailed practical guides to leading-edge technologies and business models in modern application development. This series will identify, define, and stimulate emerging trends in the industry, covering such rapidly evolving areas as electronic commerce, e-business, inter/intranet development, Web architectures, application integration solutions, and the intersection of business and technology. Each title will focus on a new innovation in the field, presenting new ways of thinking and demonstrating how to put breakthrough technologies into business practice.

1. The Business of Ecommerce: From Corporate Strategy
to Technology • *Paul May*

2. e-Enterprise: Architecting with Application Models
and Components • *Faisal Hoque*

3. Mobile Commerce: Applications and Technologies
of Personal Electronic Business • *Paul May*

4. Practical WAP: Developing Applications
for the Wireless Web • *Chris Bennett*

Practical WAP

Developing Applications
for the Wireless Web

CHRIS BENNETT

UNIVERSITY OF WALES COLLEGE NEWPORT
LIBRARY AND LEARNING RESOURCES ALLT-YR-YN

CAMBRIDGE
UNIVERSITY PRESS

PUBLISHED BY THE PRESS SYNDICATE OF THE UNIVERSITY OF CAMBRIDGE
The Pitt Building, Trumpington Street, Cambridge, United Kingdom

CAMBRIDGE UNIVERSITY PRESS
The Edinburgh Building, Cambridge CB2 2RU, UK
40 West 20th Street, New York, NY 10011-4211, USA
10 Stamford Road, Oakleigh, VIC 3166, Australia
Ruiz de Alarcón 13, 28014 Madrid, Spain
Dock House, The Waterfront, Cape Town 8001, South Africa

http://www.cambridge.org

© 2001 Cambridge University Press

All rights reserved.

This book is in copyright. Subject to statutory exception
and to the provisions of the relevant collective licensing agreement,
no reproduction of any part may take place without
the written permission of Cambridge University Press.

Any product mentioned in this book may be a trademark of its company.

First published 2001

Design by Susan Ahlquist
Composition by G&H SOHO

Printed in the United States of America

Typeface: Garamond 3 12/14 pt.   *System:* QuarkXPress® [GH]

A catalog record for this book is available from the British Library.

Library of Congress Cataloging in Publication Data
Bennett, Chris, 1965–
    Practical WAP : developing applications for the wireless web / Chris Bennett
        p.   cm. – (Breakthroughs in application development series ; 4)
    Includes index.
    ISBN 0-521-00561-2 (pbk.)
    1. Wireless Application Protocol (Computer network protocol)   2. Application
software.
    I. Title.   II. Series
    TK5105.5865+
    832'.6 – dc21   00-066801

ISBN 0 521 00561 2   paperback

To Sharon, my wife

About the Author

Chris Bennett has more than 20 years of software development experience and a strong background in object-oriented technologies including UML, XML, CORBA, and Java. In addition to being an international trainer and speaker, he is an IT consultant and architect for Unisys Canada, where he builds distributed Internet systems.

Contents

2   Technical Overview

3   Applications

8 Push Applications   159

PART 3 WAP IN PRACTICE

9 Design Factors   191

10 Architectures   229

11 Usability and Testing 251

12 Application Development Case Study 263

13 Future of WAP   315

Foreword

Imagine that your TV set had a satellite or cable service connection and no programming coming in to add life to the screen. Imagine going to the theater and having the lights dim and no performers appear on the stage. Or, imagine using your PC to access the World Wide Web without any sites to visit.

This is a world without content. It's an empty, boring, unprofitable world. It's not the kind of world that you want to live in, nor do I. The world that I want to live in is vibrant, full of exciting things to do, charged with energy and convenience, and appealing from all perspectives.

Content, you see, is king. Without it, technology is only a mechanism, a pipe within which nothing flows. That's what developing applications for Wireless Application Protocol (WAP) enabled devices is all about – delivering content to people on the go anytime, anyone, anywhere. Filling that pipe.

As the CEO of the WAP Forum, one of my key charters is to do whatever I can to help bring compelling, fascinating content to WAP users around the world. And that is what this book can help you do. Learning how to develop applications using WML, WMLScript, and other tools opens a door for you to a world that few developers have had access to before. It's the place where you want to be for these reasons:

- By 2004 more people will access the Internet from wireless devices than from PCs.

- By the end of 2001 every phone from every manufacturer will come standard with a WAP browser.

- Wireless phone users purchase new phones roughly every 14 to 18 months, depending on the location, meaning that in just a few short years every phone in everyone's hands will have a WAP browser.

- Hundreds of operators around the world have already deployed, or are planning to deploy, WAP services.

- Hundreds of companies have demonstrated their commitment to WAP by becoming members of the WAP Forum and contributing to the development and evolution of WAP.

As a result, it won't be very long before tens of millions of WAP-enabled devices are in the hands of potential users. And there will be only one thing limiting their usage of the phone to access the Internet: your imagination. It is up to you, the WAP developer, to deliver applications that these users will find so irresistible, so compelling, so intoxicating, that they will clamor to use them as soon as they find them and then tell everyone they know about them as if it were their own personal discovery.

You are secure in your development of WAP applications (or "WAP-plications" as I like to call them) because WAP will be around for a very long time. Just as Netscape and Internet Explorer evolved from their first iterations, WAP is already doing the same. The WAP browsers and supporting technology of tomorrow won't be the same as today's. As third-generation (3G) wireless networks become a reality, WAP will be there to provide browsers that are specifically tuned to meet the challenges of, and to capitalize on, the unique characteristics of mobile devices:

- Limited RAM/ROM

- Small screens

- Fewer keys

- One-finger navigation

- Location-based information

- Portability

- Always on, always in your pocket

These, and many other factors, will demand a microbrowser that is designed for the wireless environment.

In addition, when 3G is here, WAP will be critical to help manage the spectrum that operators are paying billions of dollars to use. Those investments demand techniques that wring out every last iota of capacity in order to be able to amortize the costs. And when 4G, 5G, 6G, and others become a reality, WAP will be here, too, because the specification is organic – it evolves to take advantage of the improvements in handsets and networks.

Even in the very near future, WAP will evolve. Soon we will migrate the specification to accommodate XHTML, the next-generation rendering language of the Internet, making it even easier for developers to write an application once and have it render properly on a variety of different devices – a scenario sure to expand in the future with browsers to be found on car screens, home appliances, cash registers, wireless devices, PCs, TVs, and so on.

But we won't forget our heritage as we migrate to XHTML and perhaps to other technologies in the future – WAP is committed to backward compatibility.

So go forth and create applications that make people say, "Wow!" Develop WAP sites that are so compelling, consumers or business-people will recognize them as their own personal killer apps. Use your imagination to conjure up new markets, new services, and new products. WAP will serve as the foundation for your community to develop these products and services around the world.

What you do with WAP – a robust, durable framework for turning these ideas into reality – is up to you. But I have faith in this community of developers. I fully expect you to turn my dreams into your reality – and I look forward to that day with great anticipation.

Keep WAPping!

Scott Goldman
CEO, WAP Forum Ltd.

 # Acknowledgments

I owe a great deal to the many people who made this book possible. Thanks to my friends at Unisys for support, understanding, and helpful feedback. In particular, I am indebted to David Morash for the application development case study and to Dianne Webber for her understanding and support. The quality of this book owes much to Richard Taylor's invaluable technical reviews. Thanks also to Lothlórien Homet and her friends at Cambridge University Press who guided me through the process and to the folks at G&H SOHO for their masterful editing and production. Most of all, thanks to my wife Sharon for her encouragement and patience.

A Note on Companies and URLs

The wireless Web is a volatile place with new companies springing up daily and established firms remaking their images at least once a year. An example of this volatility is Openwave (*www.openwave.com*). Openwave is an amalgam of Phone.com and Software.com. Phone.com is itself a metamorphosis of Unwired Planet, one of the original founders of the WAP Forum! This has an impact on a book such as this, where references to companies and their URLs can rapidly become outdated. For instance, throughout this book we use Phone.com URLs because these are valid as we go to print. Should Openwave choose to reorganize their Web presence, this may no longer be true!

Corrections and Source Code

Corrections to this book and the source code listed in Appendix B can be found on the Web at *www.wirelessweb-books.com*.

PART 1

A WAP Primer

Introduction

The last decade has seen the rapid convergence of two pervasive technologies – wireless communications and the Internet. The wireless marketplace has grown to more than 300 million users in this time, and the number of cell phones alone is expected to top 1 billion units by 2003. This marketplace is characterized by incredible growth and intense competition; price wars, falling profit margins, and subscriber turnover rates of 20 to 50 percent are the norm. It is the intense competition and the need to differentiate their offerings that has forced providers to expand into areas such as messaging and information services.

In the same period, the Internet has evolved from its military and academic roots to a communications platform that underlies our modern world. In many countries, the Internet is challenging traditional sources of information, commerce, recreation, and business integration. However, expansion of the Internet is slowed by the limited availability of land-line-based networks in many parts of the world. For example, in much of South America, cellular networks are less expensive to deploy and once installed are unlikely to be supplanted by land lines.

The marriage of these technologies to create the mobile Internet has immediate benefits and far-reaching consequences. These include an expanded audience that can access Internet services from any location covered by a cell phone network. Less obvious is the potential opened up by location-aware services and secure mobile commerce applications. Despite privacy issues, the ability to send personalized information to any mobile user from anywhere on the Internet has enormous potential. Time becomes another dimension in this truly World Wide Web as push technology allows carefully timed content to be sent to a focused target audience.

The Wireless Application Protocol (or WAP) gives us a framework to build the mobile Internet. WAP standards define an efficient protocol for Internet access over narrow bandwidth wireless networks. They also specify a complete application environment (including markup and scripting languages) that addresses the limitations of mobile devices. WAP was created by a worldwide industry forum (the WAP Forum) and is independent of vendor and underlying mobile networks, virtually assuring its acceptance.

Before diving into the WAP standards, let's put things in context. WAP was created out of a very real need for a common way to access the Internet from mobile devices. Existing Web and Internet standards do not provide adequate quality of service when extended to current mobile networks and devices. Although attempts have been made to tailor the Internet standards for the mobile world, none of these initiatives has achieved worldwide acceptance.

THE MOBILE INTERNET

Mobile messaging services and financial transactions have been common in Europe and Japan for years and access to the Web (in some form) is already an accepted component of many mobile subscription packages. The United States has been slower to adopt such services due to a relatively unregulated market and incomplete digital network coverage. However, this is changing, and by 2003 it is predicted that Internet-enabled mobile devices will dominate the conventional wireless phone by a large margin (see Fig. 1-1). In fact, researchers at International Data Corporation estimate that by 2004, wireless access will be *the* primary type of Internet connection. Obviously, the stage is set for a new Internet revolution – a move to a truly World Wide Web with access from anywhere to anywhere!

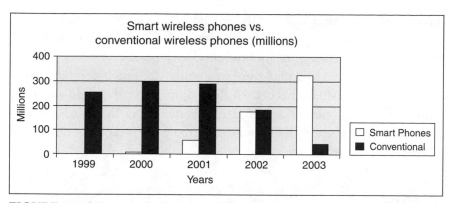

FIGURE 1-1. Smart vs. Conventional Wireless Phone Usage
(source: DataComm Research)

MOBILE APPLICATIONS ARE DIFFERENT

A note of caution – the wireless Web will not replace desktop Web access! Mobile users have different needs than their desktop counterparts. The mobile user requires rapid access to specific information. The ability to search and surf the Web will still be required, but messaging and personalized information channels take on much greater significance in the mobile world. Although it is not possible to neatly describe the entire realm of wireless Web applications, let's take a stab at breaking these applications into four categories: communications and personal information management (PIM), Internet, enterprise, and telemetry applications.

Communications and Personal Information Management

Communications applications such as messaging, e-mail, and notification currently form the nucleus of wireless data applications. Mobile providers often deliver these value-added services. PIM applications, such as scheduling and calendar services, are also used by mobile providers to differentiate their offerings. Note that although text-based data communications applications are becoming increasingly important, we should not assume they will supersede traditional voice-based communications. In fact, one of the major user interface challenges currently facing mobile developers is the awkward nature of text entry on devices that were originally designed for voice communication. A current hotbed of development is the field of voice interfaces – both recognition and synthesis – and the WAP Forum recognizes that voice will become an important interface channel to WAP applications.

Internet

General Internet applications receive the majority of media attention because such applications are accessible to the entire consumer marketplace. Mobile commerce services including ticketing, banking, and other purchases are rapidly growing. Financial institutions are in the forefront of the push toward wireless Web-based electronic commerce because of the huge cost savings that can be realized over traditional banking services. Portal services including news, weather, and stock updates are available within a new class of Internet portal – the mobile portal. Portal connections are extremely important in the wireless world due to the limited display and entry capabilities of mobile devices. It is no small task to enter a URL on the 3 by 4 keypad found on most cell phones – hence the importance of the mobile portal as a personalized access point to the wireless Web.

Enterprise

Enterprise-specific mobile services are often overlooked, but they will become increasingly critical to a business's success. Because up to 40 percent of workers spend a significant amount of their workday away from their desks, the ability to extend the office beyond the desk is of enormous benefit. Mobile access is already a reality in areas such as sales automation, transportation, and field service, where the benefits of automation are crystal clear. Mobile enterprise connectivity will become popular for other mobile professionals as businesses begin to understand the advantages of the virtual office.

Telemetry

Telemetry applications use mobile communications to send messages from one embedded device to another or to a central server. Remote installations or mobile machinery that require monitoring (e.g., cars, storage tanks, and pipelines) can send alerts without requiring costly installation of land-based telephone lines. When you stop to think about it, the potential number of mobile users in the world tops out at 6 billion or so. Think of all the machines we deal with every day that could also become mobile Internet subscribers. The Japanese mobile communications company NTT DoCoMo estimates that by 2010, approximately two thirds of their mobile connections will be from such sources (see Table 1-1).

New Possibilities

The wireless Web also enables entirely new classes of applications. Location-aware services take advantage of the user's mobility to offer applications tailored to the user's current position. Location information can be provided by the user as a postal code or address or may be automatically available from the client device (via global positioning system [GPS] or cellular network triangulation). Add push technology and time-aware services to this mix, and we turn the traditional Web upside down. Now applications can initiate a dialogue with the mobile user – making possible highly personalized location and time-

TABLE 1-1. NTT DoCoMo's Customer Predictions for 2010 (source: *The Economist,* October 9, 1999)

CONNECTED VIA MOBILE	NUMBER (MILLIONS)
Humans	120
Cars	100
Bicycles	60
Portable PCs	50
Vending machines, boats, motorcycles, etc.	30
Total	360

specific services. If you think this raises issues of privacy and confidentiality, you're right! Subscription models and explicit user permission will be the norm for these classes of application. It is in these uncharted waters that there is potential for the next "killer app."

THE REALITY

Although wireless technology holds great promise for delivering new realms of applications, the limitations of wireless networks and devices impose considerable constraints on application delivery. Wireless communications technology labors under limitations that are unheard of in the desktop Internet world. These include relatively low bandwidth networks, air time-based pricing models, and device limitations imposed by the constraints of portability.

The prevalent ("second") generation (2G) digital cell phone networks have typical transfer rates of well under 9600 bits per second, more than four times as slow as a typical dial-up desktop connection (actual 2G wireless transfer rates range from below 2000 bits per second to just under ten times this for sustained transmissions). In addition, unlike the Internet's IP (Internet Protocol) standard, there is no one digital mobile network standard. The two primary types of digital networks, circuit switched and packet switched, further complicate things, as do geographic differences; Global System for Mobile communications (GSM) dominates Europe and has the largest world share, Code Division Multiple Access (CDMA) and Time Division Multiple Access (TDMA) are common in North America, and Personal Digital Cellular (PDC) is prevalent in Japan. If this is not enough complexity for you, enhanced second-generation (2.5G) are in early deployment in some countries and third-generation (3G) mobile networks are under development. These newer networks promise bandwidth matching current high-speed desktop connections and a new fistful of acronyms! Despite the hype, realistically it will be a few years before these next generation networks enjoy widespread coverage outside major population centers.

Network technology is just one part of the wireless equation. Unlimited Internet access that is already the norm in several countries contrasts with the by-the-minute access charges of cellular providers. As digital networks evolve from the relatively inefficient connection-oriented circuit-switched networks to those that employ packet switching, this pricing model will be challenged. With packet-switched networks, users share bandwidth and will most likely be charged either a flat fee or charged based on the amount of data they transport over the network. In addition, the mobile electronic commerce value chain has not yet solidified. Who controls access to applications, collects payments, and "owns" the customers is a matter of heated debate, with mobile carriers, service providers, merchants, and financial institutions all vying for their share.

Another factor is the mobile device. Because of the inherent limitations of size and battery power, wireless devices have less powerful processors and memory, smaller displays, and limited input choices. Typical displays range from 3-line, 12-character phone displays to the relatively rich quarter-VGA interfaces provided by some hand-helds. Due to battery concerns, most displays provide only monochrome capabilities. Processors in mobile devices range from minimal microprocessors found in cell phones to the 32-bit processors that power Palm OS, Windows Pocket PC, and Symbian EPOC hand-helds. Perhaps the most significant difference between wireless and the desktop is input options, which range from the telephone keypad with soft-key support to minute QWERTY keypads and stylus-based entry.

DÉJÀ VU

In order to cope with the unique problems of mobile Internet access, a number of proprietary solutions have emerged, reminiscent of the pre-Internet era where bulletin boards were the primary mode of network connectivity. Today, most wireless connectivity solutions rely on device-specific, custom client development and a proprietary server at a central provider's site. One example is the Short Message Service (SMS), a popular wireless solution in Europe that provides two-way messaging and data access applications. Another is Phone.com's Unwired Planet (UP) architecture that makes use of a proprietary Handheld Device Markup Language (HDML) to provide thin client access from UP browsers to

Web applications via a UP gateway server. Similarly, Palm Computing's Web Clipping applications rely on an installed client and a connection to a Palm server to deliver filtered Internet content. Although these solutions work, none deliver on the promise of flexible ubiquitous mobile Internet access. Only SMS has become a de facto standard, but it is limited by very short messages (160 characters) and a complex infrastructure. Clearly what is needed is a way to provide everything that SMS, Web Clipping, and HDML offer but using technology that builds on existing standards. This is where WAP comes in.

THE WIRELESS APPLICATION PROTOCOL

The Wireless Application Protocol is a global standard for bringing Internet content and services to mobile phones and other wireless devices. The WAP standards are maintained by an industry consortium called the WAP Forum. Founded by Ericsson, Motorola, Nokia, and Phone.com (previously known as Unwired Planet) in June 1997, WAP Forum membership now exceeds 500 organizations, representing over 95 percent of the global handset market. The WAP Forum also includes members who are infrastructure providers, software companies, and content providers. The goal of the WAP Forum is to address the problems of wireless Internet access, ensuring that such access is not limited by bearer, vendor, or underlying network technology. WAP has been accepted as a de facto industry standard, and it is estimated that 95 percent of smart phones shipped to the United States and western Europe in 2003 will be Wireless Application Protocol (WAP) enabled (source: "Unwiring the IP Network with Global Standards WAP and Bluetooth," Strategy Analytics Inc., May 1999).

OVERVIEW OF THIS BOOK

The remainder of this book focuses on WAP (versions 1.1 to 1.3) and how to develop applications using the WAP standards. In the remainder of Part 1 we explore the ins and outs of the WAP specifications, look at client devices, and examine current alternatives to WAP. We define what makes an application suitable for a mobile audience and provide an overview of WAP-based application areas. This part concludes with a look at the tools we can use to build and deploy applications.

Part 2, "The WAP Development Standards," provides an in-depth exploration of Wireless Markup Language (WML) and its accompanying scripting language, WMLScript. We also cover push technology, which is a key component in messaging and time-critical applications.

Part 3, "WAP in Practice," gets down to business with advice on designing applications, architectural choices, usability and testing, and a complete development case study that follows a WAP application from concept to deployment. We wrap up with a look at the future of WAP.

How to Use This Book

Part 1 provides a comprehensive technical overview of WAP and should be read by all readers. Part 2 contains tutorial-style guides to WML, WMLScript, and push development. These chapters are a must-read for developers, and the push chapter, in particular, will be of interest to architects and technical managers. The design factors and architectures chapters in Part 3 are aimed at architects and developers. The remaining chapters, "Usability and Testing," "Application Development Case Study," and "Future of WAP," should be useful to all readers.

A Note on Examples

Most of the examples in this book were created as static WML pages and rendered using the UP SDK 4.0 simulator available from *updev.phone.com*. This simulator emulates the Phone.com browser, which is licensed to several phone vendors worldwide and popular in the United States. Some examples were produced using the Nokia 7110 simulator that comes with the Nokia 2.0 Toolkit. All examples were tested on both simulators, and major differences are noted in the text. We discuss these tools and other simulators and toolkits in Chapter 4.

Technical Overview

The WAP world is a complex blend of standards, devices, networks, and applications. In this chapter we summarize WAP from a technical viewpoint. To do this, we must explore WAP standards, identifying those that are relevant to general application development. We examine the layered WAP protocol that provides efficient communication over a wireless network and look at the Wireless Application Environment (WAE) and its languages for markup (Wireless Markup Language, or WML) and scripting (WMLScript). We take a brief look at WAP client devices including WAP phones, palmtops, and hybrids. Finally, to place WAP in context, we outline some technical alternatives that can also be used to provide wireless Web services.

The problems solved by WAP include the following:

- **Protocol mismatch:** Unlike the Internet, mobile networks (e.g., GSM and TDMA) are not inherently IP based; they do not support the protocol of the Internet.

- **Device limitations:** Mobile devices (cellular phones, pagers, and palmtops) are not ideal Web clients.

- **Usability:** Usability is an issue, particularly with the limited size of mobile phones and pagers.

It is not simple to integrate mobile networks with the Internet. The wired Internet provides a universal address space based on IP addresses and assumes a more stable environment than that found in mobile networks. In contrast, mobile networks typically employ non-IP device identifiers and use a variety of technologies to communicate with clients. To bridge this gap, it is necessary to use some sort of translating gateway to join the mobile client and the Internet. This is the solution adopted by WAP and other wireless Web solutions including NTT DoCoMo's I-Mode service, Palm's Web Clipping, and the Short Message Service (we discuss these alternative solutions later).

In addition to a gateway to the Internet, we need a data protocol that takes into account the narrow bandwidth and relatively unreliable connections typical of mobile networks. These networks are characterized by incomplete coverage (due to natural or human-made obstacles, or base station positioning). Physics dictates how rapidly we can communicate with mobile devices – bandwidth equals power, and more bandwidth means shorter device battery life. Data protocols for the wireless Web are typically custom, non-IP-based protocols or optimized versions of the Internet's protocols.

Not only must the mobile device be capable of talking to the translating gateway via the selected data protocol, but it must also be able to host Web applications. These applications must use the input and output facilities of the device in an effective way, be this by voice recognition and response or miniature QWERTY keyboards and color VGA screens. Mobile device application environments range from subscriber identity module (SIM) cards, through downloaded application skeletons (used in Palm Web Clipping applications), to the thin client browser model. The latter is used by WAP and I-Mode and employs a so-called microbrowser capable of rendering suitable Web content and perhaps executing scripts.

Usability is arguably the greatest challenge facing mobile application developers. WAP directly addresses some usability issues, but the challenge of building usable applications for mobile devices goes beyond anything a technical specification contains (see further discussion in Chapter 11).

The wireless Web requires new network protocols, a new application environment, and some way to address the usability challenges presented by mobile clients. The next few sections explain how the WAP standards try to address these challenges.

WAP Standards in Context

The Wireless Application Protocol is defined by approximately forty documents that describe a protocol and application environment uniquely suited to mobile networks and devices. The WAP Forum releases a new version of these documents every six months that can be downloaded in Adobe PDF format from the technical section of the WAP Forum site (*www.wapforum.org*). Many of these documents are specifications that contain the full details of a standard; these are usually written for a mixed audience of mobile network providers, device manufacturers, and application developers. This, added to the sheer number of standards, makes it difficult for people new to WAP to make sense of the protocol. Before we dive into the standards, it will help to look at a typical WAP configuration.

Network Architecture

At the heart of the WAP network architecture is the WAP gateway (see Fig. 2-1), which acts as a mediator between a mobile client and a Web server. Although other configurations are possible, including intranet deployment and integration of the WAP gateway and Web

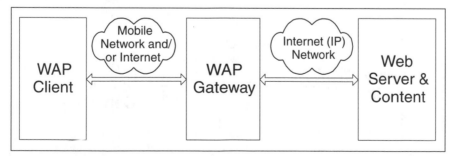

FIGURE 2-1. WAP Network Architecture

server, the WAP gateway remains the interface between the mobile device and content sources.

The WAP client (e.g., a cell phone) does not communicate directly with a Web server as is the case in the Web model (see Fig. 2-2); instead, the WAP client talks to a WAP gateway that acts as a mediator between the client and the Web server. This gateway translates between the WAP and Web protocols (and performs other functions we cover later in this chapter). The gateway communicates with the Web server on behalf of the WAP client.

JUST THE GOOD STUFF – WAP DEVELOPMENT STANDARDS

Developing WAP applications does not require a full understanding of all standards. Of general interest to WAP developers are those that involve the WAP client and the Web server. Only a small subset of the standards are required for normal application development, and those useful to the first-time developer are listed in Table 2-1. This table also identifies the chapters where we cover material related to each standard.

The standards applicable to more advanced application development (including push applications) are described in Table 2-2. Much of the material from these standards is explained in the remaining chapters of this book. Refer to the chapter cross-reference column in both tables.

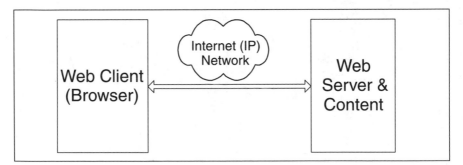

FIGURE 2-2. Web Network Architecture

TABLE 2-1. Basic Application Development Standards

TYPE OF SPECIFICATION	SPECIFICATION NAME	DESCRIPTION	CHAPTER CROSS-REFERENCE
Overviews	*Wireless Application Protocol Architecture Specification*	Provides an oveview of the WAP architecture. This is an excellent supplement to what is described in this chapter.	This chapter
	Wireless Application Environment Overview	Gives a background to the Wireless Application Environment (which we explain later in this chapter) and insights into the philosophy of WAP.	This chapter
Language and Library Specifications	*Wireless Markup Language Specification*	Describes the Wireless Markup Language including a complete WML document type definition.	Chapters 5 and 6
	WMLScript Language Specification	Defines the scripting language that supplements the Wireless Markup Language.	Chapter 7
	WMLScript Standard Libraries Specification	Outlines the functions available to WMLScript programs including language, string, dialog, floating point, browser, and URL libraries.	Chapter 7

TABLE 2-2. Advanced Application Development Standards

TYPE OF SPECIFICATION	SPECIFICATION NAME	DESCRIPTION	CHAPTER CROSS-REFERENCE
Security	*WMLScript Crypto Library*	Application-level security routines accessible from WMLScript (e.g., digital signing of data)	Chapters 7 and 9
Telephony	*Wireless Telephony Application Interface Specification*	Describes public *WMLScript* calls that are available from any WAP deck (e.g., dialing a voice call)	Chapter 7
Client Device Profiles	*User Agent Profiling Specification*	Sets out mechanisms for describing the capabilities of mobile devices	Chapter 9
Push	*Push Architectural Overview*	Outlines how push messaging applications work	Chapter 8
	Push Access Protocol Specification	Defines the protocol between the content Web server and the push gateway	Chapter 8
	Push Message Specification	Describes the format of a push message	Chapter 8
	WAP Service Indication Specification	Covers push messages that provide indirect push functionality	Chapter 8
	WAP Service Loading Specification	Describes push messages that provide direct push functionality	Chapter 8
	WAP Cache Operation Specification	Specifies cache control messages that can be pushed to or pulled by a client application	Chapter 8

HOW WAP STACKS UP – THE PROTOCOL STANDARDS

Why can't we simply use Web and Internet protocols over mobile networks? The answer lies primarily in the differences between the two types of networks: Unlike the Internet, most mobile networks do not support IP addresses, and many impose limits on packet size; due to low bandwidth, mobile network protocols must minimize network roundtrips and simple recovery from interruptions is mandatory, given the realities of current cellular coverage. To provide these and other features, WAP protocols define a new layered model that is loosely based on Internet protocols (see Fig. 2-3). These protocols describe a layered stack similar to the Web/Internet protocols of HTTP, TCP/IP, TLS, and UDP. Taking a look under the hood, as it were, of the WAP protocol stack helps answer a number of questions that will probably come up during your first development effort.

Figure 2-3 provides one possible comparison of the WAP and Web protocols (due to differences in functionality between the layers in the two protocols, it is not possible to provide an exact one-to-one mapping). Application developers are mainly concerned with the top (application) layer, which contains the Wireless Application Environment (WAE). The WAE contains the languages for markup (Wireless Markup Language, or WML) and scripting (WMLScript) as well as wireless telephony functions (WTA). WML is logically equivalent to Hypertext Markup Language (HTML) used for Web page layout, and WMLScript is a cousin of ECMAScript (or JavaScript). Push standards are also included within the WAE.

A session layer (described by the Wireless Session Protocol, or WSP) supports the application layer. This layer provides similar functionality to Hypertext Transfer Protocol (HTTP), but adds support for sessions, data encoding, and push mechanisms. WSP provides session maintenance over an unreliable connection and can resume a session even after a long break in communication. This is useful in dealing with lost connections and high latency and also helps reduce the air-

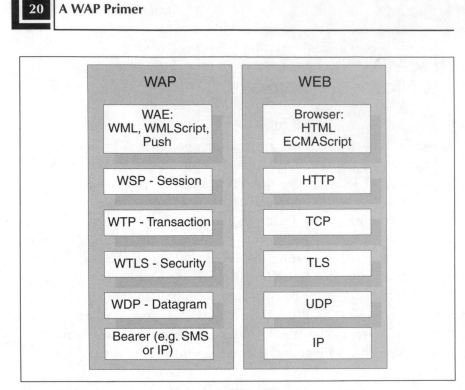

FIGURE 2-3. WAP and Web Protocols Compared

time used by a data connection. The WSP allows efficient binary encoding of previously defined content types (to save bandwidth) and supports various flavors of push applications (where a server initiates a session with a client).

The transaction layer (described by the Wireless Transaction Protocol, or WTP) lies below the session layer. This layer provides a reliable transactional transmission protocol similar to TCP/IP, but optimized to allow reconnection and to minimize handshaking (to reduce network traffic). Like TCP/IP, the Wireless Transaction Protocol layer uses various means to ensure that the packets sent by the underlying packet transmission protocol are transmitted reliably, without corruption or loss.

The Wireless Transport Layer Security (WTLS) protocol is an optional layer based on the Transport Layer Security (TLS) protocol (formerly referred to as Secure Sockets Layer, or SSL). WTLS defines security mechanisms for public key encryption and authentication, use of digital certificates, as well as support for compression. This layer ensures the security of information passing between the mobile device and the gateway. Note that TLS is usually used to secure requests and responses between the WAP gateway and the Web server.

The Wireless Datagram Protocol (WDP) is based on the Internet's User Datagram Protocol (UDP) and specifies a low-level protocol for rapid packet transmission. This low-level protocol is implemented on a given mobile network bearer's technology or on top of Internet Protocol (IP) where this is available. When WDP is sent over the air, a bearer-specific protocol mapping is used. It is this that provides the mobile network independence, which is one of the most important advantages of WAP. It is important to understand that WAP protocols can be used both over the air and/or over an IP-based network such as the Internet. When WAP protocols are used over an IP network, the WDP layer is simply implemented as UDP. The scenario most often discussed in WAP Forum literature assumes that the WAP gateway is co-located with the mobile provider. However, information sent over the air using the WAP protocol can also be forwarded (via an Internet gateway such as a remote access server) to a WAP gateway running anywhere on a local network or the Internet (refer to Fig. 2-4).

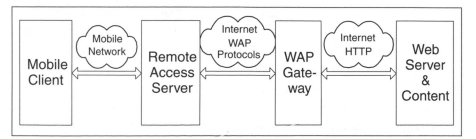

FIGURE 2-4. WAP Access Using a Gateway Not Co-Located with a Mobile Provider

This scenario assumes that the mobile network is a circuit-switched network (i.e., the mobile client dials in and establishes a connection via a modem pool to a remote access server). The remote access server (RAS) provides a point-to-point connection much like that established when you dial up an Internet service provider from a desktop PC. This RAS may be hosted by a mobile operator, at a third-party Internet service provider, or within an organization's own IT infrastructure. Similarly, the WAP gateway can be hosted by any of these parties, and its location typically depends on the degree of security required by the client and content provider. Most residential users will use a setup hosted by their mobile operator, whereas corporate users may access a separate corporate WAP gateway and may even dial into a corporate RAS.

THE WIRELESS APPLICATION ENVIRONMENT

The wireless protocols that describe the WAP protocol stack are key to the success of WAP, but it is the Wireless Application Environment standards that are most relevant to application developers. The Wireless Application Environment (WAE) provides a vendor-neutral application architecture based on Internet standards. Its specifications outline an application programming model that supports browsing and scripting as well as extensions that allow cellular network operators to offer network services within WAP. Like the protocol stack specifications, WAE standards are tailored to suit the requirements of mobile devices and networks.

The WAE architecture model contains much that will be familiar to Web developers including the use of URLs to name resources and standard content formats (e.g., WML, WMLScript) to distinguish between classes of data. However, despite similarities, the WAE architecture is fundamentally different from current Web standards. The need to optimize content for wireless delivery and display has resulted in changes in virtually every area. The integration of cellular services and support for push-type messaging has also created a completely new suite of standards.

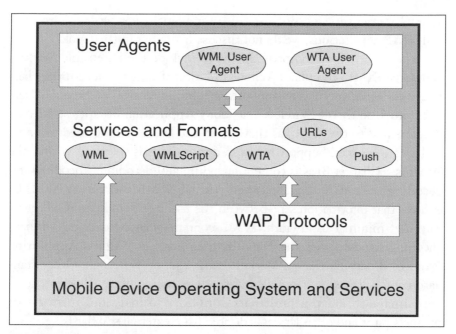

FIGURE 2-5. Wireless Application Environment in Context

Figure 2-5 outlines the components of the Wireless Application Environment, dividing these into user agents and services/formats. This figure is based on material from the WAP Forum's Wireless Application Environment Overview (available at *www.wapforum.org*). User agents are simply applications that run inside a WAP-capable device such as a mobile phone. The WAP standards support independent user agents to allow for expanded device functionality and to ensure that special services such as mobile network access are isolated from regular Internet services.

The WML user agent is conceptually similar to a Web browser and includes support for Wireless Markup Language interpretation and display (much like a Web browser renders HTML). The Wireless Telephony Application (WTA) user agent is an application that collaborates with a mobile provider's WTA server to provide mobile network value-added functionality. Although this user agent works with WML, it interfaces with local client or mobile provider resources and does not access Internet services. Because this user agent is not accessible to general WAP applications, we do not discuss it further in this book.

The services that comprise the WAE include the Extensible Markup Language (XML) compliant Wireless Markup Language, a scripting language (WMLScript) and its supporting libraries, as well as telephony services provided by the Wireless Telephony Application libraries. URLs are fundamental to the WAE, as they are to the Web, and are used to name and locate services. Support for push applications is specified within the WAE (see Chapter 8) as is content encoding and decoding. Encoding and decoding of content (e.g., between textual WML and binary WMLC) ensures that information sent between the user agent and the WAP gateway uses minimal bandwidth. WML content is encoded using a binary encoding standard with the ironically long name of Wireless Application Protocol Binary Extensible Markup Language, or WBXML. Other standard content encodings include byte code encoding of WMLScript, standard image formats, a multipart container format, and formats for business cards and calendar data adopted from external standards.

ANATOMY OF A WAP REQUEST

We are now ready to take a look at the anatomy of a typical WAP request. Figure 2-6 shows the client, gateway, server trio. The client hosts a WAE User Agent (e.g., a WML browser) and makes an encoded request to the gateway using WAP's Wireless Session Protocol (WSP). This request is analogous to a Web browser sending an HTTP request that specifies a URL. The difference is that the request is directed to a WAP gateway, which acts as a proxy. The gateway translates the client request into a standard HTTP Post or Get, which is sent to the resource named by the request URL. This resource (a Web server) satisfies the request by supplying WML content, which is returned to the gateway as an HTTP response, as it would be in the case of a normal Web request. The gateway encodes the response's content and headers and returns this, using the layered WAP protocol, to the client where it is decoded and displayed. Note that information may also be encrypted between client, gateway, and server.

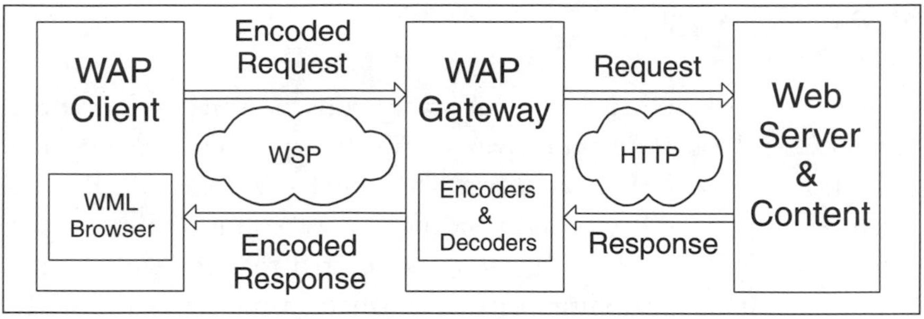

FIGURE 2-6. Anatomy of a WAP Request

You may have noticed in the previous discussions that the WAP gateway is a key component in almost every aspect of a WAP request and response. Because of this, the gateway is an issue that must be considered in many WAP applications. Here are some areas over which the WAP gateway has control:

■ **Access to the Web:** The gateway can limit general Web access to sites approved by the gateway owner by refusing a connection to a given URL.

■ **Access to mobile users:** If the gateway has push capabilities (i.e., it is a push proxy gateway), it can dictate whether or not a push application can establish a dialogue with a given mobile user (see Chapter 8 for an explanation of these terms).

■ **Security:** In order for a secure connection to be established, a gateway must support both WTLS to the mobile device and TLS to the WAP application.

■ **Device profiles:** The gateway must be capable of processing user agent profiles if these are to be used by a WAP application.

■ **Caching and cookies:** The gateway performs caching of headers and cookies and determines whether or not cookies are supported.

We look into these issues throughout the remainder of the book.

WAP CLIENTS

Now that we have a high-level understanding of the WAP specifications, let's look at the most tangible part of WAP – the mobile devices that provide access to WAP applications. The Wireless Application Protocol attempts to provide device independence by assuming minimal device capabilities. WML and WMLScript are tailored to work with limited display and input capabilities as well as small memories and relatively slow processors. The standards assume a minimum device display of 3 lines by 12 characters and input capabilities that allow navigation and alphanumeric entry. However, a wide range of devices currently support WAP and an even greater diversity is just around the corner.

The majority of WAP devices can be divided into WAP phones, palmtop computers, and hybrids that combine features from both these groups (see Fig. 2-7). WAP phones combine data capabilities with digital and/or analog cellular voice functionality; the current terminology for these phones is somewhat confused as we discuss in the sidebar "Mobile Device Terminology." Because WAP browsers will be integrated with the majority of digital handsets in the next few years, these devices will be the most common client for residential (i.e., noncorporate) users.

FIGURE 2-7. WAP Clients

Mobile Device Terminology

The current terminology for these devices is somewhat confused, probably as a result of rapid evolution in this area. The term *smart phone* has been applied both to phones that are data capable and to phones that have additional features more common in a palmtop. I refer to the former simply as WAP phones and the latter as hybrids. Similarly, there are a number of names for sub-laptop computers including Pocket PC, hand-helds, and palmtops (e.g., Microsoft PocketPC/CE, Symbian EPOC, Palm OS). These devices have some form of operating system or equivalent (e.g., a Java virtual machine) in common and extensibility through software and hardware. I refer to these devices as palmtops. ◨

Palmtop computers (e.g., the Handspring Visor and the Symbian EPOC-based hand-helds) can usually be extended to provide wireless modem functionality and can function as WAP user agents. A growing number of palmtops (e.g., the Palm VII and RIM's Blackberry devices) are provided with integrated wireless access. Palmtops are generally favored over other devices by organizations that want to provide employee access to corporate data.

Hybrid devices (sometimes called communicators) offer phone functionality with the improved display and input facilities provided by palmtops. Hybrids try to provide the best of both worlds and, at first glance, represent the logical evolution of the mobile Internet client. However, the rise in popularity of local area radio links (e.g., Bluetooth) may remove the need for this physical integration. Separation of the input device, display, and radio frequency (RF) unit makes good ergonomic sense. Specialized wearable devices and "body networks" may be the future of mobile computing.

Other WAP devices that are not immediately obvious are laptop and desktop computers. A portable computer equipped with a wireless link (e.g., via a plug-in modem card) can be used to access WAP content; here the limitations of display and entry are not an issue, but limited battery life and network bandwidth must still be dealt with. This computer makes use of a software browser that will typically be a stand-alone browser or simulator. However, WAP browsers are also available that execute within a Java virtual machine or run within the environment of a

Web browser. It is also possible to run these same browser applications on a desktop machine with a dial-up or direct Internet connection. This setup can be particularly useful during development and when exploring and evaluating WAP services (to save on airtime charges).

General features of WAP-capable mobile devices are described in Table 2-3. Information about current devices that provide WAP support is available from the vendors (including Ericsson, Nokia, and Phone.com) as well as from independent WAP sites.

TABLE 2-3. WAP Devices

TYPE	DISPLAY SIZE	DATA ENTRY	WML RAM	PERIPHERALS	COMMENTS
WAP Phone	90 by 50 pixels is typical, which equates to better than 4 lines of 12 characters	Phone Keypad	1300 bytes plus	External keyboard possible	Advantages are portability and cost. Most common WAP device now and in near future. Examples include offerings from Nokia, Ericsson, Qualcomm, etc.
Hybrid (palmtop + phone)	Up to palmtop resolution	Keypad, stylus, or touch screen	Similar to high-end phones	Probably not needed – tries to provide most functions "out of the box." Hand-held + cell phone connected by local radio link may be better alternative.	Like any compromise these are larger than the smallest phones and less versatile than stand-alone PDA. Some of these try to do it all with integrated GPS, audio, Bluetooth, and HTML browsers. Examples include the Qualcomm PDQ Palmtop, Nokia Communicator, and Ericsson R380.

THE COMPETITION – ALTERNATIVES TO WAP

A discussion of WAP technology would not be complete without a look at some of the alternatives to this technology. There are currently a number of solutions that take an approach similar to WAP as well as solutions which provide a "heavier" mobile Internet client. Refer to the sidebar "Thin and Thick Clients." We examine solutions that are currently available including Short Message Service, Phone.com's HDML, HTML, NTT DoCoMo's I-Mode, and Palm's Web Clipping service.

TYPE	DISPLAY SIZE	DATA ENTRY	WML RAM	PERIPHERALS	COMMENTS
Palmtop	100+ by 100+ pixels; up to quarter-VGA	Stylus, keyboard, or touch screen	Limited by free RAM (typical max 2 MB to 8 MB)	Expandable – printers, bar code readers, Bluetooth plug-ins. Note that cell modem is required and may be a peripheral or require an external link to cell phone.	Advantages are the relatively large display and long battery life. Superior data entry and larger RAM for caching of WML decks. Disadvantages are high cost, no voice capabilities, learning curve, and size. Examples include platforms based on Symbian EPOC, Windows CE and Pocket PC, and Palm OS.
Laptop	VGA (640 by 480 or better)	Keyboard	Limited by free RAM (max to 512 MB or better)	Extremely flexible. Like a palmtop, requires a wireless modem (typically a plug-in card).	A possible alternative to locating an Internet hookup on the road.

Thick and Thin Clients

A spectrum of client/server solutions for mobile computing ranges from *thin client* (where the client typically contains little business logic) through *thick client* (where a complete application runs on the client).

Thin: The majority of application processing is carried out on a server, and a client browser renders content from the server and may execute scripts. This is the solution category in which WAP lives (where a WML browser processes WML and WMLScript). Other thin client solutions include the following:

- Short Message Service (SMS)
- Phone.com's HDML
- Web browser (HTML and ECMAScript – e.g., MS Mobile Explorer)

Medium: A client controller must be installed, but gets remainder of content and layout from server:

- Palm's Web Clipping applications
- AvantGo's channel-based service

Thick: The client contains GUI and business logic and must be installed or downloaded. You will sometimes see this type of client referred to as a *fat client,* although this is no longer politically correct. Examples include:

- Virtual Machine-based clients such as various implementations of Sun's Java 2 Micro Edition (J2ME) standard
- Microsoft's Pocket PC nonbrowser applications, Symbian EPOC applications

THE SHORT MESSAGE SERVICE

The Short Message Service (SMS) has been available in Europe since 1991 and was introduced into North America by Bell and Nextel. This is a point-to-point mechanism for transmitting short messages to and from wireless handsets. The service makes use of a short message service center (SMSC), which acts as a store-and-forward system for guaranteed delivery of short messages (see Fig. 2-8).

Initial applications of SMS focused on eliminating alphanumeric pagers by permitting two-way general-purpose messaging and notification services, primarily for voice mail. As technology and networks matured, a variety of services were introduced, including electronic

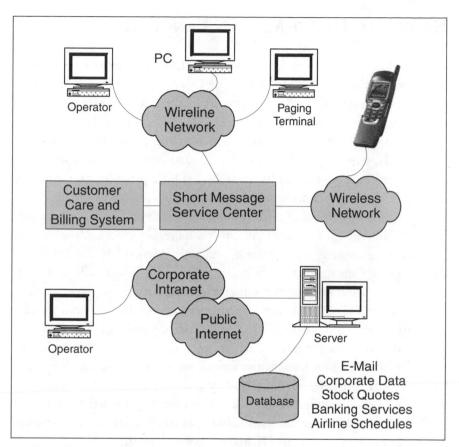

FIGURE 2-8. Short Message Service Overview

mail and fax integration, paging, banking, and information services such as stock quotes.

It is interesting to note that although SMS has some major limitations (including a maximum message size of 160 characters and no support for images), it has become a pervasive and useful tool enabling a wide range of applications. SMS has much in common with WAP, including a focus on network operator value-added services and customer care, support for push (notification) applications, and general information service access.

HANDHELD DEVICE MARKUP LANGUAGE

Handheld Device Markup Language (HDML) is the precursor to WAP's Wireless Markup Language. HDML was created by Unwired Planet (now Openwave/Phone.com) to provide an HTML-like markup language optimized for mobile devices. HTML and HDML share the same parent language (Standard Generalized Markup Language, or SGML), but HDML uses a simplified tag set, a card and deck metaphor, and explicit navigation and history models. HDML provides tags that are useful for creating a compact user interface. The ability to organize this user interface into decks of cards provides an efficient way to reduce network traffic and split up content into manageable pieces. Variables are used to share content across a deck, and only one card is displayed at a time. The explicit navigation model ensures that a device will be able to display navigation options to the user regardless of how a particular card is laid out. In HTML, the larger screen areas and ability to scroll using a pointing device allow navigation items (buttons and links) to be freely scattered throughout a page. The limitations of mobile devices make this type of navigation layout impractical. In addition to explicit navigation, HDML provides explicit history maintenance; the card history model has been extended beyond the page history provided by a regular HTML browser to allow programmable operations on the history stack.

Creating applications in HDML allows you to support a number of phones that run Phone.com's UP browser. This is a reasonable short-term option (or adjunct) to WAP development in North America, where a large percentage of data-capable phones use this microbrowser. Because Phone.com is a primary supporter of WAP, many of the features of HDML have found their way into the WAP specifications. HDML has become an evolutionary dead end, replaced by its XML-compliant cousin, WML.

HYPERTEXT MARKUP LANGUAGE

It is possible for mobile devices to provide regular HTML Web browser functionality (in fact, this is what Microsoft's Mobile Explorer does). The primary disadvantage of this approach is that HTTP and

TCP/IP provide a less than ideal solution for cellular communications. These protocols assume more bandwidth and a longer-lived, more stable connection than is common in cellular networks (for a more complete discussion of these issues, refer to the discussion on the WAP protocol stack earlier in this chapter). Another potential difficulty is that HTML has evolved into a markup language suited for PC monitor displays, and HTML pages typically contain layout, navigation, and graphics that are unsuited for display on resource-limited devices. Despite the technical difficulties, the appeal of being able to access the full breadth of Web resources makes this an attractive option.

Note the various subsets of HTML including Handheld-Friendly HTML (used by AvantGo's channel-based Web service) and I-Mode's Compact HTML or CHTML (HTML 1.0 plus a subset of later HTML versions with extensions). For information on Handheld-Friendly HTML, AvantGo provides a style guide for developers (see *www.avantgo.com/developer*). Information on Compact HTML can be found at the World Wide Web Consortium's site (*www.w3.org*).

I-MODE

The Japanese Telecommunications company NTT's DoCoMo subsidiary offers a service named I-Mode. I-Mode runs over only one type of cellular network – Personal Digital Cellular (PDC), a Japanese-only packet digital cellular network. It uses a similar architecture to WAP with a dedicated server to handle translation between cellular and Internet networks. It supports both pushed and regular access of CHTML (described earlier). I-Mode is proprietary to DoCoMo (Japan's largest ISP) and has been extremely successful with millions of subscribers accessing applications that include entertainment, banking, messaging, and ticket reservation.

WEB CLIPPING

Palm Computing (*www.palm.com*) comes at the problem of limited devices and network bandwidth from a different angle. Palm's Web Clipping solution uses a client/server architecture where a skeleton

Palm Query Application is predownloaded to a Palm or compatible device (typically using direct PC synchronization). This application then provides links (where dynamic information is required) to limited Web pages called Web Clippings. Requests and responses are transmitted over a wireless packet data network using Palm Computing's Palm.net service. All communications are processed by a special proxy server that communicates with the requested Web resource using HTTP (much as a WAP gateway does). The proxy server directly retrieves pages that are marked via a special tag:

```
<meta name="PalmComputingPlatform" content="true">
```

This indicates that the page has been tailored to a Palm device. Other Web pages are "clipped" to reduce their size and ignore unsupported tags. Refer to Figure 2-9 for an overview of this process.

When building a Palm Query Application, a developer creates a set of HTML pages centered around an index page. These pages are compiled into a .pqa application file using freely available Palm Application Builder software. Typically, this application contains at least one link to an Internet URL identifying a CGI script, server page, or servlet. Although these sources of dynamically generated content are usually created with the constraints of a Palm device in mind, this content can also be served to regular HTML browser clients. This requires the use of a special tag to inform the Palm clipping proxy

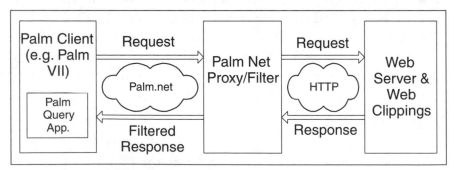

FIGURE 2-9. Web Clipping Overview

server of non-Palm content (e.g., large color images) as well as care in limiting page size and markup.

Web Clipping development has a number of parallels to WAP application development. Images are allowed, but discouraged in Web Clippings. The concept of a base WAP deck is analogous to the preinstalled Palm Query Application in that once installed (or downloaded) a set of pages can be locally navigated until dynamic content is required. Suggested size limits on clipping pages of less than 1 kilobyte (preferably 400 bytes) are similar to those of WAP applications targeted at basic devices. Finally, the subset of HTML 3.2 supported by Web Clipping is similar to the markup supported by Wireless Markup Language. Refer to Chapters 5 and 6 for a full explanation of the WAP features discussed here.

Advantages of Palm's approach to Internet access are that both the on-device Palm query application and the downloaded clippings are written in a subset of HTML 3.2 with a few extensions (note that nested tables, image maps, frames, cookies, and JavaScript are not supported). Thus with some care, experienced Web developers can create Palm mobile applications with a short learning curve. Tools are available for development and testing including a Palm Query Application Builder and a Palm VII simulator for use in testing applications. The disadvantages of this approach are that it is available only on Palm OS devices and requires the application user to subscribe to a special service (Palm Net) where a per-kilobyte download fee is paid in addition to airtime charges.

We have not discussed heavier client approaches including installed applications and Java-based solutions. These technologies are not direct competitors to WAP, being analogous to PC applications or Java applets in the desktop world. We discuss Java-based technologies in Chapter 13 and show that WAP and Java applications can coexist much as thin client Web applications and Java do today, on the desktop.

Although all of the approaches we have discussed provide some form of wireless Web services, WAP has the striking advantage of being vendor, device, and network neutral. This neutrality is what will assure its long-term survival.

In this chapter we have learned what WAP is and why it has great potential. Unlike current alternative technologies, WAP runs efficiently on many underlying transport mechanisms and is independent of device and manufacturer. We explored the WAP specifications, identifying those relevant to application developers. These specifications define a layered mobile network protocol and a complete Wireless Application Environment. We looked briefly at WAP client devices and outlined some alternatives to WAP for mobile Internet service delivery, learning why WAP is superior for truly international thin client wireless Web applications. In Chapter 3, we look at WAP applications and learn which applications are appropriate for the wireless Web.

Applications

What makes a good WAP application? This is the critical question to ask before you embark on a WAP development effort. Applications and content that make sense on the desktop may be candidates for a WAP conversion or extension. However, many applications require bandwidth, text entry, or display capabilities that just do not exist in the wireless world. Also, users should have a compelling reason to access the application while on the move or away from their desk: The application must be useful! To answer the question of what constitutes a useful WAP application, we start with the potential users.

MOBILE USERS

So who is going to use your application? There are four main classes of mobile users: mobile workers, mobile professionals, residential users, and remote devices.

Truck drivers, couriers, and public safety workers (ambulance drivers, police officers, and inspectors) are mobile workers – workers whose jobs mandate mobility. In many fields, these workers already use some form of mobile application; couriers may use automated waybills, and inspectors often carry handheld data entry devices. However, these applications are usually proprietary and may be based on private networks and custom devices.

Professionals are white-collar workers whose jobs require some amount of travel, including salespeople, managers, and consultants. These professionals are often early adopters of technology – the first to take to cell phones and laptops. This attitude, combined with the growing trend toward the virtual office, will fuel strong growth in this segment.

Residential users represent the largest user group and the segment with the longest term potential. The acknowledged convenience of the cell phone and exposure to mobile applications in their work role will drive initial acceptance. In addition, many application providers that currently use the Web to deliver services to residential users are eagerly embracing the wireless Web channel.

Although you probably would not immediately think of a machine as a user of the wireless Web, remote devices that require monitoring and maintenance fall into this category. These include storage tanks, pumping stations, pipelines, and generators that can use a wireless data channel to transmit alerts and status updates. By adding remote control functionality (e.g., programmable logic controllers) it is possible to make adjustments to, and even carry out maintenance on these devices using the same wireless channel.

CRITICAL SUCCESS FACTORS FOR WAP APPLICATIONS

In order for a WAP application to be successful it must be seen as having value for its potential users. An application is valuable if it is relevant (i.e., solves a problem or provides a desired service) and if it improves the convenience of this service. Applications that have particular relevance to the mobile user are those that take advantage of one or more of time, location, and personalization.

Time

Like Web applications, mobile applications are often more valuable when they are accessible outside normal hours of business; accessibility increases the convenience of a service. From another angle, applications that deliver time-dependent services such as stock alerts or notifications are also good mobile application candidates. Unlike the desktop, wireless Web clients can accompany us anywhere and time-aware applications can help us stay on top of things without having to always be looking at our watches.

Location

Location independence is the key differentiator of mobile applications – access from anywhere to anywhere. If an application is useful away from the home or workplace desktop, then it is a mobile application candidate. Location awareness is another facet of mobile applications. The mobile device is a personal device, and the device's location is usually its owner's location. Taking the network administrator's view, mobile users are simply nodes on a highly fluid network. The position of these nodes can be used to great effect by applications that have a geographic component such as restaurant finders or navigation services.

Personalization

Because the mobile device is a personal device, the individualized services of the Web including Web portals and instant messaging become even more compelling in the wireless Web world. Personal preferences, security information, digital identities – all of these can be used to advantage by mobile applications. The limited displays of mobile devices increase the importance of personalization to ensure the relevance of displayed information.

It is likely that the majority of future wireless Web applications will be forced to consider all of these points in order to remain viable. In a nutshell, the killer mobile service will provide access from anywhere at any time and deliver a service that is both timely and tailored to the user's desires and location!

Other Considerations

In addition to the points just outlined, applications that push information to their users may be appropriate mobile applications. Consider if your application requires the ability to initiate a dialogue with the user or push the information (e.g., notifications and alerts) to that user. Similarly, applications with a communications focus (e.g., messaging, dispatch, and groupware) are good candidates.

The type of user interface required by your application is also important. Ask yourself if it is possible to deliver your application using a relatively limited textual interface. Images are possible but not supported across all devices, and entry of large amounts of text is not feasible on many devices.

Now that we have considered what makes a good wireless Web application, let's take a look at some application categories. As mentioned in Chapter 2, we can (somewhat arbitrarily) divide wireless Web applications into communications and personal information management (PIM), Internet, enterprise, and telemetry applications.

COMMUNICATIONS AND PIM

Communications applications are perhaps the most obvious type of mobile application. These applications are popular with both residential and business users. E-mail has, to date, been the most widely implemented wireless Web application, enjoying popularity that parallels its enthusiastic adoption during the early years of the Internet. Business users typically access corporate mail servers (e.g., Microsoft Exchange or Lotus Notes/Domino), and residential users often access free e-mail accounts or a specified mail server through a wireless portal. E-mail can also be sent directly to a cell phone or special-purpose e-mail terminal by mapping a traditional Internet e-mail address to a selected mobile device identifier. E-mail services are usually bundled with a mobile subscription package.

Instant messaging services that allow Web users to check the availability of people, communicate instantly, and use a chat-like environment to carry on a conversation are rapidly making their way on to the wireless Web. Yahoo! has introduced a location-aware service as a pilot in the U.K. where users can locate their friends both online and physically. Equally important is the capability for mobile instant messaging to provide the platform for other services such as stock notifications, auction alerts, and mobile gaming. Mobile chat rooms are a logical extension of one-to-one instant messaging, allowing virtual mobile communities to participate in online discussions.

Another communications trend is unified messaging, which collects communications from a variety of sources into a single logical inbox. The large array of communications channels, ranging from voice to fax and e-mail to paging and instant messaging, provides an obvious case for a single window of access. The mobile device is a logical choice for accessing this "universal" inbox, and implementations of unified messaging often offer additional access channels including Web access and e-mail redirection.

One barrier to widespread use of mobile communications applications is the difficulty of entering text on a typical mobile device. However, a number of solutions are either currently available or on the horizon; these include smart word recognition (e.g., T9 technology where the device attempts to find the most likely word based on the letters typed on a handset keypad), voice interfaces, external keyboards, and stylus-based entry. Voice recognition has made great strides in the past decade, and current applications do a far better job of recognizing natural speech than their predecessors. Speech recognition and synthesis are currently available through server-side processing (e.g., voice portals), but it is only a matter of time before this technology will be available in handsets. Fluid integrated speech and text interfaces may become the norm for mobile communications.

Personal information management (PIM) including calendars, address books and task lists is offered in the now ubiquitous Personal Digital Assistant (PDA) as well as most office-type applications (e.g., Microsoft Outlook). The advantage of moving these applications onto the wireless Web is that they can then be accessed from anywhere and even shared between multiple users (facilitating work group scheduling). This greatly simplifies synchronization between devices and users by centralizing the information that is currently spread between server-based or desktop systems and PDAs.

LPG's WAPoffice provides a good example of a communications package that supports wireless and Web access to e-mail, addresses, and calendar information. This Finnish product (*www.lpg.fi*) is targeted at enterprises and portals that require a mobile communications interface to Interactive Mail Access Protocol (IMAP4) or Post Office Protocol (POP3) mail servers. It also offers calendar and address book access. Figure 3-1 shows a series of screens from this application. Screen *a* shows the main menu of the e-mail application, screen *b* shows an e-mail message under construction, and screen *c* shows the month view of the calendar application.

INTERNET

When we use the term *Internet application* we describe services aimed toward residential users or "consumers" (as opposed to enterprise applications that are targeted at business users). This area is extremely broad, encompassing applications that are currently accessed through Web channels as well as services uniquely suited to the wireless Web that leverage the location/time/personalization trio. Following closely on the heels of the e-commerce Web phenomenon comes mobile electronic commerce, or m-commerce. Mobile commerce applications include financial, shopping, and advertising services and are at the forefront of general Internet mobile applications.

FIGURE 3-1. LPG WAPoffice Communications Application

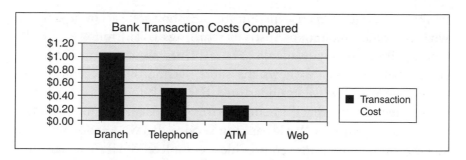

FIGURE 3-2. Relative Costs of Banking Transactions (source: "M-Commerce: Enabling the Wireless Internet Value Chain," Nortel Networks 1999)

Financial Applications

Banking and brokerage services are some of the earliest Internet mobile applications to achieve a degree of consumer acceptance. In Europe in particular, online banking has become the norm with more than 90 percent of banks offering this service. Huge cost savings have driven this evolution, and the move to mobile service delivery promises a far wider audience than desktop access. As Figure 3-2 shows, online banking costs the bank less than 2 percent of traditional brick and mortar transactions (2 cents versus more than a dollar U.S.).

Obviously, the easier a bank can make it for you to bank via the Web, the better for its bottom line. Mobile banking functions include the following:

- public information such as exchange and interest rates

- private information including balances, interest, and transaction summaries

- transactions such as fund transfers and bill payments

BAWAG (Bank für Arbeit und Wirtschaft AG) is the first Austrian bank to deploy a WAP financial solution. It initially rolled out a mobile banking solution (see Fig. 3.3) as an extension of its Web banking service. Screen *a* in Figure 3.3 shows an account balance with the total amount in Austrian schillings (ATS) followed by the amount immediately available. These values are converted to euros (EUR) below. Screen *b* shows the short version of an account statement and begins with an underlined Back link followed by a list of transaction date/currency/amount entries. Less than two months after going public with its WAP banking service, BAWAG added mobile stock brokerage functions to provide a complete WAP financial solution. We look at the BAWAG solution from a technical standpoint in Chapter 10.

Mobile brokerages are another obvious application area that offers value through convenient access and by delivering time-sensitive information directly to the mobile user. As with online banking, large cost savings can be realized over traditional (stockbroker-based) trades that cost as much as $70 U.S. per trade versus under $20 for an online trade. Online brokers are extending their services to the wireless Web offering functions such as these:

- public information, including stock quotes

- portfolio maintenance

- pushed alerts for price movements and order execution

- transactions (including buy, sell, and cancel)

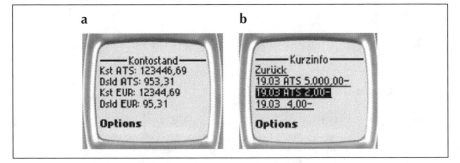

FIGURE 3-3. BAWAG Mobile Banking

Payment and Security

Because mobile devices are usually used by one person, they are logical candidates for storage of personal information. This information may be stored in integrated Subscriber Identification Modules, or SIMs (although these are not yet available in the majority of WAP devices); these smart cards provide a tamper-proof repository for digital identification (e.g., digital certificates and private keys) as well as electronic cash, preferences, and membership information.

Payment applications can use stored cash or take advantage of identity information to enable secure account or credit card payment. Mobile providers can also take advantage of their relationship with their subscribers to offer integrated payment solutions. These solutions can take advantage of the subscriber's account and current billing mechanisms to pay for third party services.

Security applications use a stored identity and a user-entered PIN to:

◼ provide secure-payment

◼ gain access to buildings or facilities

◼ digitally sign documents (to ensure nonrepudiation)

Security functionality will also underpin mobile applications where user identity and security of information is important (such as financial and mobile commerce services). Acceptance of this will be slowed by cultural inertia as well as technical issues such as the limited storage capability of current SIMs.

Shopping

From ordering a pizza to buying a CD, mobile shopping promises to extend Web channels and enable new location and time-aware transactions. Web e-tailers of books and CDs have extended their virtual storefronts to the mobile market, and novel services that tailor the shopping experience to the shopper's location are being trialed. The latter includes services that allow price comparisons of a product from

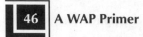

within a participating store as well as applications that offer special offers to subscribers while they are within a participating shopping center.

Auctions

Online auctions have become phenomenally successful, and mobile auctions promise to go one better, improving on the convenience and timeliness of this service. Subscribers to a mobile auction service can receive a notification when a bid is required on a specified item. The mobile user can take appropriate action, accepting the new price or declining to bid. Subscribers can also receive notifications of newly available items or confirmation that they have obtained a given item successfully.

Advertising

Advertising underlies much of the commercial Web. Although the techniques common on the Web (including banner ads) may have a hard time making the move to the tiny display of a mobile phone, the potential for one-to-one marketing is far greater on the wireless Web. One-to-one marketing can make good use of time, location, and personal preferences. As support for push messages and an "always connected" network model become more the norm, carefully timed, location-specific applications will become common. Banner advertisements have already found their way onto the screens of handheld computers where graphics and increased display size make them more feasible.

Ticketing and Reservation

Ticketing services represent some of the earliest WAP applications. They rely on increased convenience, bypassing lengthy Interactive Voice Response (IVR) interfaces, and avoiding trips to the agency or outlet. Event tickets (e.g., concert, cinema, and opera) are already a reality in Europe, and transport ticketing including bus, train, ferry, and airplane tickets offers another major application area. Electronic tickets for airlines are one option that is particularly simple where the airline and/or agency already has in place a Web interface to its reservation system. Loyalty/membership programs are frequently integrated with ticket applications, and both of these are natural candidates for inclusion in mobile portals.

Membership and Records

These applications assume that the mobile user has an identity card (e.g., a SIM) integrated with his or her device. This opens up the possibility of storing membership and loyalty information in a way that permits easy integration with m-commerce services. Also, the user's medical or employment records could be stored in the mobile device, making these available to trusted applications.

Locators and Navigation

Location-based services help the user find a specified service in a given location. These either rely on the user to enter a location (e.g., a postal code) or use some form of automatic locating device such as GPS. Services to locate gas stations and restaurants are already available, and the more sophisticated services permit entry of a range or radius to search and provide directions or navigation information to assist in finding the location. Route planning and traffic information systems are currently under development for use in vehicles. These offer similar functionality to the satellite-based systems now available in high-end automobiles.

Government Services

Government service delivery via the wireless Web offers the promise of easy access to a relatively large segment of the population. Current Web services have an audience typically limited to less than 50 percent and as few as 3 percent of the population. The ability to renew a vehicle license, pay a fine, or obtain a business license online via a mobile phone has potential political and financial dividends that are not likely to go unnoticed by politicians. Governments that are currently considering or in the process of implementing Web-based services will probably extend these to the wireless Web to achieve the common mandate of access to all.

ENTERPRISE

Enterprise applications are targeted at business users and typically extend the employee-only corporate intranet to palmtops and other mobile devices. Such services typically improve the efficiency of a business operation, reducing duplicate entry of information, providing timely access to critical data, and integrating processes that would otherwise be impossible to coordinate. Enterprise applications may also target customers and partners by mobile-enabling existing extranet services.

Supply Chain Integration

Integration of business processes along the supply chain is currently carried out by Enterprise Resource Planning systems such as SAP. While these systems are being extended to the Web, adding a mobile channel will improve the timeliness and ease of access to critical information. For example, a sales representative could check factory availability or current status of an item from a customer's premises.

Job Dispatch

Mobile devices provide an intuitive channel for highly distributed mobile work flow. The mobile employee can retrieve schedules and review tasks on the move; automatic or human dispatchers can push detailed alerts to these workers while updating a centralized scheduling system. Workers can provide real-time status updates for inspections, emergency situations, and field service. The improvements in productivity, reduced administrative work, and efficiency of scheduling and dispatch will provide a rapid return on investment for such applications. We examine an application that provides mobile employee work flow in the development case study in Chapter 12.

Customer Relationship Management

Customer relationship management (CRM) applications will be critical to the success of mobile operators and other service providers. The cost of ensuring customer satisfaction using current external-facing CRM methods such as IVR and toll-free numbers is quite large (annual customer care for mobile operators has been estimated at more than 10 euros per subscriber, according to Phone.com). Internal CRM is a form of sales force automation with the advantage of being able to access customer information (personal details or a history of transactions or complaints) in the field.

Sales Force Automation

Salespeople are a highly mobile segment of the work force. Their success may hinge on being able to provide clients with what they need in a competitive and convenient fashion. The mobile application can improve both ends of this process by providing up-to-the-minute contact status, market intelligence, and sales forecasts. Order entry, product availability, and even online payment services can provide a competitive edge to the suitably equipped agent. The PayLink and ProductLink applications from e-plicity.com (*www.e-plicity.com*) offer mobile point of sale and catalog applications. Merchants can use PayLink to process orders, accepting credit or debit card as well as cash or account-based payment. Payments are immediately submitted for approval and fed into the company's financial processing software in real time. ProductLink extends PayLink to provide a complete product catalog with access to real-time inventory and pricing information. Figure 3-4 shows some screen captures of PayLink that illustrate a fast-food delivery service. Screen *a* shows a list of addresses to which food must be delivered. Screen *b* displays the details of an order and screen *c* shows the total order cost and provides the patron with a chance to tip the delivery person. Not shown are payment processing and receipt screens.

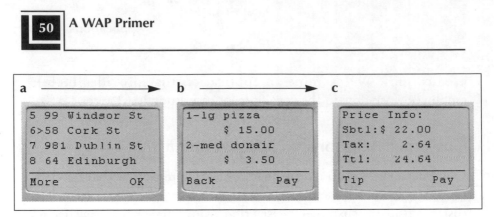

FIGURE 3-4. PayLink from e-plicity.com

TELEMETRY

Communication with mobile users has its analog in the world of machinery and devices. Whether it is a transport truck crossing the nation or a pipeline transporting gas through the wilderness, the benefits of staying in touch without wires is obvious.

Potential telemetry clients and applications include:

- Trucks – position reporting, fleet tracking
- Pipelines – remote monitoring
- Security systems – intrusion reporting
- Vending machines – inventory reporting
- Cash machines – transaction link, status reporting

Telemetry applications that currently rely on private networks will face stiff competition from the lower cost solution offered by public cellular and IP networks. Applications that require a fixed phone line can also realize a rapid cost saving by converting to a mobile connection. This is obviously the case in remote installations or where additional land-line connections are not available; however it may also be true where infrequent use cannot justify a dedicated Public Switched Telephone Network (PSTN) connection.

Fleet management is already a popular application of telemetry, and reduced cost of installation and yearly service charges is driving a new wave of development in this field. Monitoring of fixed machinery such as pipelines and pumping stations is a reality in Finland where the water industry uses Nordic Mobile Telephone to monitor and control pumping stations. The use of a mobile link for a security system has a benefit even where a PSTN connection is feasible. It is harder to prevent the transmission of a cell phone than it is to cut a telephone line! Vending and cash machines are often installed in locations where traffic is high and telephone outlets are scarce (airport lobbies, shopping malls, etc.). Using mobile links (and secure communications in the case of a cash machine) these devices can be deployed wherever there is a supply of power.

MOBILE PORTALS

Mobile portals are often extensions of their desktop counterparts, although mobile providers are now moving into this area, taking advantage of their strengths in communications. Portals are a natural fit in the mobile world. Web portals provide a filtered, customizable view of the Web and often bundle communications (free e-mail) with news, weather, stock, and user-selectable information. Personalization, communications, and focused delivery of selected information make the portal the ideal entry point for the mobile user. In fact, portals can be viewed as a tailored aggregation of communications, PIM, Internet, and possibly enterprise applications – covering the majority of possible WAP applications.

At least three flavors of Web portal are currently available, and it is reasonable that these will all make the transition to a wireless existence. These are the Internet portal – a general compendium designed to appeal to most consumers; the enterprise portal – a window into a particular company, organization, or government entity; and the industry portal – a cross-enterprise site that usually facilitates business-to-business commerce and appeals to a vertical segment of the population (e.g., the pharmaceutical industry). Figure 3-5 illustrates the concept of the mobile portal and Figure 3-6 shows a possible architecture for such a portal.

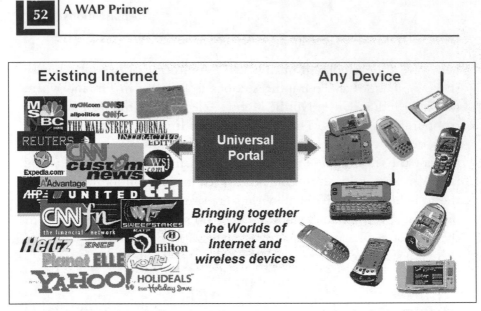

FIGURE 3-5. The Mobile Portal Concept

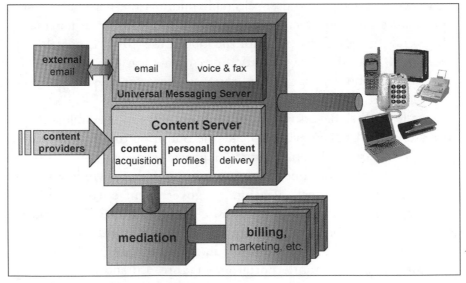

FIGURE 3-6. A Mobile Portal Architecture

Note the messaging server providing unified messaging with multiple channels and the content server that provides content acquisition, personalization, and delivery. M-commerce facilities are enabled by marketing (e.g., targeted marketing and cross-selling), billing engines, and mediation.

This architecture is implemented by a product from Unisys called the Active Content Gateway. Other mobile portal products include Alcatel's Nextenso and Oracle's Portal-to-Go.

THE REST OF THE ICEBERG

Unfortunately it is far from feasible to cover all possible WAP applications, and, in fact, this is what makes WAP development so interesting. It has been said that we have the networks, devices, servers, and users – now all we need is the ideas – and the creativity to build the applications that take advantage of this technology! An understanding of the technology and some areas to which it can be applied are a good start; with a spark of imagination and a little luck, you may be the next mobile dot-com millionaire! The remaining chapters provide design and development guidance and will give you much of what you will need.

Tools

It is possible to develop dynamic WAP applications with only a text editor and a Common Gateway Interface (CGI) scripting language such as Perl or PHP. However, you can make your job easier (and produce better applications) if you add a few WAP tools to your development toolbox. Because WAP applications are also Web applications, Web tools play a major role in building WAP applications. General-purpose Web tools that you can use include the following:

- ▣ Web servers (configured for the WAP MIME types)

- ▣ Servlet engines (e.g., Tomcat or JRun)

- ▣ XML parsers and XSL processors (for parsing and generating WML)

- ▣ Customizable editors (e.g., EMACS, vim, and IBM's XEENA XML editor)

- ▣ Languages including Perl, Java, PHP, and C++

- ▣ Application servers that support XML and enable integration with legacy data

- ▣ Integrated development environments (IDEs) that support Java Server Pages, Active Server Pages, Enterprise Java Beans, servlets, or other server-side technologies

WAP development is different from Web development with new languages, a wider range of target client devices, and the presence of a

WAP gateway between your application and the client. These factors mean that it is often better to use special-purpose tools for:

- Editing

- WML display and WMLScript execution

- WAP device emulation

- Syntax checking and script debugging

- Generation from languages (e.g., libraries or APIs)

- WAP content serving (e.g., WAP-enabled application servers)

- WAP gateway functionality (e.g., encoding/decoding)

- Image creation

- Testing

We look at the tools that support these functions and recommend a basic application development toolkit. We also briefly examine a tantalizing alternative to WAP development – HTML to WML translators.

Many of the tools discussed require developer registration to download. Vendors often provide a developer-specific Web site that may include useful documentation and even discussion groups for their products. The WAP world is rapidly evolving, so any discussion of tools that provides specific recommendations will soon become outdated. However, we provide URLs for the tools we discuss, and a good search engine (such as Google – *www.google.com*) will help you find a tool should its URL change.

EDITORS

Although Wireless Markup Language shares many tags with HTML, it is different enough to need its own editors – HTML development tools will not work with WML unless they have been extended to do so (see the sidebar "An Extended Web Site Development Tool").

An Extended Web Site Development Tool

One HTML Web site creation tool that has made the transition to WAP is Macromedia's Dreamweaver (*www.macromedia.com*). Nokia WML Studio for Macromedia Dreamweaver is an extension to Dreamweaver, which allows you to create WML content. The extension runs within the Dreamweaver HTML editing environment and claims to provide a WYSIWYG ("what you see is what you get") environment including a WML parser with visual error feedback and a preview function. ▣

General text editors including EMACS (*www.gnu.org/software/emacs*) and vim (*www.vim.org*) have plug-ins that provide WML syntax highlighting. Besides these, WML editing options include:

▣ WML text editors

▣ Prompt-driven editors

WML text editors provide a level of sophistication above general text editors including WML-aware display and syntax checking. WAPtor is one such product, which provides tag and attribute-aware editing and a browser preview window (*www.waptop.net*). It uses color to distinguish among elements, attributes, text, and comments, and it also highlights syntax errors. Figure 4-1 shows a WAPtor editing screen and associated WML tag help window. Note that not all versions of this editor include the highly useful WML tag help that is found in version 2.1, pictured. WMLEdit, available at *www.hoiley.com*, provides similar capabilities to WAPtor.

The WAP software development kits (SDKs) from Motorola, Ericsson, and Nokia include WML and WMLScript editors. We discuss SDKs in more detail later.

Prompt-driven services for WAP site creation are available online from DotWAP (*www.inetis.si/english*) and EasyWAP (*www.wappy.to*). These Web services allow you to build simple static WAP decks without WML knowledge and are usually associated with free (advertising-supported) WAP hosting. To build a site, you fill in a series of prompts for card titles

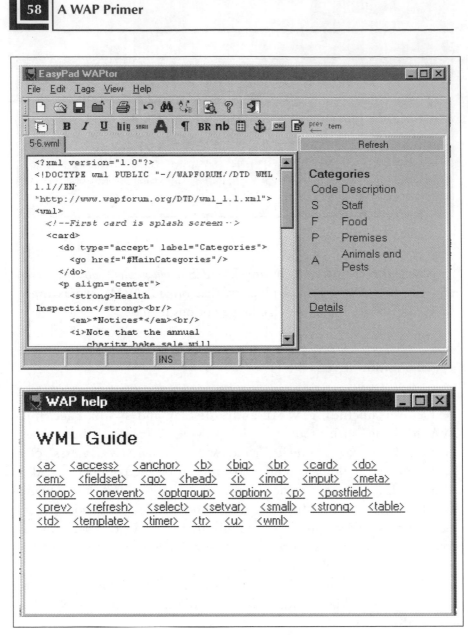

FIGURE 4-1. WAPtor WML Editor Version 2.1 Showing WML Tag Help

and content. External links and images are usually supported, but input and scripting are not. Obviously, these editors are not a serious option for application development but may be used to create a quick WAP presence.

WAP Browsers and Device Emulators

One of the most important items in your toolbox is a WAP browser or emulator. During development it may not be possible to use the actual target device (e.g., a cellular handset) or to access a wireless carrier. However, a variety of alternatives are available including online (Web-based) browsers and Windows applications. Browsers are also available for palmtops and other desktop platforms.

Web-based browsers include the Wapalizer browser from Gelon (*www.gelon.net*), which converts WML to HTML on the fly for display in a Web browser. This browser emulates a number of phones including Nokia 7110 and Ericsson R320. Wapsilon (*www.wapsilon.com*) provides similar functionality and also includes a PDA-style browser. One nice feature of these browsers is the ability to view source code in a separate window – useful for obtaining real-world sample code to improve your own WML. The Multi Media Mode (M3) Gate browser available from *www.numeric.ru/m3gate/* is produced by a company with the catchy name of Numeric Algorithm Laboratories. This product integrates with your Web browser to provide automatic display of WML and execution of WMLScript when a WAP site is specified. It can also run as a stand-alone Windows program and provides a skin that emulates a generic palmtop client (pictured in Fig. 4-2). This tool must be downloaded and installed prior to execution.

The SmartPhone emulator is another Web-based tool that uses a small Java applet to provide WML display and WMLScript execution. The Web edition relies on a server-side application (Java Servlet), which is hosted by the makers of the emulator (Yospace – *www.yospace.com*). This servlet provides a gateway-like functionality to encode the WAP content for efficient processing by the applet. A stand-alone developer edition is available for Windows, UNIX, and Mac-OS. A JavaBean version is also available that provides a complete WAP environment in a component. These products have a license fee.

The Web browser Opera (*www.opera.no*) supports both HTML and WML browsing, and Netscape and Microsoft browsers are likely to follow suit. WinWap (*www.winwap.org*) is another stand-alone Win-

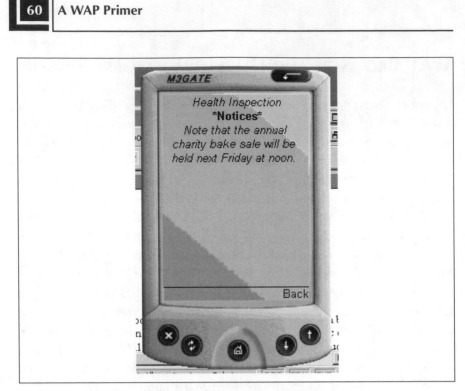

FIGURE 4-2. M3Gate Windows-Based WAP Emulator

dows browser that (in its registered version) supports connections to WAP gateways as well as direct HTTP and file access to WML decks.

Palm OS browsers are available from a number of vendors including AU-Systems (download from *www.wapguide.com/wapguide*) and MobileID (*www.mobileid.com*). These particular browsers are based on Ericsson's WAP browser, which is also embedded in Ericsson's WAP phones and hybrid devices. The MobileID browser is associated with a portal and e-mail service that allows you to receive and send e-mails from your Palm Pilot or compatible handheld device. The KBrowser from 4th Pass (*www.4thpass.com*) is a cross-platform browser available for various models of Palm, Pocket PC, and other devices. It is based on the Java 2 Micro-Edition Kilobyte Virtual Machine (KVM). WAP browsers are also available for Psion's Symbian EPOC hand-helds (the revo and 5 ms). Refer to *www.psion.com* for more information.

The majority of microbrowsers that power WAP mobile phones are provided by Phone.com, Nokia, Motorola, and Ericsson. Emulators for these are usually included with the SDKs provided by the vendor. Phone.com (*updev.phone.com*) provides an emulator for the many phones that use its browser, and "skins" are available to mimic the appearance and behavior of these devices. Nokia's SDK (*www.forum.nokia.com*) includes an emulator for their 7110 phone as well as a generic Blueprint phone. Motorola's emulator (*www.motorola.com*) emulates a Motorola Timeport, and Ericsson (*www.ericsson.com/developerszone*) provides emulators for their R320 and R380 handsets. Design guides that explain device capabilities and provide design suggestions are available at these vendors' Web sites. Microsoft's Mobile Explorer microbrowser has been adopted by Sony and Benefon. An emulator for this dual mode (HTML and WML) browser is available at the Benefon Web site (*www.benefon.com*). This browser will also be available on Pocket PC-based hand-helds.

Be warned that simulators do not perfectly emulate real-world devices. For example, unlike the Nokia 7110 handset that it emulates, early versions of the Nokia simulator do not display wireless bitmapped images on a separate line. Deck size limitations imposed by real devices may not be enforced by simulators, and the behavior of simulators is different depending on whether you serve content directly (via HTTP) or whether you configure the simulator to use a WAP gateway. Despite the availability of skins from some vendors, the underlying software is usually a generic version of that vendor's product and cannot be expected to mimic the device's behavior exactly. The lesson here is always try your applications on real devices before deployment.

Syntax Checkers and Debuggers

WAP gateways parse and encode the WML and WMLScript content before sending it to the WML browser. Unlike WML browsers, which are very forgiving when it comes to missing tags and mixed upper- and lowercase spellings, WAP gateways assume that the content they receive has the correct syntax. If they cannot recognize a tag, perhaps because you used uppercase text instead of lower, the gateway will probably simply give up and display a cryptic error message to the user! Therefore you must have a simple way to validate the syntax of your WML. You can use syntax-aware editors to check static (hand-made) decks, but dynamically generated WML requires another approach. Phone.com's SDK includes a WAP phone simulator supported by a console window in which WML syntax errors are displayed. Using this environment, you can load and test local files, URLs served by a local Web server, and URLs accessed via the Internet. The simulator provides functions to display content and also provides a reasonable level of debugging when WML syntax is not valid. The Phone.com SDK supports WMLScript and provides some syntax checking for this, although its support for run-time debugging is limited. Nokia's SDK provides a Java-based IDE with views for syntax errors, variables, history, and push information. Ericsson's toolkit offers similar functionality in a less integrated environment with tools that support WML syntax checking and WMLScript validation.

Online testing services are also available to validate your WML. Anywhereyougo.com offers a service that checks the content type header, validates the WML against its Document Type Definition (DTD), measures deck size, and warns you when your code uses elements that are not commonly supported. The deck to be validated must be available at an Internet-accessible URL.

LIBRARIES

Libraries for Java, PHP, Perl, Python, and other languages ease the task of dynamically generating WML. Enhydra (*www.enhydra.org*) is an open source application server that supports WML generation and includes Java packages for WML element and attribute manipulation.

Phone.com provides Perl and C functions for WML generation (see *www.phone.com/products/upsdk.html*). HTML and WML Hybrid Adapted Webserver (HawHaw) is a PHP library that provides WML, HTML, and Handheld Device Markup Language (HDML) generation from the same source code. HawHaw (*www.hawhaw.de*) determines at run-time which language is required by a browser's request and automatically generates markup in that language.

WAP-ENABLED APPLICATION SERVERS

Because WML is an XML language, vendors that support an XML channel to their server can claim to support WAP application development (e.g., BEA's WebLogic Server available from *www.bea.com*). A number of servers provide additional support for WAP including Oracle's Portal-to-Go and Enhydra (mentioned earlier).

Portal-to-Go (*www.oracle.com/products*) uses an intermediate XML markup language to define a view of specified data. Adaptors translate content from sources such as databases or HTML pages into a simple XML markup language. Java applications or XSLT processing is then used to transform these pages into a target device language such as WML. This approach is valuable in environments where disparate sources of information in various formats must be personalized and channeled to a variety of devices.

WAP GATEWAYS

WAP gateways are needed to do end-to-end application testing with real client devices. Test gateways are available from vendors including Ericsson, Nokia, and Infinite.com. Ericsson (*www.ericsson.com/developerszone*) has a freely downloadable demo gateway with limited capabilities. Nokia's developer gateway may be downloaded from the Nokia developer's forum on a trial basis (there is a cost for the registered version, available at *www.nokia.com/corporate/wap*). Infinite.com's WAPlite is a fully featured WAP gateway (*www.waplite.com*) priced for development and/or enterprise use. Both Ericsson and Phone.com (*updev.phone.com*) offer access to their development WAP gateways for registered developers. WapHQ provides a publicly available gateway accessible via dial-up in the U.K. and also via the Internet (*www.waphq.co.uk*). An extensive list of public and private WAP gateways is available in the technical area of WAP-

drive.net (*www.wapdrive.net*). For those who appreciate the free things in life, an open source WAP gateway is available from Kannel (*www.kannel.org*). At the other end of the spectrum are production gateways which are typically big-ticket items (see sidebar "Production Gateways").

WIRELESS BITMAP TOOLS

Tools to create wireless bitmaps and convert other image formats to WBMP format are available as online services, plug-ins to popular image editing programs, and as stand-alone applications.

ImageMagick (*www.imagemagick.org*) is a general image converter that runs on most platforms, with libraries for C, C++, Perl, and Java. Teraflops (*www.teraflops.com*) provides a handy online tool that converts GIF, JPEG, and BMP files to WBMP format and allows you to preview and download the results as well as an online tool based on ImageMagick libraries. Figure 4-3 shows the Teraflops converter in action. Screen *a* shows a portion of the Teraflops Web converter Web page with the name of an image about to be converted. Screen *b* shows the JPEG prior to conversion, and screen *c* shows the converted WBMP.

Production Gateways

Although not required for development, production gateways are available in two main flavors – carrier grade gateways for use by mobile networks (Cellcos) and enterprise gateways suitable for corporate applications (e.g., sales support or employee e-mail and calendar access). WAP gateways are costly and typically run on high-end hardware. Even enterprise gateways from the major vendors have large price tags, making gateway ownership a nontrivial decision. In order of worldwide installed base, Phone.com, Nokia, and Ericsson are the most popular vendors of production gateways. Materna (www.materna.com), Motorola, and CMG (*www.cmg.de* – a German-language site) also offer production gateways. Phone.com's gateway supports the largest number of underlying cellular networks, which may explain its popularity. However, it also implements the largest number of non-WAP-standard features (e.g., alerts) that require a client browser from Phone.com to work correctly (note that these features may not be enabled by all operators and should not be relied on for applications that will be generally accessible). ◧

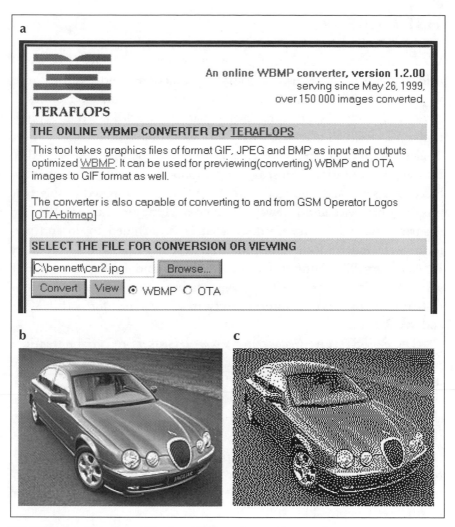

FIGURE 4-3. Teraflops Wireless Bitmap Image Conversion

RCP *(www.rcp.co.uk)* provides plug-ins for Adobe Photoshop and JASC Paint Shop Pro that support WBMP editing as well as a stand-alone WBMP converter. A stand-alone Java-based converter is available from Gingco *(www.gingco.de/wap)*. This product allows scaling and adjustment of image intensity during conversion.

TEST TOOLS

WAP emulators, development gateways, and actual handsets or hand-held computers can be used to carry out functional and usability tests with varying degrees of realism. One of the most common pieces of advice in FAQs and on mailing lists is that you should test your applications on a variety of gateways with a full range of potential target clients. That being said, an emerging class of tools are specifically designed to test WAP applications. Most of these products are extensions of Web-based regression and load testing tools and are not designed to solve the problems of device and gateway differences. However, they are useful in ensuring that your software does what it is designed to do and performs well under a load. Two products currently available are Mercury Interactive's WinRunner and LoadRunner and Empirix's e-TEST suite. Mercury Interactive (*www-heva.mercuryinteractive.com*) also offers real-time performance monitoring software and services for both I-Mode and WAP.

The e-TEST suite (*www.empirix.com*) lets users record interactions with a WAP application using Phone.com's simulator (discussed later). It monitors HTTP/HTTPS communications (with planned support for WSP and WAP gateways) and records these interactions as visual test scripts. These scripts can then be used to perform function/regression testing where scripts are played back, and any differences between the expected output and the current response are recorded. They can also be used for load testing and for monitoring of performance following deployment. For more details on this type of testing, see Chapter 11.

SOFTWARE DEVELOPMENT KITS

Software development kits (SDKs) usually combine a WAP editor, an emulator, and some means of checking and debugging WML and WMLScript. Some SDKs include APIs for dynamically generating WAP content. The major WAP gateway vendors supply toolkits free of charge to developers, and if you are developing applications for that vendor's mobile devices and gateway then this is probably all you need. Table 4-1 summarizes the capabilities of toolkits from Nokia, Phone.com, Ericsson, and Motorola. We cited URLs for these vendors earlier in the chapter.

All SDKs are available for Windows platforms and typically require a workstation class machine with 64 megabytes of RAM and more than 20 megabytes of free disk space. Documentation and sample code are available for all toolkits.

An alternative to the SDKs available from the handset vendors is the WAP Developer Toolkit from Dynamical Systems Research. This product provides a WAP browser and WML and WMLScript encoders, decoders, compilers, and interpreters. Its primary attraction is that it is

TABLE 4-1. WAP SDKs Compared

VENDOR	EDITOR	EMULATOR	SYNTAX CHECKING AND DEBUGGING	DOCUMENTATION	API
Nokia	Yes – WML, WMLScript, WBMP images, and push	Yes – supports Nokia 7110 and generic emulation	Yes – syntax checking, context display (variables and history), push message display. Excellent full-featured debug mode.	SDK Developer's Guide, WML and WMLScript References, Designer's Guide, User's Guide	No
Phone.com	No	Yes – Phone.com browser with skins for several models including Japanese phones	Yes – console window provides WML syntax errors but not as advanced as Nokia's	Getting Started guides, WML and WMLScript references, SDK Developer's Guide, WMLScript Developer's Guide	Yes – Perl and C functions
Ericsson	Yes – integrated with emulator; WML and WMLScript help	Yes – includes Device Designer, which is used to create device skins and set user interface behavior	Yes – WML and WMLScript syntax checkers. Useful debug information.	User's Guide, Installation Guide, and Design Guidelines	Yes – Perl functions
Motorola	Yes – WML and WMLScript editing as well as VoxML	Yes – integrated with Editor. Emulates Motorola Timeport. Also supports VoxML for voice interfaces	Yes – a transcript window displays source, communications, and debug messages	Users Guide, Developers Guide, WML Language Guide	No

written completely in Java, making it a truly cross-platform option, whereas most toolkits are designed for a Windows platform. This toolkit runs on various flavors of Unix and Macintosh platforms and is available from wap.net (*www.wap.net*).

HTML TO WML CONVERTERS

HTML to WML converters offer the tempting promise of a painless migration to the wireless Web. These tools convert existing HTML pages or entire sites to WML. This is not a trivial task because WML is very limited when compared to HTML, and the microbrowsers are a tiny fraction of the size of desktop Web browsers. Another often over-looked factor is that the content of a typical Web site may not be ide-ally suited to mobile access; a great deal of information is displayed on one Web page and that information may not be relevant to a specific user. Despite these obstacles, a number of vendors offer tools or ser-vices to convert Web content to WML. The following types of conver-sion may be supported:

- Markup language conversion – converts HTML tags to WML equivalent (e.g., frames and image maps are translated to links)

- Filtering – removes tags that are unsupported

- Image conversion (JPEG or GIF to WBMP)

- Content-specific filtering (uses templates to translate selected portions of the source document)

Spyglass/OpenTV Prism (*www.opentv.com*) offers a CORBA-based server that provides dynamic translation of HTML to WML transla-tions. This middleware integrates with Web servers or WAP gate-ways. This is not an inexpensive solution: Integration requires external consulting services from Spyglass/OpenTV.

Deck-It by Pyweb (*www.pyweb.com*) provides a service and tools that support transcoding of HTML to WML. This technique takes HTML content, which may contain embedded tags, and dynamically creates WML content. The embedded tags indicate to the transcoder how the HTML content should be modified for the mobile Web. The transcoding server runs at Pyweb's site, and WAP clients access a URL at this site. The server then retrieves the associated HTML page and translates it to WML before returning it to the client.

Phone.com includes a simple converter with its WAP gateway that performs text, link, input form, and title extraction and splits the content into appropriately sized decks. Other converters are available from Poqit.com (*www.poqit.com*) and Oracle (Portal-to-Go, discussed earlier, under application servers).

RECOMMENDED TOOLKIT

A minimal development toolkit includes these elements:

- At least one software development kit (e.g., Nokia's SDK), although for international development, two or possible three toolkits are mandatory. These provide emulators and a means to prototype and test WAP services. To get a feel for how your applications will look on widely different handsets, develop and test on both the Phone.com and Nokia SDKs. If you are developing for palmtop clients, use an emulator such as Wap-silon or, better still, an actual device.

- A WML/WMLScript editor if this is not provided with your SDK (e.g., if you are using Phone.com's SDK). An editor is useful when learning WML and for prototyping user interfaces.

- Emulators for as many of the phones you intend to support as possible. The emulators provided with the SDKs are probably your best starting point.

- A developer gateway is required if you are deploying an application that uses a dedicated gateway (e.g., a mobile financial service)

You may also wish to acquire a library for the language that you intend to develop in, although this is not mandatory because WML can be created using standard text output statements. As we discuss in later chapters, XML can play an important role in a multichannel interface. XML tools, including Java parsers and style sheet processors, are available from Apache (*xml.apache.org*) and Sun (*www.sun.com/xml*), among others.

That concludes our look at the tools of the trade. You might download and install at least one of the SDKs mentioned here before you move on to the next section. The Phone.com SDK is a simple starting point because it does not require preinstalled Java. The Nokia SDK has superior editing and debugging facilities and may be a better all-round choice for development (especially in Europe). Having an SDK available will let you try your hand at WML and WMLScript as we cover these topics in the next few chapters.

PART 2

The WAP Development Standards

5 | Wireless Markup Language

O nly a subset of the WAP standards is applicable to general application development. In this part (Chapters 5–8) we look at three areas of WAP that the developer needs to know in order to build practical applications. Wireless Markup Language (WML) is a display markup language that provides the thin client user interface to WAP. WMLScript is a scripting language that extends WML so you can validate user input, display dialogue boxes, and access local resources. The WAP push standards support a different application paradigm where the server initiates an application with a client. Push applications have great potential, and although device and gateway support for push is currently very limited, this will soon be a high demand area.

WML is the HTML of the wireless Web. Like HTML, WML is a display markup language that supports layout, input, and navigation as well as inclusion of images and scripting. Unlike HTML, it addresses the limitations of wireless devices. In this chapter we consider how WML solves some of these device limitations. We then walk through a tutorial, illustrating the basic language concepts through a series of related examples. The version of WML covered here is 1.3. Most devices support WML 1.1 so be sure to note functionality that has been added since WML 1.1 was released. (See the sidebar "WML Versions." Chapter 6 provides further information on WML, and a WML tag reference is provided as Appendix A.)

WML Versions

Functionality that has been added since WML 1.1 is as follows:

- The preformatted text block `<pre>`, which was added in WML 1.2, has a revised set of contained elements in WML 1.3.
- An encoding type attribute was added to the `<go>` element in WML 1.2.
- The access key shortcut (`accesskey`) attribute found in input fields and links was added in WML 1.2.
- A cache-controlling attribute and entity (`cache-control`) was added to the `<go>` element in WML 1.3.
- Mixed case and abbreviated variable escaping modifiers are deprecated. Only "`noesc`," "`escape`," and "`unesc`" are valid for escaping variables.

We explain these elements and attributes in this chapter and in Chapter 6.

SIZE MATTERS

WML addresses many of the limitations of wireless devices. Specifically, it helps cope with small displays, lightweight processors, and slow connections.

Limited display size means that navigation links may not be visible because the physical display window may be significantly smaller than the total page. Small displays also dictate a special approach to user interface design: The typical computer monitor is more than one hundred times the size (in pixels) of the average WAP phone display (e.g., the Nokia 7110 – Europe's benchmark first-generation WAP phone has just over 4000 pixels versus a standard 800 × 600 SVGA display of 480,000 pixels).

Processors devoted to display and script processing in mobile devices are usually at least an order of magnitude slower than desktop processors, due in part to battery constraints. This means that heavyweight number crunching is not practical, and minimizing client-side processing is advisable.

In the current generation of digital networks, multisecond delays and sub-10 kilobit/second transfer rates are the norm. Download delays play a major role in user satisfaction, and an interface that is slow will not win many friends.

So, what does WML provide that deals with these problems? WML gives us:

- ▣ An explicit navigation model – ensuring that devices will be able to present navigation options in an appropriate way.

- ▣ A deck and card metaphor for user interface layout – providing both a sensible way to divide an interface into manageable sections and a more efficient way to retrieve content over a slow connection.

- ▣ In-client validation of field input – input masks reduce the need for custom validation routines and their associated processing load.

- ▣ Navigation and selection mechanisms – providing "hints" to the device, allowing the device to fit the intent of the page developer to the capabilities (e.g., soft keys) of a device.

A LITTLE HISTORY AND A LOT OF ACRONYMS

WML has two parents: Handheld Device Markup Language (or HDML) and XML. HDML was created by a U.S. company called Unwired Planet (now Phone.com) and was based on HTML. Because HDML was developed prior to the popularity of XML, it is not an XML-based language. When WML was created, HDML formed the basis of this new language, but it was modified to conform to the XML specifications.

Because WML is an XML language, an understanding of XML concepts and terminology will make the rest of this chapter easier to swallow (see the sidebar "An XML Primer"). In general, WML syntax is more rigid than that of HTML. At the start of any WML document, you must provide a prologue that identifies both the version of XML on which your deck is based and the name and location of the corresponding WML document type definition (DTD). When creating tags, attributes, or variables, make sure their case is correct (typically all tags and attributes are lowercase), and when displaying text, place it inside a `<p>` (paragraph) block. Attribute values must be quoted and certain characters must be escaped because they have a special meaning in WML. We discuss these constraints in more detail later in this chapter.

An XML Primer

Extensible Markup Language, or XML, specifies standards for defining custom markup languages. It was created specifically for Internet use and designed to be readable by humans, yet easily processed by programs. XML has become a very popular way to define structured data. For example, there are languages defined using XML that facilitate communication of financial data, mathematical proofs, and even musical scores! XML can also be used to create display markup languages; a good example of this is XHTML, which is a revision of HTML to conform to XML standards. WML is also an example of an effective use of XML to create a simple and concise display markup language.

XML content is contained within XML documents (a WML deck is an example of an XML document). In addition to marked-up content, an XML document can contain a header that references a document type definition (DTD). The DTD is where the syntax of an XML document is defined and contains a complete list of tags that are valid within the specified language. An example of a document type definition is the WML DTD, available at the WAP Forum site (as an appendix to the Wireless Markup Language specification). You may also hear the term *schema* used to describe a method for defining XML syntax. Schemas are an alternative to DTDs, providing a richer and more flexible way to define XML syntax. The WML language is currently defined using a DTD, so this is what we focus on. We examine DTDs in more detail as soon as we look at an XML document.

Consider the following XML document:

```
1. <?xml version="1.0"?>
2. <!DOCTYPE AccountStatement
     "http://www.bigbank.com/DTD/acctstmt_1.0.xml">
3. <!--Customer Account Statement-->
4. <AccountStatement>
5.  <Account type="Savings">
6.    <LastName>Bennett</LastName>
7.    <FirstName>Chris</FirstName>
8.    <Identifier>BEN1453</Identifier>
9.  </Account>
10. <Transactions>
11.   <Withdrawal>
12.     <Date>June 23, 2000</Date>
13.     <Amount>200.00</Amount>
```

```
14.     <Location>Bayers Road</Location>
15.   </Withdrawal>
16.   <Deposit>
17.     <Date>June 30, 2000</Date>
18.     <Amount>1000.00</Amount>
19.     <Source>Unisys</Source>
20.   </Deposit>
21.  </Transactions>
22. </AccountStatement>
```

Line 1 specifies the version of the XML standard to which this XML document conforms. Line 2 references an external document type definition located at a (hypothetical) URL. Line 3 is a comment; all comments in XML begin with "<!--" and end with "-->." Line 4 begins an account statement that contains account information (lines 5 to 9) and two transactions – a withdrawal and a deposit – beginning at line 10 and running to line 21. The account contains last name, first name, and identifier tags, each of which contains text data. Note that case is important, and a tag named Deposit is not considered the same as deposit in XML. Also, note that all tags have matching close tags (e.g., <Deposit> is closed by </Deposit>).

The document type definition for this XML is:

```
<!--DTD for customer account statements -->
<!ENTITY % Transaction     "Withdrawal|Deposit">
<!ENTITY % CoreTransInfo  "Date, Amount">
<!ELEMENT AccountStatement (Account, Transactions)>
<!ELEMENT Account (LastName, FirstName, Identifier)>
<!ATTLIST Account
             type  CDATA #REQUIRED>
<!ELEMENT Transactions (%Transaction;)*)>
<!ELEMENT Withdrawal    (%CoreTransInfo;, Location)>
<!ELEMENT Deposit       (%CoreTransInfo;, Source)>
<!ELEMENT LastName       (#PCDATA)>
<!ELEMENT FirstName      (#PCDATA)>
<!ELEMENT Identifier     (#PCDATA)>
<!ELEMENT Date           (#PCDATA)>
<!ELEMENT Amount         (#PCDATA)>
<!ELEMENT Location       (#PCDATA)>
<!ELEMENT Source         (#PCDATA)>
```

In this DTD, three types of things are used to define the correct syntax for account statement documents: entities, elements, and attributes. Entities, such as the Transaction entity, provide a form of macro substitution, allowing logical groupings of things such as elements and attributes to be defined once and referenced throughout the DTD. In this case, a transaction may be either a Deposit or a Withdrawal. Another entity, CoreTransInfo, defines core transaction elements (Date and Amount) that are contained in both deposits and withdrawals. If we were to define a new transaction type such as Transfer, this would also make use of `CoreTransInfo`, adding its own unique elements such as `From` and `To`.

Elements define the allowable tags in an XML document and may themselves include other elements. An account statement element contains one `Account` and one `Transactions` element and an account must contain a `LastName`, a `FirstName`, and an `Identifier` element. An account must also have a 'type,' which is identified as a required attribute within the `ATTLIST` (attribute list) line. Note that in an XML document, attributes values are always quoted (e.g., line 5 in the Account Statement document).

Transactions can contain zero or more `Transaction` entities (the asterisk specifies the zero or more cardinality, and a plus (+) would have indicated one or more). Note that prior to evaluation, an XML processor would replace the `Transaction` entity with the `(Withdrawal|Deposit)` element clause. Each `Deposit` and `Withdrawal` element contains the core transaction elements (expanded to `Date`, `Amount`) as well as their own unique elements. Each `Withdrawal` contains a nested element named `Location`, and each `Deposit` contains a nested `Source` element.

`PCDATA` refers to parsed character data. This is simply textual information that may contain embedded elements. `FirstName`, `Date`, and `Source` are all examples of elements that contain only textual information. `PCDATA` is used only within elements, whereas `CDATA` is used within attributes to designate a text type. Note that extra white space within XML documents is not treated as significant and is usually ignored during processing.

There are a number of reserved characters in XML. These include the tag delimiters (< and >) as well as the ampersand (&), which is used when referring to entities, and the quotation mark and apostrophe, which can be used when specifying string literals such as attribute values. To use these literals in text (in both elements and attributes), replace them with their equivalent character entities as follows:

- `quotation mark` `&quot;`
- `ampersand` `&amp;`
- `apostrophe` `&apos;`
- `tag delimter <` `&lt;`
- `tag delimeter >` `&gt;`

For more information on XML, refer to the W3C web site (*www.w3.org*) or the XML industry portal (*www.oasis-open.org*).

DIVIDE AND CONQUER

WML is easier to understand if we divide it into some logically related pieces:

◨ Deck and card architecture

◨ Layout and presentation (text and images)

◨ Navigation

◨ Input

We introduce these in order and build an example of a WML deck for a hypothetical health inspection department that illustrates these items. The complete WML deck (in its final form) is available in Appendix B.

We cover these more advanced topics in Chapter 6:

◨ Deck declarations (templates, access control, and metadata)

◨ Variables, parameters, and context

◨ Events, tasks, and history

◨ Grouping

A DECK OF CARDS

In the HTML world, a Web page is the common unit of organization, and dividing a page into subsections can be done implicitly through intrapage links. WML takes an explicit approach to this, specifying the deck as the fundamental unit of organization. A deck is defined by `<wml></wml>` tags and contains one or more cards (`<card></card>`). When a client requests a WML deck, the complete deck is returned. The `wml` element can contain `class`, `id`, and `xml:lang` attributes; these attributes are found in many elements and are discussed in the sidebar "Common WML Attributes."

In addition to cards, a deck can also contain a head and a template. The head (`<head></head>`) provides a holder for access control and meta tags (discussed in Chapter 6). The template provides a place where deckwide navigation instructions or event handlers can be specified. Again, we defer a discussion of this until we have

```
<?xml version="1.0"?>
<!DOCTYPE wml PUBLIC "-//WAPFORUM//DTD WML 1.1//EN"
  "http://www.wapforum.org/DTD/wml_1_1.dtd">
<wml>
  <card>
     <p>Health Inspection</p>
  </card>
</wml>
```

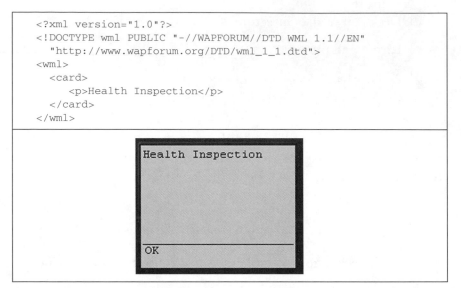

FIGURE 5-1. A Simple WML Deck

introduced navigation and events. Figure 5-1 shows a very simple
WML deck that displays a single line of text inside a paragraph
(<p></p>) and does not offer any navigation or input options. Note
the prologue line that references the WML 1.1 DTD available at a
WAP Forum URL. Although we cover WML version 1.3 in this
book, the DTD used in the examples is version 1.1. This is the version of WML most widely supported by commercial WML browsers.

Displaying Your WML

The examples in this chapter (and your own decks) can be displayed most
easily using a simulator such as the UP Simulator from Phone.com or the
Nokia simulators provided with the Nokia WAP Toolkit. We discussed these
products in more detail in Chapter 4, but for a quick start, you can download
the Phone.com SDK from *updev.phone.com* (registration for the developer
program is required). The UP SDK is available for Windows and the download
is (currently) about 4 or 5 megabytes. Once this is installed, you can execute
the simulator, which will look something like the following (the appearance

can also be customized using skins – information is available on the Phone.com site):

To load a local file, type in the file's URL using the following format:
`"file://C:/dir1/dir2/file.wml"`
where `"C"` is the drive letter, `"dir1/dir2"` is your directory path, and `"file.wml"` is the name of your WML deck. If your file has syntax errors, these will be displayed in a separate MS-DOS window; otherwise your deck should be displayed and you will be able to use the keyboard or the mouse to select options and work the keypad.

When using the UP simulator without an Internet connection, you should be careful to specify a WML version that is supported locally (e.g., WML 1.1). Specifying a later version of WML (e.g. 1.3) may cause problems when the simulator attempts to retrieve the associated DTD using its URL.

A lighter alternative to the UP simulator is the M3Gate emulator (for Windows) described in Chapter 4. This product integrates with your Web browser (with the benefit of being able to select WML links from HTML pages) and can also run as a stand-alone application. It emulates the behavior of a Nokia 7110 handset. ■

Refer to *www.wapforum.org/DTD/* for a list of official WAP Forum DTDs. Further WML sample code in this chapter will leave out these prologue lines for the sake of brevity, but they are required in a valid WML deck. The sidebar "Displaying Your WML" explains how to use a simulator to check out examples from this book or your own code.

In addition to the common attributes (explained in the sidebar "Common WML Attributes"), the `card` element may contain a `newcontext` attribute that is set to true when you want to clear out the current context (for more on contexts, see Chapter 6). The `ordered` attribute is used to provide flexibility to the WML browser. If this attribute is set to false, the browser has the option of rearranging items on the card in order to suit the device's display capabilities.

LAYOUT AND PRESENTATION

WML gives us a number of simple ways to lay out a card. The fundamental unit of layout is the paragraph. The `<p></p>` tags define a standard paragraph, and attributes allow us to define word wrap (`mode="wrap"` or `"nowrap"`) as well as paragraph alignment (`align="left,"` `"right,"` or `"center"`). Default text alignment is to the left, and default word wrap is that of the previous paragraph. Just about anything goes within a paragraph including text, line breaks, text emphasis (e.g., `bold`, `italic`), tables, images, and various navigation tags.

WML version 1.2 introduced a variation on the paragraph – the preformatted paragraph (defined by `<pre></pre>`). This is a limited block of text (images are not allowed) that permits text emphasis, line breaks, links, and input. The primary difference between `<pre>` and `<p>` is that a WML 1.2-compliant user agent will try to leave the white space and hard-coded layout as close as possible to the original (e.g., by disabling automatic word wrap and using a fixed pitch font). Because preformatted paragraphs are not supported in WML 1.1, be careful that your target devices support them.

Common WML Attributes

Because attributes are useful when describing elements, it should come as no surprise that there are some attributes that appear with most WML elements. The `id` attribute is used to give a unique identifier to any element. This type of attribute is also found in other markup languages including HTML and various XML-based languages. Because `id` provides a unique identifier by which to reference an element, no element can have more than one such attribute. The value of this attribute must start with a letter or "_" and contain only letters, numbers, ".", "-", and "_". The primary use of `id` in WML is as a card identifier that can be used for navigation within a deck. However it is possible that further use will be made of this for styling and manipulation of markup such as that provided by Dynamic HTML and the W3C Document Object Model in the HTML world. The `id` attribute is available in all WML elements.

The `class` attribute can be used to associate an element with a class or classes to which this element belongs (e.g., `<p class="warnings">` `...</p>` could specify that this paragraph belongs to a class of markup known as "warnings"). The value of the `class` attribute may be a single class name or a space-separated list of classes. Classes are useful when performing server-side manipulation of WML (e.g., in a system where multiple markup languages are generated, classes could assist in element transformation). Classes could also be used in client-side styling as they are in HTML (using cascading style sheets, or CSS). Despite a potential here for flexible device-tailored styling, the WAP specifications do not currently specify support for client-side style sheets such as CSS. Like `id`, the `class` attribute is available in any WML element.

The `xml:lang` attribute allows you to identify a natural or formal language in which text has been written. This language is often identified by a code such as the two-letter International codes specified in ISO 639 (see *www.w3.org/WAI/ER/IG/ert/iso639.htm*) or the codes assigned by the IANA – the Internet Assigned Numbers Authority (you can find more information on IANA in Chapter 7). For example, `<wml xml:lang="de">...` `</wml>` defines a deck within which all content and attributes should be in German. The `xml:lang` attribute is found in all WML elements which can contain text.

Although not found with all elements, the `title` attribute is commonly used to provide a short name that can be used when displaying the element. It is generally used in cards because WML browsers often render the card title as a physical heading, although you should not rely on this being displayed (e.g., the Nokia 7110 does not render card titles). ◧

Text may be any character data with the exception of XML-reserved characters such as angle brackets and ampersands (refer to the sidebar "An XML Primer" for a complete list of reserved characters in XML). In addition, because WML makes use of the dollar sign ($) this must be escaped with a second dollar sign ($$) in order for it to appear in text. The other two character oddities are the nonbreaking space and soft hyphen (and ­). The raw character equivalent of these (e.g., A0 hex or 160 decimal for a nonbreaking space and AD hex or 173 decimal for a soft hyphen) can cause problems with some gateways including Nokia's. We look at the nonbreaking spaces and soft hyphens in Chapter 6 when we discuss WML character entities.

PLACING THE RIGHT EMPHASIS

Text can be spiced up using emphasis tags and line breaks. Line breaks are inserted in text using the <br/> tag. Note that this is an empty element (see the sidebar "Empty Elements") and unlike HTML, WML requires you to explicitly terminate the br with a forward slash.

Emphasis tags allow you to change the appearance of text (note that there is no explicit support for fonts). The options are defined in Table 5-1.

TABLE 5-1. Text Emphasis Options

TAG	DESCRIPTION
<em>	Emphasis
<strong>	Strong emphasis
<b>	Bold font
<i>	Italic font
<u>	Underline
<big>	Large font
<small>	Small font

The WML specification recommends the use of `<strong>` and `<em>` elements because these are likely to be supported on most devices (a user agent may treat `<b>`, and `<big>` as if they were `<strong>` and, similarly, may treat `<i>` and `<u>` in the same way as `<small>`). This makes it unwise to rely too heavily on bold, italic, and underline tags within your applications.

Let's take a look at an extension of our first deck to add some text, paragraph alignment, line feeds, and emphasis. Note that the XML prologue has been left off for brevity:

```
<wml>
  <card>
     <p align="center">
       <strong>Health Inspection</strong><br/>
       <em>*Notices*</em><br/>
       <i>Note that the annual
          charity bake sale will
          be held next Friday at
          noon.</i>
     </p>
  </card>
</wml>
```

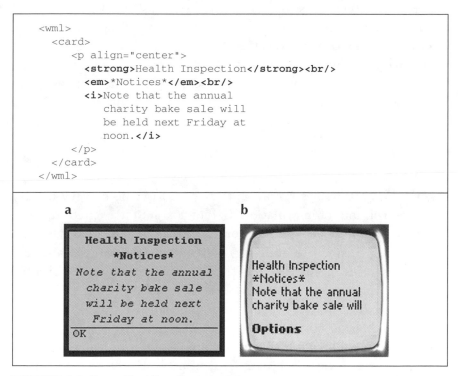

FIGURE 5-2. Some Text Emphasis and Layout

Empty Elements

An empty element is one that contains no text or nested elements. Empty elements are specified by a single tag of the form `<tagName [attributes]/>`. Note the trailing slash and the optional attributes (empty elements can contain attributes). Empty elements are common in XML languages, and WML contains a number of these including `<br/>`, `<img/>`, and `<input/>`. ▣

Note that the Phone.com UP Simulator 4.0 pictured in Figure 5-2a supports italic emphasis, but does not distinguish between `<em>` and `<strong>`. Depending on the version of browser and capabilities of the device, handsets that use the UP Browser from Phone.com may not show text with different emphasis. Unlike the Phone.com user agent, the Nokia 7110 simulator (pictured in screen *b*) does not support paragraph centering or emphasis tags. This Nokia simulator is included with Nokia's WAP Toolkit version 2.0.

TABLES

As with HTML, tables (`<table></table>`) can be used to display rows and columns of information. Before you get too excited, remember that mobile screens range from less than 1 percent of the area of a desktop display to about 25 percent for the larger handheld computers. This means that realistically your tables will be limited to two or three columns on most devices (WAP phones that allow only 12 to 20 characters in one row can only comfortably display a name and value on each line). Of course, it is possible to send these devices wider tables, but the way these are dealt with will depend on the device. The user will probably be forced to scroll to see the larger tables or the device will wrap the text, resulting in scrambled formatting. Also be aware that older devices may not support tables, and those that do may display them in unexpected ways (e.g., one table cell per card or all cells lined up above each other!).

Tables also have limits that are not encountered in HTML. For example, it is not legal to nest tables, and each table must explicitly define its size in columns. The latter is done using the `columns` attribute (e.g., `columns="2"`) where the number of columns *must* be greater than zero. Other attributes of tables include `align` and `title`. The `title` attribute (e.g., `title="My Table"`) may be used by the user agent to label the table. The `align` attribute determines how each column's text or images are aligned. This is done using a single character for each column. For example, a three-column table that required left alignment for column 1, center for column 2, and right for column 3 would have an align tag: `align="LCR"` where the first character `L` (short for left align) applies to column 1, the second character `C` (center align) applies to column 2, and the third character `R` (right align) applies to the third column. `D` is used when you want the default encoding (which the WML specification does not define, leaving this to the user agent manufacturer).

As in HTML, table rows and columns are specified using `<tr>` and `<td>`. A table must contain at least one row, and a row at least one column. Columns can contain text, text emphasis, line breaks, images, and links. Figure 5-3 displays a card with a simple two-column table that lists the various categories of health hazards a health inspector might encounter and provides a code for each.

Note that in Figure 5-3a, the description on the last table row is not completely displayed. We specified that the paragraph within which the table is placed should not do any word wrapping. The description of "Animals and Pests" is too long to be displayed, so this user agent uses a banner-like approach, alternating display of the first half of this row with that of the second half. This approach is specific to Phone.com browsers, and different vendors may use other methods.

Note also the `columns` table attribute. If this is left out, the WML deck will not parse and the user agent will display a (probably cryptic) error message. Screen *b* shows the same WML deck on a Nokia 7110 simulator. This should serve as a warning to use tables sparingly because the Nokia 7110 does not recognize the table rows and columns and simply places cell contents one after the other, each on their own line.

```
<wml>
  <card>
    <p mode="nowrap">
      <strong>Categories</strong>
      <table columns="2">
        <tr><td>Code</td><td>Description</td></tr>
        <tr><td>S</td><td>Staff</td></tr>
        <tr><td>F</td><td>Food</td></tr>
        <tr><td>P</td><td>Premises</td></tr>
        <tr><td>A</td><td>Animals and Pests</td></tr>
      </table>
    </p>
  </card>
</wml>
```

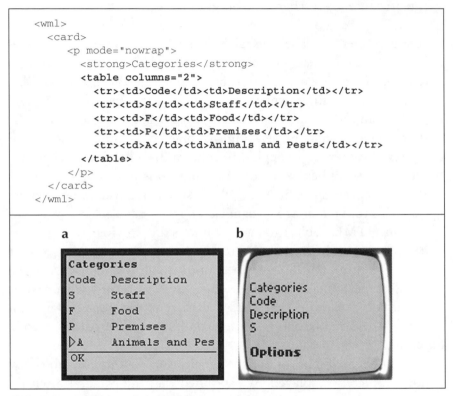

FIGURE 5-3. A Two-Column Table

IMAGES

The last area of layout and presentation we examine is images. WAP does not yet support the JPEGs and GIFs that are common in the Web world. Limited device displays and processing, coupled with low bandwidth currently makes it too expensive to send and render these types of images. Instead, bitmapped images called Wireless Bitmaps

(WBMP) provide basic monochrome image display. Online, stand-alone, and plug-in converters are freely available to convert BMPs, JPEGs, and GIFs into wireless bitmaps. These are discussed in more detail in Chapter 4.

Images are inserted into paragraphs, table columns, or links using the <img> tag. Like the line break tag, image is an empty tag and all of its values are specified as attributes. Attributes specify where the image is located, what text to display if images are not supported, and various layout options. There are two possible sources for images – a server URL and a local client-side URL. The server-side URL is specified in the form src="my_image.wbmp" and is a required attribute. The client-side URL is specified using the localsrc attribute, which references a vendor-specific well-known image name (e.g., local-src="paperclip" for a phone.com device). If you specify this attribute (and it is available on the mobile device), it will override the src attribute. An alternate attribute (e.g., alt="MyImage") must be provided to support both retrieval errors and user agents that cannot display images. This ensures that something can be displayed as a placeholder for the missing image.

Image layout options include image physical size and surrounding white space (relative to the display size) as well as alignment relative to where the image is inserted in the card (images can appear above, in the middle of, or below this insertion point). Size is defined by height and width attributes in terms of percentage of the physical screen (e.g., height="50%") or pixels (e.g., width="45"). White space is defined by the vspace and hspace attributes, again in terms of a percentage of the physical display area or number of pixels to the left and right or above and below (e.g., hspace="5"). The align attribute defines the image's position relative to its insertion point in the card, with a default of "bottom" (e.g., align="middle"). Figure 5-4 shows a simple image on a Health Inspection "splash" screen. Note that, used to directly read files, the Phone.com simulator expects a black and white bitmap image (not a wireless bitmap), whereas the Nokia 7110 processes wireless bitmaps. Screen *a* shows the Phone.com rendition of this image (note that the align attribute is ignored), and screen *b* shows how the Nokia 7110 simulator renders a WBMP equivalent of "inspect.bmp."

```
<wml>
   <card>
      <p>
         <strong>Health Inspection</strong><br/>
         <img src="inspect.bmp" alt="Inspection" align="middle"/>
      </p>
   </card>
</wml>
```

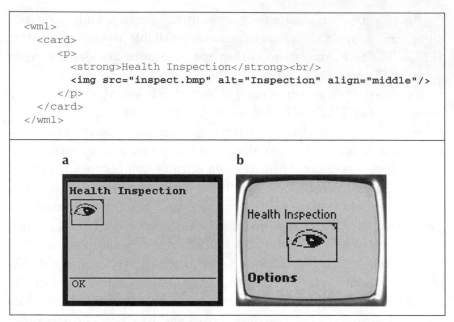

FIGURE 5-4. Use of the Image Tag

NAVIGATION

In all the examples we have looked at so far, we have not provided any facilities for navigating within a deck or for requesting a new deck from a server. WML provides a surprising number of ways to navigate within and between decks. Before we discuss these, we need to understand two terms — the event and the task. An *event* is some sort of occurrence that causes a task to execute. An event may be as simple as a key press or selecting an on-screen link. These user-initiated events are the easiest to understand and are commonly used to do navigation. Another type of event occurs indirectly and is called an *implicit event.* Some examples of implicit events include card entry and countdown timer events. A *task* is something that is executed because of an event (e.g., navigation to another card within a deck).

Now that we've got the terminology down, let's look at how to navigate in WML. The most common ways to create user navigation are the <do> and <a> elements. The <do> element provides a general

way for the user to act on the currently displayed card and is somewhat similar to (although more versatile than) the 'SUBMIT' INPUT
element in HTML. Although <do> can be used to submit the contents of a form to a server, it can also be used to navigate to another
card in a deck, return to the previously displayed card, and even
refresh the current card's contents.

The <do> element is an event element and does not work on its
own — it must contain a task element in order to carry out an action.
The <go> task element is used for both intercard navigation and for
making server requests. Figure 5-5 shows how the <do> and <go> elements work together to provide intercard navigation. The do-go event
handler is rendered by the mobile device as a "Categories" widget,
here displayed at the bottom of the screen. A browser button located
immediately below the screen is used to select this action. You can
place do-go event handlers anywhere within a card and depending on
the user agent, these will be rendered in position or displayed at the
top or bottom of the display area.

Within the WML, note the use of the '#' character to designate
that the target ("MainCategories") is a card within the current
deck. The <do> element has a type attribute set to "accept." This
attribute is used by the browser when determining how best to display a <do> element. The "accept" type is used for primary actions,
and later in this chapter we look at how the "options" type can be
used to specify lists of navigation choices. Note, also, the use of comments as defined by XML (<!--comment text...-->) and '...',
which indicates that markup has been omitted to improve clarity.

When users need to access information that is selected based on
their input or is otherwise unavailable within the current deck, they
must be able to request a new deck. This is done via a do-go event
handler that references another deck URL. Figure 5-6 lays out a modified version of the second card from the previous example. This time,
the href attribute of the go element refers to the URL, which (we
presume) will generate an appropriate WML deck. A "Details" widget
is displayed at the bottom of the screen, associated with a selection
key on the mobile device's keypad. It is possible to pass data to the
specified URL using post fields or by adding parameters explicitly to

the URL (we discuss post fields in Chapter 6). Note the method attribute used to specify whether the request should be made using a "get" (submission data will be included in the request) or a "post" (submission data will be sent separately). The method attribute is not mandatory, since "get" is the default value and is included in this example, simply for illustration, because no data is being passed.

```
<wml>
  <!-First card is splash screen->
  <card>
    <do type="accept" label="Categories">
     <go href="#MainCategories"/>
    </do>
    <p align="center">
      . . .
    </p>
  </card>

  <!-Second card displays categories->
  <card id="MainCategories">
    <p mode="nowrap">
      <strong>Categories</strong><br/>
      Staff<br/>
      Food<br/>
      Premises<br/>
      Animals and Pests
    </p>
  </card>
</wml>
```

a ────────▶ b

```
Health Inspection
    *Notices*
Note that the annual
  charity bake sale
  will be held next
   Friday at noon.
Categories
```

```
Categories
Staff
Food
Premises
Animals and Pests
OK
```

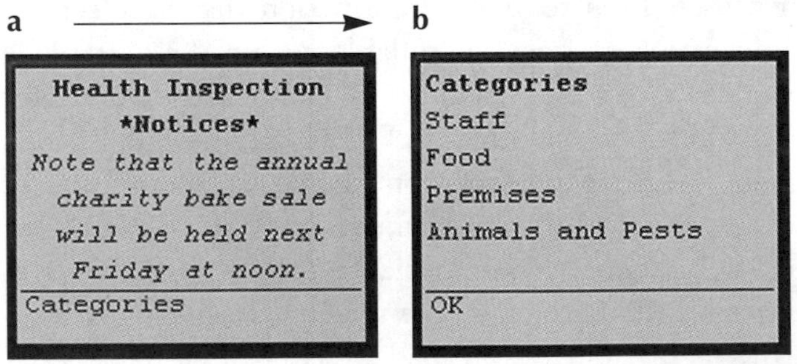

FIGURE 5-5. Card Navigation

```
<!--Second card displays categories-->
<card id="MainCategories">
  <do type="accept" label="Details">
    <go method="post" href="http://gov.ns.ca/health/inspect"/>
  </do>
  <p mode="nowrap">
    . . .
  </p>
</card>
```

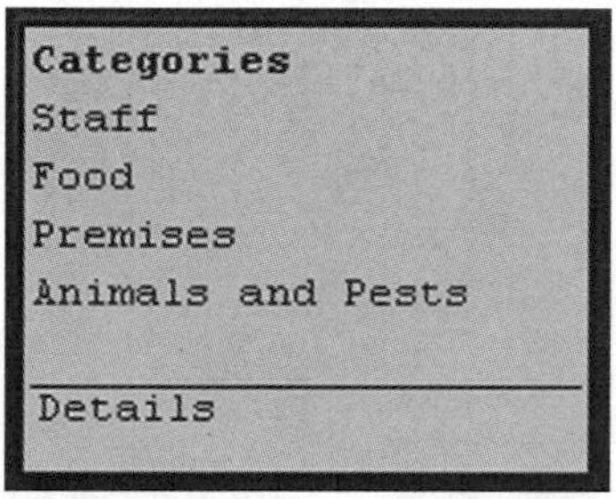

```
Categories
Staff
Food
Premises
Animals and Pests

Details
```

FIGURE 5-6. Deck Navigation

When you have a number of possible navigation choices from a single page, you can use a series of do-go event handlers, specifying type="options" for each as shown in Figure 5-7. Note that this will not work well on some devices (e.g., Nokia handsets). For specifying navigation options that work well on the majority of devices, use lists of links (which we discuss later).

How the user agent deals with multiple do-go event handlers is vendor dependent, but the type attribute serves as a hint to the user agent that will help it do appropriate rendering. In Figure 5-7, the Phone.com simulator provides a "Menu" widget (screen *a*) that when selected displays a list of options (screen *b*).

Links are another way of navigating between cards and decks. One main difference between links and <do> elements is that links are usually rendered in-line, whereas <do> elements are most often assigned to a labeled key at the bottom or top of the display. WML provides two ways to create a link, one a shorthand for the other.

```
<!-Second card displays categories->
<card id="MainCategories">
  <do type="options" label="Staff">
    <go href="http://gov.ns.ca/health/staff"/>
  </do>
  <do type="options" label="Food">
    <go href="http://gov.ns.ca/health/food"/>
  </do>
  <do type="options" label="Premises">
    <go href="http://gov.ns.ca/health/premises"/>
  </do>
  <do type="options" label="Animals">
    <go href="http://gov.ns.ca/health/animals"/>
  </do>
  <p mode="nowrap">
    . . .
  </p>
</card>
```

FIGURE 5-7. Do-Go Event Handlers Using Options

The <anchor> element is the most flexible way to create a link, and the <a> element is a shorter version that contains an implicit <go> element. Consider the following WML:

```
<anchor title ="Staff">Staff Details
  <go href="http://gov.ns.ca/health/staff"/>
</anchor>
```

This will create a link that displays "Staff Details" as the link anchor and links to the "staff" URL. The optional title attribute is used to display additional information about the link such as a tool

```
<!-Second card displays categories->
<card id="MainCategories">
  <p>
    <strong>Categories</strong><br/>
    <a href="http://gov.ns.ca/health/staff">Staff</a><br/>
    <a href="http://gov.ns.ca/health/food">Food</a><br/>
    <a href="http://gov.ns.ca/health/premises">Premises</a><br/>
    <a href="http://gov.ns.ca/health/animals">Animals
        <img src="animal.wbmp" alt=" "/>
    </a>
  </p>
</card>
```

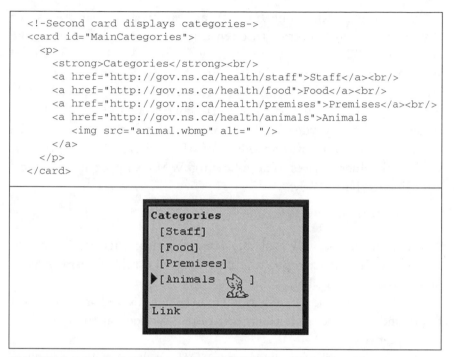

FIGURE 5-8. Links including Embedded Image

tip. An equivalent to this, using the shorthand version, would be as follows:

```
<a title ="Staff" href="http://gov.ns.ca/health/staff">
  Staff Details
</a>
```

The `<a>` tag is preferred to the `<anchor>` because it can be encoded more compactly for transmission to the mobile device. Figure 5-8 provides similar functionality to that shown in Figure 5-7, but uses links for navigation.

The "Link" label references a soft key. When the user presses this, the device attempts to navigate to the target URL of the selected link. The cursor keys are used to select a different link. Note the use of an embedded image within the last `<a>` element – this is not supported by the Nokia 7110 (although the image can be placed outside the link tag).

Because more than one link can appear on a card and it is not always convenient to scroll through a number of links to reach the desired one, WML allows you to specify an access key that can be used as a shortcut to a link. This is done by adding the `accesskey` attribute to the `<a>` or `<anchor>` element. Because most mobile phone keypads are limited to numeric characters and '#' and '*', these are probably your best choice in access keys. Note that the `accesskey` attribute was added in WML version 1.2, so it will not work with older devices. The following WML snippet maps a local deck link to the "1" key:

```
<a href="#card2" accesskey="1">Next</a>
```

The mobile device will probably label the link with its associated access key. In our example, the mobile device might display "`[1]` `Next`" as the link's label.

In this brief look at navigation we have not covered variables, post fields, and a number of optional attributes. We look at these in detail in Chapter 6.

Up to this point, we have seen WML decks that let us look at information and move from card to card, but we have had no way to enter information for use by a WAP application. As in HTML forms, WML provides a way to enter text and to select from lists of items. The variety of input types is more limited in WML with two primary text `<input>` variations (regular text and password) and a `<select>` list that allows either one or multiple `<option>` items to be chosen.

TEXT ENTRY

Entry of text is provided by the `<input>` tag, which, like its HTML counterpart, allows the user of an entry screen to enter data that will be associated with a name when submitted to a server for processing. A simple input field that allows entry of a user ID follows. Note that the `name` attribute specifies a variable that will contain the user's input. This variable can be preset to a specified value that will appear in the input field when it is displayed:

```
<input name="userid"/>
```

TABLE 5-2. Format Masks for Input

N	NUMERIC CHARACTER
A, a	Alphabetic character (A = uppercase, a = lowercase)
X, x	Numeric or alphabetic character (X = uppercase, x = lowercase)
M, m	Any character (M means that uppercase is assumed and m that lowercase is assumed, but in either case, any characters may be entered)
\	Leading backslash specifies character literals that will be displayed and included when the field is submitted for server processing (e.g., a 7-digit phone number with a '-' separator can be specified as: `format="NNN\-NNNN")`.
*	Leading asterisk (*) specifies 0 or more characters. The * must be followed by a formatting character such as M or x (e.g., a password with a minimum of four characters can be specified as: `format="mmmm*m"`
0, 1, 2,...,N	Leading number specifies 0..N characters. The leading number must be followed by a formatting character (e.g., a 7-digit phone number could be specified as: `format="3N\-4N")`.

As with HTML inputs, there are a number of ways to constrain what the user can enter in a field. The `maxlength` attribute can be set to a number that determines the maximum number of characters which may be entered in this field. The `emptyok` attribute may be set to `"true"` or `"false"`, and this attribute is usually used where an optional input field has set a format mask (described later). The `format` attribute (not available in HTML) provides a simple way to implement a format mask, limiting user entry to a specific set of characters and/or numbers while allowing embedded constants to improve the readability of input fields. The formatting rules are specified in Table 5-2.

Password Inputs and Security

Note that the WAP specifications do not require that password input fields be encrypted prior to transmission to a server. Password entry over a nonencrypted (i.e., non-WTLS) link should only be used for applications requiring minimal security. In addition, not all WML browsers mask entry of password characters. When toggling through multiple character choices on a handset keypad, the device may display each character choice, allowing an observer to see the password being entered. ⬚

Other input attributes include `value`, which is used to specify a default value to which an input will be set on its first use, and the `type` attribute, which may be either `"password"` or `"text."` The default input type is `"text,"` and `"password"` is used when the input should not be echoed to the user (see the sidebar "Password Inputs and Security").

The `size` attribute specifies how wide (in characters) the entry area should be and as with anchors, the `title` attribute can be used by a user agent to identify the field (e.g., via a tool tip). Although not mandatory, input can use the `tabindex` attribute to specify where it lies in the order of selectable elements on the current card. As with anchors, inputs may specify an `accesskey` attribute to provide a keyboard shortcut to the field (see the explanation of anchors earlier for more information).

SELECT LISTS

Select lists allow a user to choose one or more items from a list. Each item in the list is specified by an `option` element. A simple select list follows:

```
<select name="fuel" value="gas" multiple="true">
        <option value="gas">Natural Gas</option>
        <option value="electric">Electric</option>
        <option value="propane">Propane</option>
        <option value="wood">Wood</option>
</select>
```

This list provides four options, setting the default value to the first option (`"gas"`) via the `value` attribute of `<select>`. The `multiple` attribute is set to true so that users can choose more than one item in the list; if the `multiple` attribute is not specified, it defaults to `false`. Each option has a value that will be added to the variable `"fuel"` (specified by the `select` element's `name` attribute). The text that appears inside the `option` element will be displayed to the user in the select list. Because this is a multiple select list, when more than

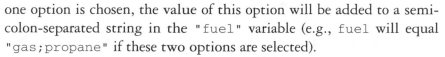

one option is chosen, the value of this option will be added to a semi-colon-separated string in the `"fuel"` variable (e.g., `fuel` will equal `"gas;propane"` if these two options are selected).

Other attributes that are part of the `select` element include `iname` and `ivalue`; `iname` specifies a variable name for the index or indexes of the selected options, and `ivalue` provides a default index or indexes for this variable. Like `<input>`, `<select>` uses the `tabindex` attribute to specify where it lies in the order of selectable elements on the current card.

The `option` element is used to specify the items in a select list. A `select` element contains one or more options, and each option typically defines a value that will be used to set the `select value` attribute. Options may also specify a `title` and/or an `onpick` attribute. When the user selects an option which contains an `onpick` attribute, the URL specified by this attribute is invoked (i.e. an "onpick" event occurs); in the case of multiple select lists, the "onpick" event occurs on both selection and deselection of the option. An `option` may also specify an event handler by nesting an `onevent` tag (see Chapter 6).

Let's take a look at an example that shows us how we might use both `<input>` and `<select>` elements. Figure 5-9 shows a WML card for a hypothetical kitchen inspection form. The Phone.com simulator displays each `input` and `select` element separately as shown in the three screens. Note the use of a format mask to ensure that at least one digit is entered for the light level field (screen *a*). The "Number of Fans" input (screen *b*) is optional as indicated by the `emptyok` attribute. Cooking fuels are selected via a multiple-choice list. In our example (screen *c*), the user has selected cooking fuels of both natural gas and wood.

That concludes our introduction to Wireless Markup Language. We looked at decks and cards, layout and images, navigation, and user input. We saw how WML is similar in some ways to HTML, and Table 5-3 "Comparison of HTML 4 and WML Tags" tries to make this more concrete. In Chapter 6 we continue our study of WML.

```
<!-Kitchen Inspection->
<card id="Kitchen">
  <do type="accept" label="Submit">
    <go href="http://gov.ns.ca/health/kitchen"/>
  </do>
  <p>
    <strong>Kitchen</strong><br/>
    Light (lux): <input name="light" format="N*N"/>
    Number of Fans: <input name="fans" emptyok="true" format="*N"/>
    Cooking Fuel
    <select name="fuel" value="gas" multiple="true">
      <option value="gas">Natural Gas</option>
      <option value="electric">Electric</option>
      <option value="propane">Propane</option>
      <option value="wood">Wood</option>
    </select>
  </p>
</card>
```

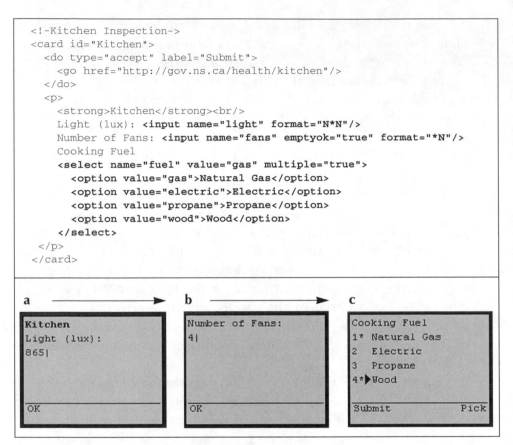

FIGURE 5-9. Submit and Input Elements

TABLE 5-3. Comparison of HTML 4 and WML Tags

WML TAG	MEANING	HTML TAG	COMMENTS
a	anchor short form	A	
access	access control	N/A	
anchor	anchor long form	A	
b	bold emphasis	B	
big	big emphasis	BIG	
br	line break	BR	Note in WML (XML) vs. in HTML
card	card	BODY or FORM	No exact correspondence. Multiple forms in one HTML page are a similar idea to multiple cards in a deck.
do	do event	INPUT of type SUBMIT	BUTTON or INPUT of type SUBMIT is similar to <do><go> event handler of type "accept."
em	emphasis	EM	
fieldset	set of display and input fields	N/A	HTML supports many ways to divide a page and group items that have no direct WML equivalent (e.g., lists, frames).
go	go task	N/A	See <do> tag.
head	header section	HEAD	
i	italic	I	
img	image	IMG	
input	input field	INPUT	WML inputs are equivalent to HTML INPUTs of type "TEXT" and "PASSWORD." WML provides separate tags for selection lists (see <select>), uses explicit post fields in place of HIDDEN inputs, and do-go event handlers in place of SUBMIT and RESET INPUTs.
meta	metadata	META	WML adds 'forua' attribute to signal that this information is for the mobile device (discussed in Chapter 6).
noop	do nothing	N/A	
onevent	event handler	N/A	
optgroup	set of options	N/A	

(continued)

TABLE 5-3 *(continued)*

WML TAG	MEANING	HTML TAG	COMMENTS
option	selection option	OPTION	
p	paragraph	P	
Pre	preformatted paragraph	PRE	
postfield	field to be passed on a POST	Similar to INPUT of type= "HIDDEN"	See <input>.
prev	previous-card task	N/A	
refresh	refresh-context task	INPUT of type "RESET"	Only approximate because HTML does not support variables.
select	select list	SELECT	
setvar	set variable assignment	N/A	Variables not supported by HTML (except through scripting extensions).
small	small emphasis	SMALL	
strong	strong emphasis	STRONG	
table	table	TABLE	
td	table data (cell)	TD	
template	deck template	N/A	
timer	timer event handler	N/A	Note that meta tag for client pull can do a timed transfer to another card.
tr	table row	TR	
u	underline emphasis	U	
wml	deck	HTML	

Wireless Markup Language – Beyond the Basics

In the last chapter, we looked at the basics of Wireless Markup Language (WML) including decks and cards, layout, input, and navigation. We now continue our exploration of WML and extend the health inspection system example to illustrate these additional WML features:

- Variables, parameters, and context
- Events, tasks, and history
- Deck declarations
- Grouping
- Named character entities
- Character sets, encoding types, and caching

VARIABLES, PARAMETERS, AND CONTEXT

Variables, parameters, and context are the ingredients for maintaining state within WML. Variables hold data values within the client and are maintained by the WML browser context. Parameters export this client state to the server. Navigation history, which we discuss separately, is also maintained in the browser context.

Variables

Variables allow us to pass information from card to card, both in and between decks. Variables are automatically defined and set when a value is entered in an input field or an item is selected from a select list. For example, `<input name="light"/>` will create and populate the `light` variable with the user-supplied text. Variables can also be set explicitly by the `setvar` attribute inside task elements such as `go`, `prev` or `refresh`. In WML, the contents of variables are treated as strings.

To define a variable, simply use its name. To access its contents, use the dollar sign reserved character (e.g., `$var` or `$(var)`). Brackets are required when the variable is not clearly separated from surrounding markup. For example, if the variable `prefix` has a value of `"Mac,"` the WML string `$(prefix)Donald` would yield the resultant `"MacDonald"` after variable substitution.

Variables must begin with a letter or underscore (`'_'`) and may contain underscores, letters, and numbers. In WML, variables may be referenced anywhere character data is legal (between tags) and also within certain attributes (e.g., `href`). Variables cannot be referenced within attributes such as `length` or `name` where the attribute values must be fixed before processing.

The following example illustrates setting the variable `progress` inside a `go` task element in order to provide information about how we arrived at the Step2 card. In the WML for the Step2 card, we refer to the contents of the variable by prefixing the variable name with `$`, as in `$progress`.

```
<go href="#Step2">
  <setvar name="progress" value="Step 1 completed"/>
</go>
.
.
<card id="Step2">
  <p>Progress: $progress</p>
.
.
</card>
```

This style of coding might be used when a user can arrive at the `"Step2"` card from several different paths. Here the `"Step2"` card displays `progress` to remind users how they arrived. Note that the `setvar` element is an empty element and other than the common attributes (see sidebar "Common WML Attributes" in Chapter 5), requires that you specify a `name` and a `value`.

Variables live locally in the WML client, accessible both from WML cards and WMLScript programs (which we cover in Chapter 7). In order to make client data available to the server programs we need to understand parameters, but first we look at how variables can be altered through conversion and escaping.

Variable Conversion and Escaping

When variables are referenced within text, the value of the variable is extracted at run-time (in the user agent) and inserted into the text. At this point, the variable may be converted to or from a URL escaped (or encoded) format (see the sidebar "URL Encoding"). What type of conversion implicitly occurs depends on the context of the text. Variables within `href` attributes will be automatically encoded prior to transmission, whereas variables in paragraph text will not be escaped. You can control variable escaping using one of three methods: `"noesc,"` `"escape,"` and `"unesc."` The `"noesc"` modifier is used when you wish to override automatic escaping, the `"escape"` modifier is used to URL escape variables in a context where this would not normally occur, and the `"unesc"` modifier allows you to convert a previously escaped variable to its original format.

URL Encoding

Before transmitting data to a gateway, the microbrowser encodes the information using a scheme called URL encoding (specified by the MIME type application/x-www-form-urlencoded). The encoding scheme consists of the following:

▣ URL-encoding certain nonprintable characters including character codes between `00` and `20` and `7F` and `FF` hex. Special characters like percent signs (%), single quotation marks (`'`), and question marks (`?`) are also encoded. These characters are replaced with a percent sign followed by the hexadecimal value of the character (e.g., `%40` is @ and `%25` is %).

▣ Replacing spaces with plus signs (+).

▣ Separating each name and value with an equals sign (=).

▣ Separating each name/value pair with an ampersand (&). ▣

Figure 6-1 illustrates variable referencing and conversion. This deck sets up some variables using `setvar` (in the first card) and then displays them using various forms of variable escaping. The screen shots show the second card, which displays a simple variable and an e-mail address in both URL escaped and unescaped forms.

```
<wml>
  <card>
    <do type="accept" label="Set Vars">
      <go href="#card2">
        <setvar name="simpleVar" value="One (1)"/>
        <setvar name="urlEscaped"
                value=
                  "name=C.+Bennett&amp;email=chris.bennett%40unisys.com"
        />
      </go>
    </do>
  </card>
  <card id="card2">
  <p>
    Simple: $simpleVar<br/>
    URL Esc:<br/>
    $(urlEscaped)<br/>
    Escaped: $(simpleVar:escape)<br/>
    Unescaped:<br/>
    $(urlEscaped:unesc)<br/>
    No Escape:<br/>
    $(simpleVar:noesc)
  </p>
</card></wml>
```

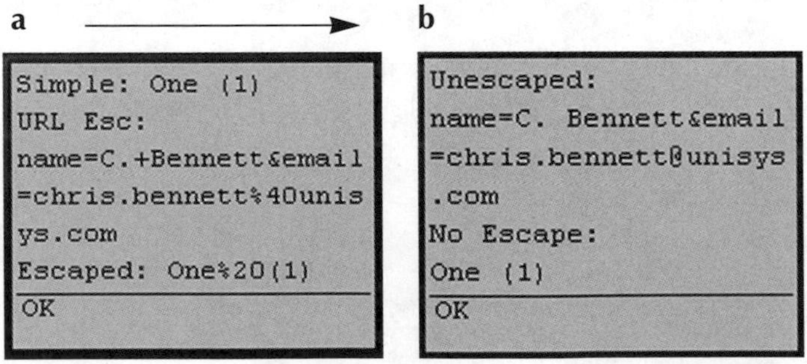

a ⟶ b

```
Simple: One (1)          Unescaped:
URL Esc:                 name=C. Bennett&email
name=C.+Bennett&email    =chris.bennett@unisys
=chris.bennett%40unis    .com
ys.com                   No Escape:
Escaped: One%20(1)       One (1)
OK                       OK
```

FIGURE 6-1. Variable Conversion and Escaping

Parameters

Parameters pass information between the mobile device and a server during a URL request. The postfield element is used to define and set parameters and may be used inside go tasks:

```
<go href="myScript">
  <postfield name="progress" value="Step 1 completed"/>
</go>
```

The code here results in a "GET" request (the default HTTP method in WML) that runs "myScript" on the server. As in an HTTP GET, the progress parameter is appended to the URL and passed to the server. If "post" had been used as the method attribute, an HTTP POST request would invoke the named URL, passing the progress parameter separately. Like setvar, the postfield element is an empty element whose name and value are set using the attributes name and value. Note that values can also be passed to a server using links (the anchor or a element) and are set as part of the href URL attribute (e.g., <a href="myScript.cgi?progress=$progress">). The & named character entity (described toward the end of this chapter) must be used to separate multiple variables.

Context

WML uses a single browser context to save all state. This includes the navigation history (a linked set of URLs that records the user's recently visited cards) and all variables that have been set within this history. Once set, a variable is available to any card, until the context is reset or the variable explicitly cleared. The context can be reset using the newcontext card attribute (e.g., <card newcontext = "true">). A word of warning: it has been reported that on some devices, setting newcontext to "true" may only reset the history, leaving the variables untouched.

Cached Pages

Not to be confused with the context is the cache of WML decks and cards maintained by the browser. This cache reduces network overhead by allowing recently used cards to be locally retrieved. However it does present a problem when you want to ensure that fresh content is always retrieved from the server (e.g., when content is time critical). One way to solve this problem is through the use of the cache-control attribute of the <go> element (new in WML 1.3). When this is set to "no-cache," the browser will pass the URL request through to the origin server, adding an HTTP "cache-control" header with this value to the request. Another way to ensure that pages are not cached is to use the <meta> tag, discussed later.

EVENTS, TASKS, AND HISTORY

As discussed in Chapter 5, there are two types of events – explicit (user-initiated) and intrinsic events. Intrinsic events occur as an indirect result of a user action or as a result of a countdown timer expiring. These are the types of events that a user directly initiates:

- Clicking a soft key
- Selecting a link
- Entering a text URL or choosing a bookmarked URL (note that this is a browser action and not strictly part of WML)
- Selecting or deselecting an option in a list (note that technically the WAP WML specification considers this an intrinsic event)
- Filling in an input field

The following events occur indirectly or without user intervention:

- Transition into a card (both forward and backward)
- Timer expiration

When events are triggered, the following different actions may occur:

- Navigation to a new card or deck
- Context reset
- Context variables updated (note that context history is updated whenever navigation occurs)

Table 6-1 describes the relationship between events and tasks that result from these events. Some of the terms in this table may be unfamiliar and we explain them later in this chapter.

We have already discussed the do-go event handlers and links, but have not yet looked at intrinsic events and handlers. In the previous chapter, we also glossed over the tasks that can be done following a do event or link selection.

TABLE 6-1. Events and Their Results

EVENT	CONTEXT RESET	CONTEXT VARIABLES UPDATED	NAVIGATION
User clicks soft key (<do>)	Yes (when task is refresh)	N/A	Yes (when task is go or prev)
User clicks a link (<a> or <anchor>)	Yes (when task is refresh)	N/A	Yes
User types a URI or selects a bookmark (this is user agent dependent)	Yes	N/A	Yes
User selects or deselects an option in a list (<select>)	No	Yes – variable(s) associated with select are updated	Yes (when onpick attribute is set or onevent element used)
User fills in a field (<input>)	No	Yes – variable associated with input updated (when this happens depends on the user agent)	No
A card is entered (forward or backward)	Yes (when a card is entered for the first time and newcontext is true)	Yes (when task is refresh and setvar is used)	Yes (if onenterforward or onenterbackward attribute of card or template is set)
A countdown timer expires	Yes (when task is refresh)	Yes (when task is refresh and setvar is used)	Yes (if ontimer attribute of card or template is set)

Intrinsic Events and the onevent Tag

Intrinsic events are handled using the onevent tag or by making use of one of the equivalent shorthand attributes. Three intrinsic events can be handled at the deck or card level:

 ontimer (a countdown timer expires)

■ onenterforward (a card is entered)

■ onenterbackward (a card is returned to)

These can be handled using the onevent element as in:

```
<card id="Step1">
  <onevent type="onenterbackward">
    <go href="#OutOfSequence"/>
  </onevent>
  ...
</card>
```

or by using the shorthand notation:

```
<card id = "Step1" onenterbackward="#OutOfSequence"> ... </card>
```

These event handlers can be used to redirect a user to a warning card should they navigate back into "Step1." The second method illustrates how the shortcut event handling attribute may be specified within the card element. A similar syntax is available for ontimer and onenterforward shortcuts.

Timers

Timers allow programmatic reaction to user idle time. A timer starts counting down when a user enters a card. When the timer counts down to zero, an event-handler, associated with the timer, is activated. Timers can be interrupted by execution of a task such as go, prev, or refresh. Timers are only declared within cards, and only one timer element (<timer/>) is allowed per card. The timeout value is specified by setting the value attribute to a number in tenths of a second. For example, value = "100" creates a 10-second timer. The name attribute can be used to specify a variable that will contain the timer's value (e.g., `"0"` upon timeout). For example, `<timer name="splashTimer" value="50"/>` declares a five-second timer with a variable named `"splashTimer"` that will contain the count-down time.

Timeout events are handled using the `onevent` element (with the `type` set to `"ontimer"`) or the shortcut `ontimer` card attribute. A timeout event is specified at the card or deck level. When set at the deck level (see "Deck Declaration" later in this chapter), the timer applies to all cards in the deck that do not declare their own timer event handler.

Figure 6-2 illustrates the use of a timer to control a splash screen (first screen) that displays for five seconds and then transfers control to the categories card (second screen) unless the user explicitly selects `"Categories"` in the meantime. Note that the `timer` element must be located before any `do` elements but is placed after the `onevent` handlers.

The `onevent` handler in Figure 6-2 can be replaced with a short-cut card attribute as in:

```
. . .
<card ontimer="#MainCategories">
  <timer value="50"/>
. . .
```

Tasks

In Chapter 5 we looked at how the `go` task may be used to navigate to specified URLs both within and between decks. In addition to `go`, three other tasks can be used to handle events specified by the `<do>` and `<onevent>` elements:

■ `prev` (go to the previous page in the history context)

■ `refresh` (update the variable context)

■ `noop` (do nothing)

Both `prev` and `refresh` can be used with the `<anchor>` element to provide links supporting history navigation and context refresh. Note that the `<a>` anchor shorthand cannot be used for this purpose.

```
<wml>
  <card>
    <onevent type="ontimer">
      <go href="#MainCategories"/>
    </onevent>
    <timer value="50"/>
    <do type="accept" label="Categories">
      <go href="#MainCategories"/>
    </do>
    <p align="center">
      . . .
    </p>
  </card>

  <!–Second card displays categories–>
  <card id="MainCategories">
    <p mode="nowrap">
      . . .
    </p>
  </card>
</wml>
```

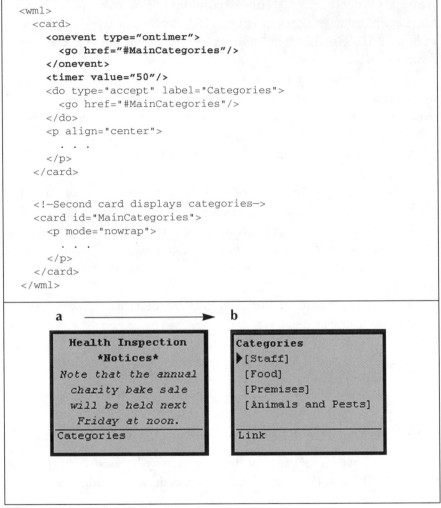

FIGURE 6-2. A Timed Splash Screen

The <prev> element provides explicit navigation through the history context. Instead of relying on the mobile device's browser Back button, you can provide a link or soft key that guides the user to the previous card on the history stack. The card history contains a list of all URLs that the user has browsed since the last time the context was reset (e.g., by typing in a new URL or setting the newcontext card attribute to true). Navigation with <prev> may include cards from different decks. Variables may be set as part of the <prev> task using a contained <setvar> element. When using the <prev> element with a <do> event handler, use the type attribute (type="prev") to assist the user agent in displaying the appropriate item. A word of caution: this does not work with some versions of the Phone.com simulator, which recognize only the full word "previous."

The <refresh> element allows you to refresh the current card, updating all displayed information with the values contained in any nested setvar elements. Execution of a refresh task also interrupts currently executing timers and restarts nonrunning timers. Figure 6-3 illustrates the use of the <prev> and <refresh> tasks in a modified version of the health inspection health deck.

```
<wml>
  <card id="Splash" ontimer="#MainCategories">

    <!—Reset timer if entered using prev task—>
    <onevent type="onenterbackward">
      <refresh>
        <setvar name="splashTimer" value="20"/>
        <setvar name="notice" value=""/>
      </refresh>
    </onevent>

    <!—Set initial notice—>
    <onevent type="onenterforward">
      <refresh>
        <setvar name="notice"
                value="The annual charity bake sale will
                       be held next Friday at noon."/>
      </refresh>
    </onevent>

    <timer name="splashTimer" value="50"/>
    . . .
  </card>
```

(continued)

(continued)

```
<!—Second card displays categories—>
<card id="MainCategories">
  <do type="prev" label="Back">
    <prev/>
  </do>
    . . .
  </card>
</wml>
```

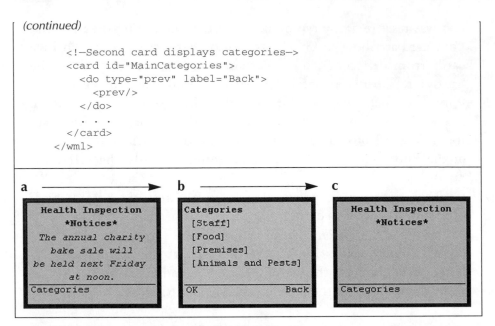

FIGURE 6-3. <prev> and <refresh> Task Elements

In the example here we added two event handlers to illustrate how the refresh task element may be used to update browser context. When the desk is first entered (screen *a*), a notice is displayed to the user. Users can explicitly move to the categories card (screen *b*) or a timed event will take them there in 5 seconds. If the first card is redisplayed (from screen *b*) via the device's Back button or the "Back" soft key, the notice will be blanked out (screen *c*). Note the reference to the "notice" variable ($notice) in place of hard-coded text. The second card adds a prev event handler (which to display on the Phone.com simulator had to be coded as <do type="previous"...>), that takes the user back to the previous card. This will be the first card if this is the first visit to this deck. The use of explicit backward navigation is vital for devices that do not have a Back key (e.g., the Nokia 7110).

The `<noop>` element, which appears somewhat useless on first acquaintance, serves an important function for deckwide templates and card-specific events. Using the `<noop>` element in a card event handler is a simple way to override a deckwide handler. This ensures that a particular navigation option is *not* available to the user on a specified card. We discuss templates in the upcoming section, and Figure 6-4 illustrates both templates and the `noop` event.

DECK DECLARATIONS

In addition to cards, WML decks can contain optional `header` and `template` elements. These elements contain information of relevance to the deck as a whole.

Templates and Precedence of Event Handlers

Templates are used to define event handlers that apply to every card in a deck. This provides a simple way to implement consistent navigation such as a Home soft key on every card. A handler specified in a template can be overridden by a similar handler defined in a card. You can create both `do-go` and `onevent` handlers for both intrinsic and explicit events. Like cards, templates allow attribute shortcuts for intrinsic events (e.g., `onenterforward="someURL"`).

The most common use of templates is for default navigation. The example deck in Figure 6-4 illustrates the use of templates with an explicit `"Home"` navigation handler on every card except the first. On the first card (screen *a*) the default handler is overridden by a card-specific handler that specifies a `noop` task. Although this handler performs no real action, it has the effect of blocking the template-defined handler so that a user agent will not place a `"Home"` widget on this card. Screen *b* shows a fruit and vegetable selection list with two soft keys — one specified at the card level (`"Inspect"`) and the other inherited from the template (`"Home"`). Screen *c* shows just the inherited `"Home"` soft key because this card does not define any additional event handlers.

```
<wml>
  <template>
    <do type="accept" label="Home" name="home">
      <go href="#FoodHome"/>
    </do>
  </template>

  <card id="FoodHome" title="Food">
    <do type="accept" name="home">
      <noop/>
    </do>
    <p>
      <strong>Food Inspection</strong><br/>
      <a href="#MeatSelect">Meat</a>
      <a href="#DairySelect">Dairy Products</a>
      <a href="#FruitVegSelect">Fruit and Veg.</a>
    </p>
  </card>
  . . .
  <card id="FruitVegSelect" title="Select">
    <do type="accept" label="Inspect" name="inspect">
      <go href="#FruitVegInspect"/>
    </do>
    <p>
      <strong>Select Fruit or Veg.</strong>
      <select name="fruitVegType" value="apple">
        <option value="apple">Apple</option>
        <option value="cucumber">Cucumber</option>
        <option value="lettuce">Lettuce</option>
        <option value="tomato">Tomatoes</option>
      </select>
    </p>
  </card>

  <card id="FruitVegInspect" title="Fruit+Veg">
    <p>
      <strong>$fruitVegType Inspection</strong><br/>
      Inspection details will go here...
    </p>
  </card>
  . . .
</wml>
```

```
a ──────────────▶

Food Inspection
 [Meat]
 [Dairy Products]
▶[Fruit and Veg.]


Link
```

```
b ──────────────▶

Select Fruit or Veg.
1▶Apple
2 Cucumber
3 Lettuce
4 Tomatoes


Inspect        Home
```

```
c

apple Inspection
Inspection details
will go here...



Home
```

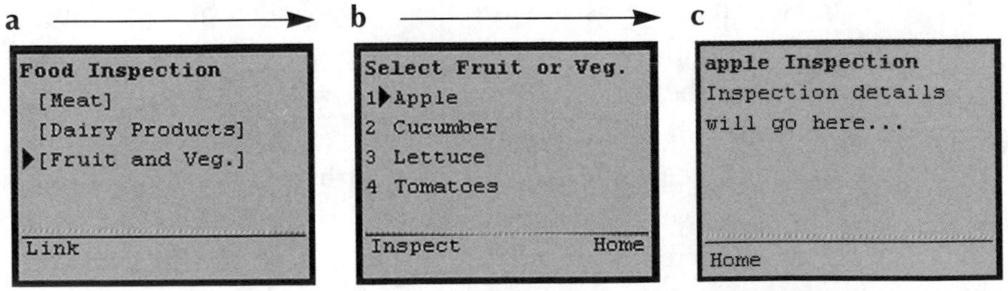

FIGURE 6-4. Template Event Handling with <noop>

The WML for this deck contains additional cards for meat and dairy selection and inspection that are not shown in Figure 6-4. These behave in the same way as the fruit and vegetable cards.

Access Control

WML allows control over the URLs that may request a deck. This control is provided by the access element. The access element is specified inside the optional head element, which, if used, must be the first element in a deck following the <wml> tag. The head element must contain either access elements, meta elements, or a combination of the two. A simple form of access control is provided by the access element's two attributes: domain and path. The domain attribute determines the URLs allowed to request a deck, whereas the path attribute is used to limit access to resources that are found under a specified directory within the selected domain. Either or both attributes may be used to limit access. The access element does not contain any other elements. Note that this type of access control relies on the WAP gateway for enforcement and does not replace server-side access control mechanisms.

Figure 6-5 illustrates deck access control. Only decks originating below the specified path (which in this case is a bit unlikely) may request this deck. The UP Simulator browser window displays the message shown (screen *a*) when a request is made from a card without access rights. Selecting "Details" displays screen *b*. Screen *c* shows how the Nokia 7110 simulator handles the same access violation.

The <go> element has an attribute that is also useful for access control. This is the sendreferer Boolean attribute, which if set to true (e.g., <go sendreferer="true"...> will result in the referring URL being sent (in the HTTP referrer header) to the resource referenced in this <go> element. This will help a server perform access control based on the requester's URL. See Chapter 9 for more discussion of security issues.

```
<wml>
  <head>
    <access path="/does/not/exit"/>
  </head>
  <card>
    <p>Should not display...</p>
  </card>
</wml>
```

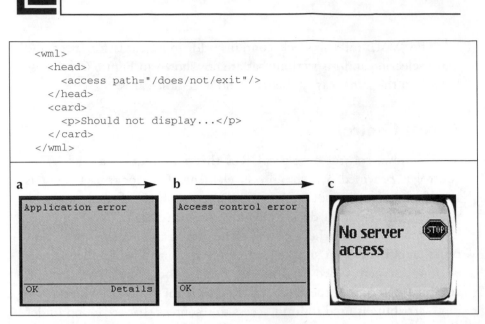

FIGURE 6-5. Deck Access Control

Meta Tags

The `meta` element provides a way to express information about a deck. Using named properties, a server may define deck metadata that can be passed as response headers (either WSP or HTTP) to the user agent. However, not all wireless devices may support `meta` tags because the WML specification does not define or require `meta` tags, nor does it explain how a user agent should use them.

If you do want to use `meta` tags, use the `http-equiv` attribute to name the metadata property. Then supply the property value using the `content` attribute. For example:

```
<wml>
  <head>
    <meta http-equiv="Cache-Control" forua="true"
      content="no-cache, max-age=0, must-revalidate,
               proxy-revalidate, s-maxage=0"/>
  </head>
  ...
</wml>
```

This code uses the cache control HTTP directive to ensure that a WML browser supporting this directive will always reload this deck from the server rather than from its cache. The `forua` attribute specifies that this metadata should be available to the user agent. Note that the value of the `content` attribute should not be split up as in this example, but be specified on a single line.

GROUPING: FIELD SETS, OPTION GROUPS

It is often useful to group items together to ensure appropriate handling by a user agent. Field sets and option groups provide this facility for fields and select lists, respectively. The `fieldset` element defines a logical boundary between fields, the term *field* encompassing a number of WML tags including text, layout, emphasis, inputs, selects, and do elements. Field sets, which must contain at least one field, can be nested to provide a hierarchy of fields. The following example illustrates the use of a simple field set to separate food packaging input from preparation area input:

```
<p>
   <fieldset title="packaging">Packaging<br/>
   Material OK?
   <select name="material" value="true">
      <option value="true">Yes</option>
      <option value="false">No</option>
   </select>
   Sealed?
   <select name="seal" value="true">
      <option value="true">Yes</option>
      <option value="false">No</option>
   </select>
   </fieldset>
   <fieldset title="Preparation Area">Preparation<nr/>
      . . .
   </fieldset>
</p>
```

Option groups (`<optgroup></optgroup>`) are used to group select list options, and, like field sets, they may be nested to create option hierarchies. Option groups must also contain at least one option.

User agents are not required to support field sets or option groups. Those that do not, will ignore the groupings and process the contained fields and options as if not grouped. Both field sets and option groups may contain `title` and `xml:lang` attributes.

NAMED CHARACTER ENTITIES

WML named and numeric character entities are required to display WML-reserved characters. For example, the 'less-than' character (<) is normally interpreted as an element start character. However, named entities provide a readable way to insert reserved characters in display text. Most WML entities are defined in the XML specifications and include the following:

- ampersand (&):   `&amp;`

- apostrophe ('):   `&apos;`

- greater than (>):   `&gt;`

- less than (<):   `&lt;`

- nonbreakingspace ( ):   ` `

- quotation mark ("):   `&quot;`

- soft hyphen (–):   `&shy;`

Recall from our discussion of variables that the dollar sign is used to reference a variable value. In order to display a dollar sign in WML text, you must use two consecutive dollar signs. For example, `"The cost is $$ $price."` will display as `"The cost is $ 100.00."` when the variable `price` has the value `"100.00."` Figure 6-6 shows how named character entities can be used.

The >, &, and < characters are used to reduce text size. The ` ` nonbreaking space is used to ensure that the words `"must"` and `"be"` are kept on the same line.

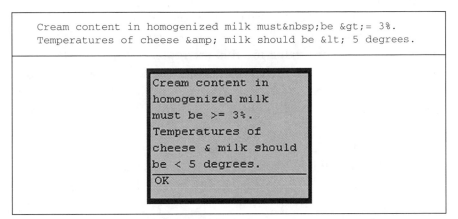

```
Cream content in homogenized milk must be &gt;= 3%.
Temperatures of cheese &amp; milk should be &lt; 5 degrees.
```

FIGURE 6-6. Named Character Entities

Note that the named character entities can also be expressed as hexadecimal or decimal numbers. For example, the named character entity " could also be written as " or ".

CHARACTER SETS, ENCODING TYPES, AND CACHING

The go element has some attributes that we have not yet discussed. These include attributes to specify acceptable character sets, encoding types, and whether client caching should be used. For more information on the related topics of internationalization and performance, see Chapter 9.

The go element can be used to specify a list of character sets that a WAP application will accept from the user agent. The term *character set* is used to refer to a method of converting a sequence of octets into a sequence of characters. These character sets are specified in a space or comma delimited field in the accept-charset attribute (e.g., <go accept-charset="ISO-8859-1,US-ASCII"...>). If present, this value determines how the user agent will transcode postfields. If not specified, the user agent will use the same character set as the last server response.

The `enctype` attribute specifies the content type to be used when posting parameters to a server (i.e., when the value of `method` is `"post"`). The default value for this attribute is `"application/x-www-form-urlencoded."` If posted parameters can contain characters other than US-ASCII characters, the WAP specifications recommend that you use an encoding type of `"multipart/form-data"` (currently the only other option).

As of WML 1.3, the `<go>` element supports a `cache-control` directive that is used to tell a mobile device not to use its cached version of a given page, but instead to fetch a new page from the server (e.g., `<go cache-control="no-cache"...>`). If the `cache-control` attribute is not set, the user agent will use its cache where possible. Meta tag controlled caching was discussed earlier.

WML Tips

Chapter 11 contains a section on usability that has a collection of tips to help make your WML user interface more usable. These tips have been gathered through experience and comments from other developers, and I strongly suggest you take a look at these before proceeding with real WAP application development!

WMLScript

WMLScript is a scripting language that extends WML to provide programmable functionality. The WMLScript version we discuss is version 1.2, and we start with a brief overview of the language basics (for further information, see the WMLScript specification available from the WAP Forum Web site). WMLScript programs rely heavily on function libraries – for numeric, string, and URL manipulation, browser state interaction, user dialogs, and even cryptographic and telephone functions. We outline the libraries and refer you to the WMLScript Standard Libraries specification and other specifications at the WAP Forum Web site for more information. A tutorial comprises the remainder of the chapter. We will see how easy it is to carry out validation, user interaction, formatting, calculations, and telephone operations using WMLScript.

A BRIEF EXAMPLE

Before we become immersed in the theory of WMLScript, let's look at a brief example that we develop further in the tutorial section. Consider the following:

```
// Calculate the area of a rectangle and go to
// the results card
extern function area(length, width) {
  var area = length * width;
  WMLBrowser.setVar("area", area);
  WMLBrowser.go("#Results");
};
```

This is a WMLScript function that accepts a length and a width parameter, calculates an area, and sets the result of this calculation in the WML browser's context. The function then returns control to the "Results" card in the WML deck from which it was called. This function is declared inside a file called calc.wmls and could be called from a deck like this:

```
<wml>
  <!--Test-->
  <card>
    <do type="accept" label="Submit">
      <go href="calc.wmls#area($length, $width)"/>
    </do>
    <p>
      Length (m): <input name="length" format="N*N"/>
      Width (m): <input name="width" format="N*N"/>
    </p>
  </card>

  <card id="Results">
    <p>
      Area is: $area sq.meters<br/>
    </p>
  </card>
</wml>
```

This WML test deck declares two cards. The first card collects length and width numbers from the user and submits these to the area function declared in the WMLScript file. The second card displays the results of this calculation, accessing the area variable that was set by the area function. The flow of control begins in the first card, passes to the area function, and then returns to the WML deck (this time to the "Results" card). We explain these concepts in more detail in the following sections.

LANGUAGE BASICS

WMLScript is an extended subset of ECMAScript (formerly JavaScript). If you are already familiar with these scripting languages, you may want to skip to the "Libraries" section. WMLScript differs from ECMAScript in many ways, due primarily to the limited execution environment provided by mobile devices. Unlike ECMAScript, WMLScript is always contained in separate compilation units (not embedded in WML). WMLScript only executes on the client side and is encoded into bytecodes prior to transmission to the client. We take a very quick look at the basics of WMLScript, defining and describing the following:

- Essential language elements

- Operators and expressions

- Statements

- Functions

- Pragmas

Much of the syntax of WMLScript will also be familiar to anyone experienced with a 'C'-type language, such as 'C', 'C++', or Java.

Essential Language Elements

Like WML, WMLScript is case sensitive. Be careful when using WMLScript library functions because some of the functions that have equivalent tags in WML use mixed case instead of WML's lowercase (e.g., the `setVar` WMLScript function is equivalent to the `<setvar>` WML element). In general, white space is not significant (except within string literals) so you can format your WML script to make it readable without affecting functionality. Semicolons are used to end statements including expressions, variable declarations, and return statements.

WMLScript implicitly supports a number of data types but does not require that variables be declared as a specific type. These are the types supported:

- Integer – 32-bit signed values.

- Float – 32-bit single precision (vs. 64 bits for ECMAScript).

- ▣ String – May be defined using single (' . . . ') or double (" . . . ") quotes

- ▣ Boolean – Initialized to `true` or `false` and contains the result of a logical test

- ▣ Invalid – A special type useful when denoting an invalid value

Variable names must begin with an alphabet character or an underscore ('_') and may contain any combination of underscore or alphanumeric characters following this initial character. Variables must be declared (e.g., `var x;`) and may be initialized on declaration (e.g., `var name="Jim";`). However because WMLScript is weakly typed, variables can be declared using a string initializer and later used to hold a float, integer, or boolean value. Strings can contain special characters using backslash encoding as in 'C' (e.g., `\n` is a newline and `\t` is a tab). Unlike 'C++' and Java, a variable can be used from the point where it is declared until the end of the function in which the variable is declared.

You can safely use the same name for variables, functions, or function parameters because each of these uses a separate name-space (i.e., an area in memory where names are stored). There are a number of reserved words (language keywords such as `name`, `var`, and `agent`), literals (such as `true` and `false`), and future reserved words (including `export` and `struct`). A complete list can be found in the WMLScript specification. 'C++' style comments are supported allowing blocks (`/* . . . */`) and single-line (`//`) comments.

Operators and Expressions

Operators allow you to assign values to variables, compare values, test truth, and perform arithmetic. For a complete list of operators, see Chapter 6 of the WMLScript specification.

Assignment operators follow the 'C' conventions allowing simple assignment (=) as well as more complex assignments that first carry out an operation and then perform an assignment. Arithmetic assignments perform an arithmetic operation on the left- and right-hand sides of the operator before doing the assignment (e.g., x += y; adds the contents of variable y to variable x and assigns the result to x. Note that this is simply a shorter way of stating x = x+y). Other arithmetic assignments include subtraction (-=), division (/=), and multiplication (*=). Integer division, modulo, and bitwise operation assignment are also supported.

Arithmetic operations include simple arithmetic (+, -, /, and *), integer division (div), modulo (%), and bitwise operations (e.g., << is a bitwise left shift and & is a bitwise AND). Unary operators (that operate on one input) include + (postive value), - (negative value), -- (pre or post decrement), and ++ (pre or post increment) as well as the bitwise NOT (~).

Logical operations include:

- logical AND (&&)

- logical OR (||)

- logical NOT (!)

For example, test = isEmpty && finished; would yield true if both isEmpty and finished were true. Note that as in 'C', when an OR or AND statement is evaluated, evaluation ends as soon as the final value of the statement is known (e.g., assuming x = 5 and y = 2, var a = x > y || firstTime; will evaluate x (5) as greater than y (2) and will not test the variable firstTime).

Comparison operators include:

- less than (<)

- greater than (<)

- equals (==)

- greater than or equal (>=)

- less than or equal (<=)

- not equals (!=)

Data types are compared as follows:

◼ Boolean: `true` is greater than `false`

◼ Integer and floating point: based on values being compared

◼ String: based on the order of character code in the supported character set (`"B"` is greater than `"A"`)

◼ Invalid: returns `invalid` if at least one operand is invalid

Conditional statements are a short way of doing an if-else test where the `?:` operator is used as it is in 'C' (e.g., `output = x > y ? "First is greater" : "Second is greater";` would assign the string `"First is greater"` to the `output` variable if `x` is greater than `y`, otherwise would assign the string `"Second is greater"` to `output`).

Three other operators are worth mentioning. The comma (,) operator is used to carry out more than one evaluation in one expression. For example, to initialize both `i` and `j` in the following for loop, you could use: `for (x=1, y=42; x < 20; x++, y-)`. This loop will begin with `x` set to 1 and `y` to 42 and then increment `x` and decrement `y` each time through the loop. The `typeof` operator allows you to access the current type of a specified variable or expression. This type is returned as a number between 0 and 4 as follows:

◼ Integer = 0

◼ Floating point = 1

◼ String = 2

◼ Boolean = 3

◼ Invalid = 4

For example, consider the following code snippet:

```
var i = 3;
var x = 14.5;
var typeOfCalc = typeof (i * x);
```

The expression `(i * x)` evaluates to a floating point result (`43.5`), so the `typeOfCalc` variable will be set to number `1`. The `isvalid` operator is used to test whether an expression is of type `invalid`, returning `true` if it is and `false`, otherwise (e.g., `isvalid (1/0);` will return `false` because division by zero is undefined).

Statements

The normal set of statements supported in any procedural language are available to the WMLScript developer. These include:

- Variable initialization

- Expressions

- `if` statements

- `for` and `while` loops

- Block statements

- `break`, `continue`, and `return`

- Empty statements

Variables can be declared and initialized or simply declared, in which case their value is automatically set to the empty string (e.g., `var str;` or `var x=78;`). Variables can be declared at any point in a function prior to their first use.

Expressions include calculations, assignments, and function calls. For example:

- `fullName = firstName + lastName;`

- `result = calcTotal(x, y);`

- `total = x * y + z;`

- `showError("Fatal Error");`

if, for, and while statements follow the 'C' syntax as shown in the following example. Note also the block statements ({ . . . }):

```
if (x > y) {
   for (var i = 0; i < x; i++) {
     .
     .
   }
   while (y < z) {
     .
     .
   }
}
```

Sometimes it is useful to be able to stop processing in the middle of a block. Three statements are available to do this:

- ▣ break, which terminates a while or for loop, resuming processing at the statement following the loop.

- ▣ continue, which terminates the current iteration of a while or for loop.

- ▣ return *returnValue*, which exits from a function with the specified *returnValue*.

An empty statement is simply a semicolon and is useful when no action is desired (e.g., when initially constructing a new block of code or function prior to adding business logic or as in the following example when you want to repeat an operation:

```
while (!isReady()) ;
```

Functions

So far we have focused primarily on statement-level syntax. To make use of WMLScript, statements are organized by function and functions are declared within compilation units. A WMLScript function is simply a named collection of WMLScript statements that returns a value. Functions accept parameters that are passed by value (i.e., a copy of the parameter is passed into the function), and when a function is called, it must be passed exactly the same number of parameters as are in its declaration. Functions always return a value (the default being an empty string). If a function needs to pass more data back to a calling function or WML deck, it uses a library call to set the specified variables (we look at this in the libraries section later). A simple function that returns the largest of three numbers follows:

```
function maxOfThree(first, second, third) {...};
```

Functions are defined in compilation units that may be libraries (defined as part of the WAP standards) or files you create. When declaring functions in a file, use the keyword `extern` to make a function available to WML decks or other compilation units (e.g., `extern function maxOfThree...`). At least one function in a file must be declared external.

Functions can be called from WML cards or WMLScript. When calling a function from WML, you need to specify:

■ the URL of the compilation unit.

■ the name of a public (i.e., externally accessible) function in the compilation unit.

■ all parameters required by the function.

For example, to call function `maxOfThree` found in a WMLScript file called `math.wmls`, you could use the following WML:

```
<wml>
  <card>
    <go href="math.wmls#maxOfThree(x, y, z)"/>;
    . . .
  </card>
</wml>
```

Note that in place of parameters, the `<setvar>` element can be used to pass information to a script from WML. Variables can be set by a script using a library function (see "Libraries" later in this chapter) to update the browser context. These can then be accessed as regular WML variables following script execution. However, it is not possible to retrieve a return value directly from the script, so a script that will be called from WML should set a variable containing the return value. This variable can then be accessed by the card to which control is returned (which can be the card that originally called the script). Note that there is no provision to call standard library functions directly from WML with the exception of the Wireless Telephony Application Interface libraries discussed in the "Libraries" section.

When calling a function from WMLScript, you must specify its name and provide a list of parameters the same length as that in the function declaration (e.g., `largest = maxOfThree(x, y, z);`). When calling a local function (that is, one within the same compilation unit), you may call this function prior to its declaration. If the function you are calling is a standard library function, you must specify the library name prior to the function name (e.g., `largest = Lang.max(x, y);` where `Lang` is the language standard library and `max` is the maximum function).

Sometimes it is useful to break up your script into separate compilation units. Perhaps you have a set of utility functions on which several compilation units rely. If you need to reference a function that is declared in another compilation unit, you must include an explicit reference to the file within which it is declared. This is done using the pragma directive `'use url'`. In addition, you must reference the external function in the same way that you refer to a location in any URL, using the `'#'` separator. For example:

```
use url myScript "http:/www.cup.org/scripts/myscript.wmls";
function doTests(x, y, z) {
  .
  .
  var largest = myScript#maxOfThree(x, y, z);
  .
  .
};
```

Note that the `'use url'` pragma assigns a name (`"myScript"`) to the URL, which is later used when accessing the `maxOfThree` function. Of course, `maxOfThree(...)` must be declared as `extern` within `myscript.wmls` to make it accessible for this call.

PRAGMAS

Pragmas are used to specify information at the level of the compilation unit. All pragmas begin with the keyword `use` and are declared prior to any function declarations. We have already seen the `'use url'` pragma, which allows a function to reference external functions within another compilation unit. Pragmas are also available for:

- Access control – Controls which URLs can invoke functions in this compilation unit.

- Metadata – Specifies information about the compilation unit that may be used by servers, the user agent, or passed as an HTTP header.

Access control is achieved in a similar way to WML deck access control, using a `domain` and/or `path` to determine which URLs can access this compilation unit (e.g., `use access domain "www.gov.ns.ca" path "/health";` will limit access to those URLs within the domain `"www.gov.ns.ca"` below the path `"/health"`). Relative URLs are supported for the domain attribute. By default, no access control is implemented for a compilation unit (all external functions have public access).

Metadata is specified using properties. Three property attributes can be specified as strings: property `name`, `value`, and `scheme` (which specifies a way to interpret the property `value`). Metadata to be passed to the server is specified using the `'use meta name'` directive (e.g., `use meta name "Author" "Arthur Dent";`). Metadata to be sent to the user agent is specified using the `'use meta user agent'` directive (e.g., `use meta user agent "ServerVersion", "1.2"`). Metadata can also be passed as HTTP headers using the `'use meta http equiv'` directive (e.g., `use meta http equiv "Keywords" "Galaxy,HitchHiker"`).

That concludes our brief tour of WMLScript language basics. While you need to understand these basics, in order to do real-world programming you also need to be familiar with the standard libraries.

LIBRARIES

The WAP standards provide a rich set of standard libraries as well as libraries to provide application-level security and access to telephony functions. We provide an overview of these libraries for your reference but defer detailed examples to the tutorial section. For further information, see the WMLScript Standard Libraries specification, WMLScript Crypto Library specification, and the Wireless Telephony Application Interface specification, all available from the WAP Forum's Web site.

Lang

The `Lang` library contains functions that directly extend the WMLScript language including integer arithmetic, string to numeric conversion, random number generation, and implementation specific values (e.g., the maximum supported integer). To access these functions from your WMLScript code, use the `Lang` library prefix (e.g., `var smallest = Lang.min(x, y);`)

Arithmetic functions (where parameters `x` and `y` are numbers) include:

- `min(x, y)`, which returns the smaller of `x` and `y`.

- `max(x, y)`, which returns the larger of `x` and `y`.

- `abs(x)`, which returns the absolute value of the specified number `x`.

These functions may return `invalid`.

String to numeric conversion routines (where parameter `s` is a string) include:

- `isInt(s)`, which returns `true` if `s` can be converted to a legal integer.

- `parseInt(s)`, which converts the contents of `s` to an integer.

- `isFloat(s)`, which returns `true` if `s` can be converted to a legal floating point number.

- ◼ `parseFloat(s)`, which converts the contents of `s` to a floating point number.

These functions may return `invalid`.

Random number generation is achieved using:

- ◼ `seed(n)`, which initializes the random number generator with the specified number `n`. If you do not specify `n` as a valid positive number a system-dependent seed will be used.

- ◼ `random(n)`, which returns a positive integer greater than or equal to `0` and less than or equal to `n`.

Both functions may return `invalid`.

Function termination is supported by:

- ◼ `exit(n)`, which ends execution of a function, returning `n` to the caller.

- ◼ `abort(s)`, which signals an abnormal exit from a function, specifying the reason in string `s`.

No values are returned by these functions.

Information about the current WMLScript interpreter is obtained using:

- ◼ `characterSet()`, which returns the MIBenum integer value (assigned by IANA) for the character set used by this WMLScript interpreter (see sidebar "IANA and MIBenum")

- ◼ `float()`, which returns `true` if the interpreter supports floating point operations.

- ◼ `maxInt()`, which returns the maximum integer that can be handled.

- ◼ `minInt()`, which returns the minimum integer that can be handled.

None of these functions return `invalid`.

IANA and MIBenum

IANA (www.iana.org) stands for the Internet Assigned Numbers Authority. In addition to IP addresses and domain names, IANA provides a central coordinating authority for numbering things in the Internet world. IANA houses the unique parameters (e.g., port assignments) and protocol values used in the operation of the Internet. The IANA character set registry contains an enumeration of Internet character sets. Each entry looks something like the following example, which declares the ISO-8859-1 extended ASCII character set with a MIB enumeration of 4:

```
Name: ISO_8859-1:1987                              [RFC1345,KXS2]
MIBenum: 4
Source: ECMA registry
Alias: iso-ir-100
Alias: ISO_8859-1
Alias: ISO-8859-1 (preferred MIME name)
Alias: latin1
Alias: l1
Alias: IBM819
Alias: CP819
Alias: csISOLatin1
```

You may well ask, what is a MIB and why should it need an enumeration? To understand MIBs, we have to start with the Simple Network Management Protocol (SNMP), which is a standard protocol used to manage Internet networks. This protocol is used in the automated management of networks including areas such as security, performance, and configuration. It uses TCP/IP for communication and offers a standard set of commands that makes multivendor interoperability possible. SNMP uses a MIB (management information base) to define the information it can obtain from a network. A MIB is a tree structure that has branches for each device or area of a network (e.g., printers or serial devices). The numbers defined as MIBenums by IANA provide a universal way to describe the character set(s) supported by a particular branch (e.g., a device) within the MIB tree. ◼

Float

This library contains basic floating point operations. Some devices may not support such operations (verify this using the Lang.float() function), in which case these functions will return invalid. Functions include those that return integers related to the specified floating point number, powers and roots, as well as implementation-specific information.

Related integer functions include:

- ▣ int(n), which truncates n returning only the integer part.
- ▣ round(n), which rounds n to the nearest integer (rounding up if two integers are equally close to n).
- ▣ floor(n), which returns the greatest integer that is not greater than n.
- ▣ ceil(n), which returns the smallest integer that is not less than n.

These functions may return invalid.

Power and root functions include:

- ▣ pow(x, y), which returns the result of raising x to the power of y.
- ▣ sqrt(n), which returns the square root of n.

pow will return invalid if x is 0 and y < 0 or if x < 0 and y is not an integer. sqrt will return invalid if n is a negative number.

Information about the WMLScript interpreter includes:

- ▣ maxFloat(), which returns the largest floating point number supported.
- ▣ minFloat(), which returns the smallest floating point number supported.

Neither of these functions returns invalid.

String

String functions provide convenient operations to access and update strings. WMLScript strings can be thought of as arrays of characters with the first character located at index 0. Functions are provided to access, modify, compare, convert to, and format strings.

Access functions that provide information about the specified string include:

- ◨ `length(s)`, which returns the number of characters in s.

- ◨ `isEmpty(s)`, which returns `true` if s contains no characters.

- ◨ `subString(s, start, length)`, which returns the portion of s starting at `start` that is `length` characters long.

- ◨ `charAt(s, index)`, which returns the character in s at position `index`.

- ◨ `find(s, substring)`, which returns the index in s where substring begins or −1 if not found.

- ◨ `elements(s, separator)`, which returns the number of elements that result when s is tokenized (split up) using `separator`. Note that `separator` may be a single character or a multicharacter string.

- ◨ `elementAt(s, index, separator)`, which returns the token in s at position `index` following tokenization using `separator`. Note that `index` begins at zero.

These functions may return `invalid`. The search functions (`find` and `charAt`) are case sensitive.

Modifying functions return a new string that is a modified version of the specified string. These include:

- ◨ `replace(s, old, new)`, which replaces all occurences of `old` substring with `new` within s, returning the newly created string.

- ◨ `removeAt(s, index, separator)`, which returns a new string created by first breaking s into tokens using `separator` and then removing the token and its separator located at `index`. Refer to the `elements` and `elementAt` functions mentioned earlier for more information on tokenizing.

- ◨ `replaceAt(s, new, index, separator)`, which returns a

new string created by first breaking s into tokens using separator and then replacing the token and its separator located at index with the string new.

◼ insertAt(s, new, index, separator), which returns a new string created by first breaking s into tokens using separator and then inserting new in front of the token at index.

◼ trim(s), which returns a new string obtained by removing all trailing and leading white spaces in s.

◼ squeeze(s), which returns a new string obtained by removing all extra consecutive white spaces in s.

These functions are case sensitive and may return invalid.

The compare(s1, s2) function uses lexicographic comparison (based on character code) to compare s1 and s2 returning −1 if s1 is less than s2, 0 if they are equal, and +1 if s2 is greater than s1. Note that you can also use the == operator to check to see if two strings are equal. The toString(value) function converts value into its string representation.

The format(s, n) function applies a format string s to n returning a formatted string using 'C'-like conventions. The format string may specify width and/or precision and must supply a type. Type can be one of d (integer), f (float), or s (string), and the format string must begin with a percent sign. For example, format ("The total value is $%2.2f", n); will return "The total is $45.78" when n is set to 45.7786. Note that to display a percent sign inside a format string, use two percent signs in a row ("%%").

String formatting may not always work as you might expect. For example Phone.com's SDK implementation does not do an implicit conversion of an integer to a float before attempting to format a number as a float (You should perform an explicit float conversion prior to formatting). Also, %2d produces 2 spaces when supplied with a zero value; to ensure that a zero is displayed, you should use %2.1d.

URL

This library contains functions that work with absolute and relative URLs. Functions are provided that get the various parts of a URL, test validity, merge two URLs, perform escaping operations, and get the contents of a URL.

Functions that get various components of a URL include:

- `getScheme(url)`, which returns the scheme (e.g., `"http"`) used in `url`.

- `getHost(url)`, which returns the host (domain) portion of `url` (e.g., `"www.mydomain.com"`).

- `getPort(url)`, which returns the server port number of `url` (e.g., `"80"`).

- `getPath(url)`, which returns the path portion of `url` (e.g., `"/scripts/myScripts.wmls"`).

- `getParameters(url)`, which returns the parameters associated with the last path segment of `url`.

- `getQuery(url)`, which returns the query portion of `url` (following `"?"`) (e.g., `"x=2&y=4"`).

- `getFragment(url)`, which returns the fragment portion of `url` (following `"#"`).

- `getBase()`, which returns an absolute URL for the current compilation unit.

- `getReferer()`, which returns the relative URL (relative to the current compilation unit) of the resource that called this compilation unit.

The functions that accept `url` as a parameter return an empty string if the URL does not contain the requested component. URL validity is tested by the `isValid(url)` function that returns true if `url` has a legal syntax. An absolute URL is returned by `resolve(base, rela-tive)`, which merges `relative` into `base`. Because URLs usually require replacement of reserved characters (e.g., `'?'` and `'/'`) prior to transmission, two methods are provided to replace reserved characters with escape sequences and to do the reverse of this:

- `escapeString(s)`, which returns a string based on `s` but with the appropriate escape sequence substitutions.

- `unescapeString(s)`, which removes escape sequence substitutions from `s` returning the new string.

To get the content of the resource specified by a URL, the URL library provides `loadString(url, contentType)`, which returns a string that matches the `url` and `contentType`. `contentType` is a MIME type that must be a subtype of `"text"` (e.g., `"text/x-vcard"`).

WMLBrowser

This library gives you access to the WML user agent context (when the WMLScript was called from WML). Most of these functions have analogs in WML, and functions are provided to manipulate variables, perform tasks, reset the context, and get the relative URL of the current card.

Functions that manage variables include:

- `getVar(name)`, which returns a string containing the value of `name` from the current browser context or an empty string if this variable does not exist.

- `setVar(name, value)`, which returns `true` if the variable named by `name` containing `value` is successfully set in the current browser context.

These functions will return `invalid` if the syntax of their input parameters is not correct.

Functions that perform tasks are:

- ▣ go(url), which has the same effect as the <go> element in WML. Following completion of the WMLScript function in which the go function is called, control will return to the WML Browser and the card refered to by url will be loaded. This url may be relative to the current deck or may be absolute.

- ▣ prev(), which has the same effect as the <prev> WML element. Following completion of the containing WMLScript function, the previous card in the WML Browser history will be loaded.

- ▣ refresh(), which has the same effect as the <refresh> WML element except that a suspended timer task will not be restarted. Refresh will occur immediately where this is supported by the device; otherwise it will occur when control is returned to the WML Browser following script completion.

Each of these functions will return an empty string if successful and invalid if not. In addition, refresh may return a string indicating a failure to do a refresh (e.g., an image could not be updated); the contents of this string are vendor defined. Note that when a new card is loaded from WMLScript, the referring URL is the URL of the card that was last displayed. For further discussion of tasks, see Chapters 5 and 6.

The newContext() function clears the entire WMLBrowser context including all variables and the card history stack. This task will return an empty string if successful and invalid if not.

The getCurrentCard() function returns the URL of the card that is currently loaded by the WML Browser. If possible, this URL is relative to that of the current WMLScript compilation unit if they share the same base URL.

Dialogs

The Dialogs library provides the following common user interface functions, which may all return `invalid`:

- `prompt(message, default)`, which displays `message` and the `default` response and returns the user's response as a string (e.g., `Dialog.prompt("Number of children: ", "0");`).

- `confirm(message, ok, cancel)`, which displays `message` and offers two options as defined in `ok` and `cancel` (e.g., `Dialog.confirm("Is that your final answer?", "Yes", "No");`). This will return `true` if the user selects `"Yes"` and `false` if he or she selects the `"No"` option.

- `alert(message)`, which displays `message` and waits for the user to confirm before returning an empty string.

Crypto

The cryptographic library is not a standard library, but it is available to public WMLScript programs from WAP version 1.2 on. Currently, it only provides support for digital signatures. Whereas the Wireless Transport Layer Security (WTLS) standard provides for client authentication during a session, the `Crypto` library adds a way to provide a lasting record of a user transaction. This is useful when there must be a foolproof way to determine that a user has approved a particular transaction (e.g., purchase of goods or services). This and other security issues are discussed in more detail in Chapter 9.

The `signText` function requests that the user digitally sign a specified string. A special digital certificate is used for this. This certificate may be stored on a smart card in the mobile device or a SIM card as used in some GSM handsets. The user is presented with the text that is to be signed and must explicitly indicate acceptance and enter a secret PIN. The function then signs the text using the user's private key. Typically, the digital signature created by this as well as the original text will be used by a server to validate the transaction; the signature may be stored for later reference.

The `signText` function has this format:

```
Crypto.signText(s, instructions, keyIdType, keyId).
```

The parameters are as follows:

- ▣ `s` is the string that will be displayed to the user and used to create the digital signature.

- ▣ `instructions` is an integer that instructs the browser to return information in addition to the signed text. The following instruction codes are supported:

    - ▣ 1 – include `s` in the result string

    - ▣ 2 – include public key hash, which corresponds to the signing key in the result string

    - ▣ 4 – include the digital certificate corresponding to the signing key in the result string

    To indicate a combination of these, simply add the codes together.

- ▣ `keyIdType` is an integer code that specifies which key should be used:

    - ▣ 0 – any signing key may be used

    - ▣ 1 – use the signing key that corresponds to the public key supplied in the `keyId` parameter

    - ▣ 2 – use a signing key that is certified by the trusted Certificate Authority indicated by the public key hash supplied in the `keyId` parameter

    The public key hashes are Secure Hash Algorithm (SHA-1) hashes and are set in `keyId` if this parameter is not zero.

- ▣ `keyId` is a string that contains one or more (concatenated) SHA-1 hashes if the `keyIdType` parameter is set to 1 or 0.

Note that this function may not be supported on many wireless devices because it requires some form of personalized locally stored security information (e.g., a Wireless Identity Module, or WIM) to be accessible to the WML Browser.

WTA Public

The Wireless Telephony Application interface provides functions to create telephony applications. Only one library in this interface is available for use by general WML decks or other WMLScript functions – that is the public library. The public library is identified by `wp` when called from WML and by `WTAPublic` when called from WMLScript functions.

When calling the public library from WML, a special URI format is used as follows:

```
wtai://wp//functionName; parameters [!result]
```

where `wtai` identifies the Wireless Telephony Application Interface, `wp` is the public library, and `functionName` is either `mc` to make a call, `sd` to send a Dual Tone Multi-Frequency (DTMF) tone sequence, or `ap` to add a number to the phone book. Parameters are passed for all these functions following a semicolon separator, and an optional variable name can be specified preceded by an exclamation mark (`!`). When calling the public library from WMLScript, a standard library function call is used (e.g., `WTAPublic.functionName(param1, param2);`). The function output is returned as a result of the function call.

Telephone numbers and DTMF digits used in telephony calls must be formatted as follows. International phone calls are prefixed by the plus (+) sign. All phone numbers simply consist of a string of ASCII digits (`"0"` to `"9"`) with no spaces or separators. DTMF digits may contain any combination of the following characters: `"*"` | `"#"` | `"A"` | `"B"` | `"C"` | `"D"` | `","` | `"0"` to `"9."`

The Public WTA library supports:

- `makeCall(number)`, which makes a voice call using the specified `number`. The number will be displayed to the user for acknowledgment prior to the call. This may also be called from WML using `wtai://wp/mc;`*number* where this URI identifies the `makeCall` function and specifies a *number*. This could be embedded in a link or `<go>` element (e.g., `<a href="wtai://wp/mc;4557175"/>`).

- `SendDTMF(`*tones*`)`, which sends a sequence of *tones* over an already active voice connection (e.g., to dial an extension). This may also be called from WML using `wtai://wp/sd;`*tones* where this URI identifies the `sendDTMF` function and specifies a set of *tones* to send. As with the make call function, this URI would be embedded in an `href` attribute (e.g., `<go href="wtai://wp/sd;543*2134"/>`.

- `addPBEntry(number, name)`, which appends a new phone book entry (`name` and `number`) to the current phone book. This may also be called from WML using `wtai://wp/ap;`*number*`;`*name* where this URI identifies the `addPBEntry` function and specifies a `name` and `number` to add. This would be specified in an `href` attribute (e.g., `<a href="wtai://wp/ap;4557175;JEREMY"/>`).

The result of these functions is zero if valid and negative if an error has occurred.

Note that not all phones support the WTA. For example, the Nokia 7110 requires that you use its "Use Number" option in the Options menu (a mechanism borrowed from SMS) to dial a number. Even though these functions were available in WAP 1.1, handsets that support this version may not provide WTA functionality.

That concludes our discussion of libraries. The next sections illustrate the use of both WMLScript and the library functions.

TUTORIAL

The following section illustrates a few common uses of WMLScript including validation, user interaction, formatting, calculations, and telephone operations. We will see how simple procedural logic and library functions can enhance an existing WML application.

When adding WMLScript to your application, you can use the following steps:

1. Decide on a name for your WMLScript compilation unit (file) and create a file with this name plus a comment header in the file that describes the file's functionality.

2. Declare public functions that are to be accessible from WML or other WMLScript as `extern`.

3. Build one function at a time, and unit test these functions using a test WML deck that invokes each function. Make use of debug statements in your code using print statements such as the Console print functions provided by the Phone.com simulator.

4. Create private functions to support the public functions.

The Phone.com UP Simulator (version 4.0) was used to test the tutorial application (it was also verified on a Nokia 7110 simulator). To run WMLScript functions, simply load the test deck that contains the calls to your functions as you would any WML deck. For example, to load a local WML deck on the C drive, you would enter something like this in the 'Go' area or the UP Simulator: `file://c:/wap/ tutorial/mydeck.wml`

Error Handling

WMLScript does not provide an exception handling mechanism like that found in Java and other heavier weight languages. Be careful when testing your WMLScript programs to "exercise" all the branches of your scripts during testing. Common coding mistakes that can lead to errors include:

 using `invalid` variables in calculations.

 dividing by zero.

 using integers where floats are expected and vice versa.

 nesting functions too deeply (the stack memory is very limited on many handsets).

Predictable errors (e.g., user errors) should be trapped and a consistently formatted error message displayed along with a means to cancel or continue as appropriate.

The Tutorial Application

The application we use for our tutorial is an extension of the health inspection system introduced in Chapter 5. We add functionality to the kitchen inspection cards to calculate the size of the kitchen and to validate the information entered about the kitchen (e.g., to ensure there are enough fans to ventilate a kitchen of the specified size). The complete WML and WMLScript for this application is found in Appendix B.

The size of the kitchen is determined from its length and width (assuming that the kitchen is rectangular). For this, we need a function called 'area' that accepts length and width parameters and sets the area in a WML Browser variable. We need to declare this function inside a compilation unit and call this file `kitcalc.wmls` where the `wmls` extension stands for WMLScript:

```
/* Health Inspection Application
   Kitchen calculations
*/

// Calculate the area of a rectangle and go to
// the results card
extern function area(length, width) {
  var area = length * width;
  WMLBrowser.setVar("area", area);
  WMLBrowser.go("#Results");
};
```

The WMLScript begins with a block comment describing this compilation unit. This is followed by the area function with its own comments. This is a public function (using the extern keyword) and accepts parameters for length and width. It allocates a variable area and assigns the results of multiplying length by width to this variable. It then sets the area variable in the browser context and returns control to the browser at the "Results" card within the calling deck (relative URL #Results). Note the use of a semicolon to terminate the function declaration ('};').

Following our own advice (see earlier), we create a WML deck (kitchen.wml) to test our new function. Initially this contains two cards — "EnterSize" and "Results." Note that the XML prologue has been omitted (see Fig. 7-1).

The "EnterSize" card prompts the user to enter the size of the kitchen, storing the input in length and width variables. Note the use of the N*N format mask attribute to force entry of at least one digit. This card defines an accept event handler that invokes the area function in the kitcalc.wmls file. The newcontext attribute ensures that the length and width variables will be cleared every time this card is displayed. The second card, "Results," displays the area browser variable, relying on the WMLScript to set this variable and transfer control to this card. It defines an event handler that allows the tester to enter another kitchen size. Figure 7-1 displays these cards. Screen *a* accepts the length input, screen *b* accepts the width, and screen *c* displays the resulting area. Note that Phone.com microbrowsers place each input item and select list on a separate physical screen even if these fields occur on a single card.

```
<wml>
  <!-Kitchen Functions Test Deck->
  <card id="EnterSize" newcontext="true" title="Enter">
    <do type="accept" label="Submit">
      <go href="kitcalc.wmls#area($length, $width)"/>
    </do>
    <p>
      <strong>Enter Kitchen Size</strong><br/>
      Length (m): <input name="length" format="N*N"/>
      Width (m): <input name="width" format="N*N"/>
    </p>
  </card>

  <card id="Results" title="Results">
    <do type="accept" label="Another">
      <go href="#EnterSize"/>
    </do>
    <p>
      Area is: $area sq.meters<br/>
    </p>
  </card>
</wml>
```

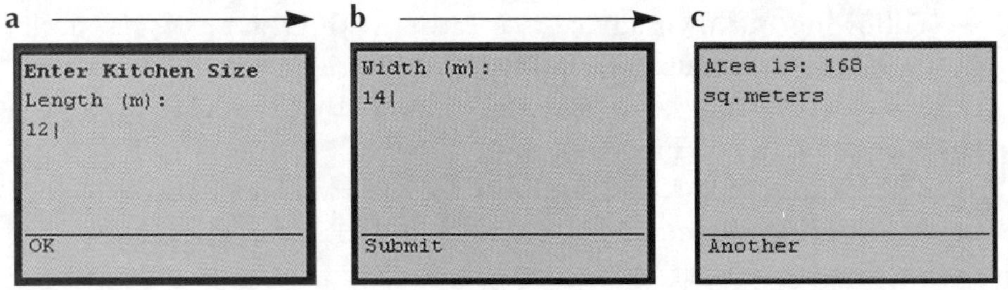

a ⟶ b ⟶ c

```
Enter Kitchen Size      Width (m):           Area is: 168
Length (m):             14|                  sq.meters
12|


OK                      Submit               Another
```

FIGURE 7-1. Area Test Deck

The next step is to create a function that validates the items a health inspector notes about a kitchen. The WML this is based on was introduced in Chapter 5. We call this function `validate` and pass it the values entered on the inspection card. For now, we just validate the lighting and ventilation values. An explanation of the validation values is included as a comment.

```
/* Validate light and fans for the specified area
   Light minimum is measured at counter level
   for preparation area (550 lux)
   Assume fan averages 500 cubic meters/hour,
   kitchen ceiling is 2.5 meters high, and we need
   8 complete air changes per hour:
      # of fans = (room volume * 8) / 500  or
                  (room area / 25)
*/
extern function validate(area, light, fans) {
  // valid values
  var validLight = 550; // LUX measured at counter height
  var validFans = Float.ceil(area / 25); // see above
  var warning = "";

  // build warning message if required
  if (light < validLight)
    warning += "Light is < " + validLight + " lux. ";
  if (fans < validFans)
    warning += "Should have at least " + validFans + " fans. ";

  // return to the appropriate card in the calling deck
  if (warning == "") { // no problems
    WMLBrowser.setVar("validLight", validLight);
    WMLBrowser.setVar("validFans", validFans);
    WMLBrowser.go("#OKResults");
  }
  else {
    // update browser context with warning
    WMLBrowser.setVar("warning", warning);
    WMLBrowser.go("#Warnings");
  };
};
```

First we declare some variables that are set to the valid minimum values for light and number of fans. To calculate how many fans are needed, the area is divided by 25 (see the code for an explanation of this number). Note the use of the ceil function from the Float library, which ensures that we always round up (e.g., 26 square meters will require two fans). The next statement initializes a warning string that is added to depending on whether the light meets the minimum standard (550 lux) and the number of fans is at least that required. The final block tests to see if we have any warnings and if there are no problems sets the valid values in the browser context so they may be displayed for reference on the "OKResults" card. If there are problems, the warning text is set in the browser context and control is transferred to the "Warnings" card.

To test this we need to add some cards to the kitchen.wml deck. First, we add a new card that allows us to select which WMLScript function to test:

```
<card id="Kitchen" newcontext="true">
  <p>
    <strong>Select Test</strong><br/>
    <a href="#EnterSize">Area</a>
    <a href="#EnterValues">Values</a>
  </p>
</card>
```

We add a new card to enter inspection values:

```
<card id="EnterValues" newcontext="true">
  <do type="accept" label="Validate">
    <go href="kitcalc.wmls#validate($area, $light, $fans)"/>
  </do>
  <p>
    <strong>Enter Values</strong><br/>
    Area (sq.m.): <input name="area" format="N*N"/>
    Light (lux): <input name="light" format="N*N"/>
    Number of Fans: <input name="fans" value="0"
                                     format="N*N"/>
  </p>
</card>
```

This card allows the tester to enter an area as well as illumination and ventilation values. It provides an event handler that passes these values to the validate function in kitcalc.wmls. Note that all values are required (using the format mask N*N ensures that at least one digit is entered) to ensure there is no problem when calling the validate routine.

We now need cards to display results for when the inspection values are all right ("OKResults") and for when there are problems ("Warnings"):

```
<card id="OKResults" title="OK">
  <do type="accept" label="Another">
    <go href="#Kitchen"/>
  </do>
  <p>
```

```
      <strong>No Violations</strong><br/>
      Light: $light, >= $validLight<br/>
      Fans: $fans, >= $validFans<br/>
    </p>
  </card>

  <card id="Warnings" title="Warnings">
    <do type="accept" label="Another">
      <go href="#Kitchen"/>
    </do>
    <p>
      <strong>Warnings</strong><br/>
      $warning
    </p>
  </card>
```

Figure 7-2 shows how these cards and the validate function work. The first five screens show a sequence of inspection data entry (screens *a* through *d*) leading to a warning card (screen *e*). The final screen (screen *f*) shows the results of a test where no violations were found (light intensity is 580 lux and there are 6 fans installed).

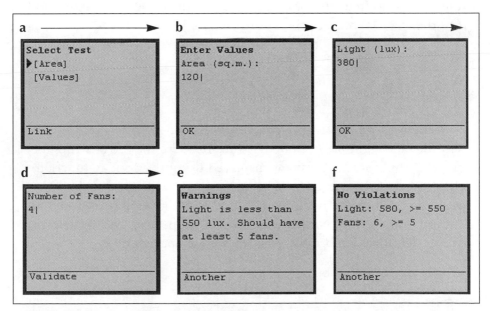

FIGURE 7-2. Validation Test Sequences

So far our health inspection example has shown how we can use WMLScript to process user input, perform calculations, and do validation. Next, we add entry and validation of the fuels that are used for cooking. This will require modifications to our test WML deck to add a multiple select list for cooking fuels and new validation output added to the "OKResults" card:

```
Cooking Fuel
<select name="fuel" value="gas" multiple="true">
  <option value="gas">Natural Gas</option>
  <option value="electric">Electric</option>
  <option value="propane">Propane</option>
  <option value="wood">Wood</option>
</select>
  .
  .
  .
Fuels: $fuel OK
```

We also need to update the kitcalc.wmls file to add a fuel validation routine and call this from the general validate function. The following lines have been added to the validate function to obtain the fuel value from the browser, set a default ("VALID") result, and call the validateFuel private function:

```
// use getVar to get fuels list
var fuel = WMLBrowser.getVar("fuel");
var VALID = "VALID";  // assume fuel OK
var validFuel = validateFuel(fuel, VALID);
```

The next group of lines has also been added to validate. The test for valid light has been updated to illustrate the use of string formatting (light intensity is now displayed using the format function). A new test of the output from validateFuel will append this function's output to the warning message if the function returned an invalid result string. Note the use of the += operator, which performs string concatenation because its operands are both strings:

```
if (light < validLight)
  warning += String.format("Light is < %d lux. ", validLight);
if (validFuel != VALID)
  warning += validFuel;
```

The `validateFuel` function accepts a string containing one or more fuels and a default return value named `VALID`:

```
// Validate fuel combinations returning a warning
// string if invalid or VALID if OK
function validateFuel(fuel, VALID) {
  var SEPARATOR = ";";
  var GASES="gas,propane";
  var gasesSelected = false;
  var WOOD="wood";
  var woodSelected = false;
  var WARNING = "Illegal to mix gas fuels and wood!";

  var nFuels = String.elements(fuel, SEPARATOR);
  for (var i=0; i<nFuels; i++) {
    var thisFuel = String.elementAt(fuel, i, SEPARATOR);
    if (String.find(GASES, thisFuel) >= 0)
      gasesSelected = true;
    if (thisFuel == WOOD)
      woodSelected = true;
    if (gasesSelected && woodSelected)
      break;
  };

  if (woodSelected && gasesSelected)
    return WARNING;

  return VALID;
};
```

Recall that the result of a multiple select list is a string that may contain multiple tokens separated by a semicolon. We determine how many fuels have been selected using the `elements` function of the `String` standard library. We use this value (`nFuels`) to construct a `for` loop that searches for gases (`"propane"` or `"gas"`) as well as `"wood."` The `String` function `elementAt` retrieves the fuel tokens one by one, and the `String.find` function determines if a fuel is a gas. The `break` element is used to exit this loop as soon as we have found at least one gas and wood. If we find a combination of gas and wood, we return a warning message; otherwise we return `VALID`. Figure 7-3 shows the new validation input and results. The inputs include substandard illumination and ventilation (input screens are the same as in Fig. 7-2) as well as an illegal fuel combination of natural gas and wood.

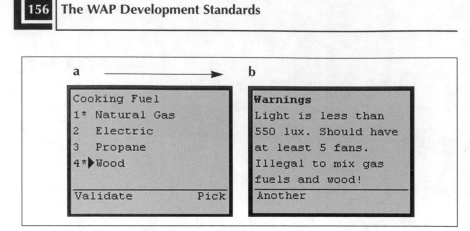

FIGURE 7-3. Fuel Validation Sequences

So far we have relied on WML cards to interact with the user. The WMLScript Dialogs library gives us another way to do this. We will alter our application to include a dialog that alerts the user to warnings if the validation function finds problems. This dialog will offer two options – a new test or reentry of the existing test. Figure 7-4 illustrates this change. One advantage of dialogs such as this is that they display well on both the Nokia 7110 and Phone.com microbrowsers.

The final modification we make to our health inspection application is to provide an option for inspectors to call their office should there be a problem with an inspection. We will modify the dialog created here to provide this option and add WMLScript that uses the WTA public library to make a voice call.

Following display of the dialog, users could choose to make a voice call to their office. A confirmation dialog will be displayed to allow users to confirm the telephone number. The WTA public library function make-Call will then initiate a voice call, suspending the WMLScript function until this call is completed, at which point control will return to the browser at the "Kitchen" card. Due to limitations of the Phone.com simulator, it is not possible to illustrate this function, but Figure 7-5 shows what a WML-based telephone call (e.g., `<go href="wtai://wp/mc;4557175"/>`) displays to the user. (Real devices with voice capabilities may display a prompt such as this prior to dialing.)

That concludes our tutorial. The kitchen deck developed to test WMLScript functions was modified for use as an application deck.

The primary change is that in the application, the user now must enter length and width of the kitchen prior to entering inspection details. The revised kitchen WML and the kitchen calculation WMLScript code can be found in Appendix B.

```
if (Dialogs.confirm(warning, "New Test", "Redo" ))
  WMLBrowser.go("#Kitchen");
else
  WMLBrowser.go("#EnterValues");
```

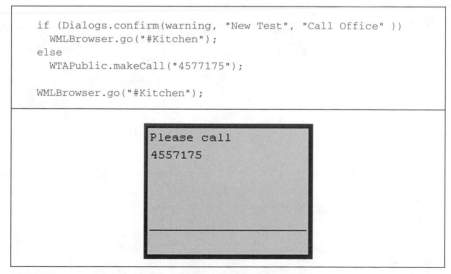

FIGURE 7-4. Confirm Dialog

```
if (Dialogs.confirm(warning, "New Test", "Call Office" ))
  WMLBrowser.go("#Kitchen");
else
  WTAPublic.makeCall("4577175");

WMLBrowser.go("#Kitchen");
```

FIGURE 7-5. Telephone Dialing Confirmation

8

Push
Applications

WAP push applications are fundamentally different from regular
WAP and Web applications. In push applications, information
is sent to a client from a server (the push initiator) without previous
user action. This is useful when an application has time-critical information that would otherwise require a user to monitor its status periodically. Examples of push applications include paging, instant
messaging, stock price alerts, and mobile auction systems.

In this chapter, we look at the components of a WAP push system
and follow a typical messaging scenario. We take a detailed look at push
messages and conclude with a simple push messaging scenario.

The WAP Forum publishes an extensive set of push-related specifications beginning with an architectural overview and covering messaging,
protocols, and the push proxy gateway's functionality. These documents
are available from the WAP Forum Web site (*www.wapforum.org*) and can
be consulted where you need more detail.

PUSH ARCHITECTURE

The framework within which WAP push takes place is illustrated in
Figure 8-1. The push initiator is a server application that communicates with a mobile client via a proxy referred to as a push proxy gateway. This proxy gateway validates and encodes a request message and
sends it to the appropriate mobile client(s). If requested to do so (by
the push application), response messages are handled in the reverse
order, providing a client/server messaging model.

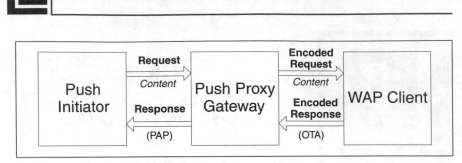

FIGURE 8-1. Push Architecture

Two protocols are used in push messaging: The Push Access Protocol (PAP) is used between the push initiator and the gateway, and the push Over the Air (OTA) Protocol is used between the gateway and the mobile client. Let's take a look at the push players, beginning with the push initiator.

The Push Initiator

The push initiator is an entity (i.e., an application running on a server) that sends push requests and receives push responses. This application communicates with the push proxy gateway over HTTP (although other transport protocols such as SMTP may be supported by future versions of the Push Access Protocol). The push application communicates with push messages, which we discuss in the next section.

Push Access Protocol

The Push Access Protocol (PAP) defines a protocol for sending and receiving messages between a push initiator and a push proxy gateway. The protocol outlines a message body layout and a set of push request and response messages. When implemented over HTTP, PAP messages are sent as HTTP Posts, and (as long as there are no problems with the connection) an HTTP response code of 202 (Accepted) is returned regardless of the result of the message. We discuss these messages and the PAP message format in the "Messages" section.

The Push Proxy Gateway

The push proxy gateway:

- accepts push requests from push applications.

- authenticates push applications (enforcing WAP network access policies).

- locates clients and resolves addresses.

- parses, encodes, and sends push messages over the air.

- handles message rejection (by the client) and errors in message format and delivery.

- informs the initiating push application of the outcome of a push message.

The gateway may also:

- tell the push application about device capabilities (using profiles).

- inform the push application of message status when queried.

- cancel delivery of an in-progress message.

The gateway may be a stand-alone application, but is more likely to be integrated with a regular WAP gateway.

Push OTA Protocol

The Over the Air Protocol supports message transmission between the push proxy gateway and client device. This protocol runs over the Wireless Session Protocol (WSP) layer in the WAP network protocol stack and supports both connectionless and connection-oriented push. In the connection-oriented case an existing session (established by a previous push or regular WAP request) may be used, or a new session may be established between gateway and client. The connectionless push relies on the client to accept requests on a well-known Wireless Datagram Protocol (WDP) port. Support is available for secure (using WTLS) and nonsecure communications. Because we are concerned with application architectures, we do not dwell on the push OTA Protocol, which is primarily of interest to proxy gateway and user agent builders. For more information on this, refer to the WAP Push OTA Protocol specification.

The Client

A mobile device that supports push applications provides a way for a push proxy gateway to send it a push message. The client can listen on a well-known port for requests or may implement a special application (the Session Initiation Application, or SIA), which accepts requests for push sessions. In addition, a currently established session can be used to send push messages. Once a push message is received, the client uses the address information to determine which client application (e.g., the WML Browser user agent) should handle the message. Not all WAP clients are capable of receiving push messages (push specifications were approved in WML 1.2). An example of a WAP 1.2 compliant handset is Ericsson's R520m model. This European handset supports the GPRS (packet-switched) network technology as well as GSM. The always-on nature of a GPRS network makes push (and data applications in general) much more pleasant to use because it essentially removes connection wait times. Ericsson's T36M model also supports WAP 1.2, but it is unclear from the vendor's literature whether these devices fully support the WAP push standards. The current version of Nokia's WAP Toolkit provides simulation of a push-capable device in its Blueprint handset simulator. This toolkit supports push message creation and can be used when developing push applications.

MESSAGES

The WAP Forum push specification suite provides a number of push message variations, including:

1. immediate loading or caching of pushed content (service loading).

2. indication of a push request that the client can accept in order to load an application (service indication).

3. query and maintenance messages.

These messages are formatted in a common way.

Message Format

A typical push message contains a header section made up of HTTP, WAP, (optional) user-defined headers, and a body section that can be of any MIME content type. A push message conforms to the generic Internet message format defined in RFC 822 (see *www.w3.org/protocols/rfc822*) and consists of one or more headers separated from an optional body by an empty line. The WAP push message may contain HTTP 1.1 headers (see sidebar "HTTP Requests and Responses") such as 'Content-Encoding', 'Content-Type' (the only header required by the push specifications), 'Cache-Control', and 'From'. For a complete list of headers, see the WAP Forum's WAP Push Message specification.

HTTP Requests and Responses

The Hypertext Transfer Protocol (HTTP) is a network protocol used to deliver resources on the Web, whether they are HTML or XML files, images, or query results. HTTP clients communicate with servers using requests and responses. The format of request and response messages is similar with both containing:

- ▣ An initial line (different for request and response).
- ▣ Zero or more header lines.
- ▣ A blank line.
- ▣ An optional message body (e.g., request parameters or an HTML page).

For a request message, the initial line consists of a method name (GET or POST), followed by a URL, followed in turn by the version of HTTP to which this message conforms. For example:

```
GET /books/wap.html HTTP/1.0
```

specifies a GET request for an HTML page located at /books/wap.html. The version of HTTP that will be used is 1.0, and the URL of the server to which this request is directed is not specified in the message. In simple cases, this initial line and a following blank line are all that is required for a valid HTTP 1.0 request. However, HTTP 1.1 requires that you include a header identifying the host name (to deal with the issue of multiple domain names residing at the same physical IP address). It is also possible (and some would say good form) to include client information when making a request. HTTP headers can be used to include the sender's e-mail address and the type of browser that is making the request, as the following HTTP 1.1 POST request shows:

```
POST /feedback/inforequest HTTP/1.1
Host: www.wirelessweb-books.com
From: gumby@felineweb.com
User-Agent: Mozilla/4.73

name=Gumby&favoriteTitle=A+Guide+To+Bluetooth
```

The first line defines a POST request that will be sent to the resource identified by "/feedback/inforequest." The host is explicitly identified in the Host HTTP header. This request is from an individual identified by her e-mail address (gumby@felineweb.com) and was sent from an HTML user agent ("Mozilla/4.73").

HTTP responses begin with an initial status line containing the HTTP version, a response status code, and an English reason phrase describing the status code. Some typical status codes include "200 OK", the infamous "404 Not Found," and "301 Moved Permanently." If an HTTP response includes a body, it will be described by one or more headers that follow the initial line. The following shows a simple HTML response returned from the POST request above:

```
HTTP/1.1 200 OK
Date: Fri 22 Sep 2000 22:23:31 GMT
Content-Type: text/html
Content-Length: 112

<html>
   <head><title>Thanks for your feedback!</title></head>
   <body>We value your opinion, Gumby!</body>
</html>
```

Headers are supplied for the date, content type (HTML), and number of bytes in content (112). The body consists of a brief HTML document. For more information on HTTP 1.1, refer to the RFC 1945 (www.w3.org/protocols/). ▣

In addition to HTTP headers, a number of WAP-specific headers are allowed:

▣ Application ID (X-Wap-Application-Id), which identifies a user agent within a mobile client (the default is the WML user agent).

▣ Content URI (X-Wap-Content-URI), which uniquely identifies this content for use when caching.

▣ Initiator URI (X-Wap-Initiator-URI), which identifies the push initiator.

It is also possible to define additional implementation-dependent message headers that can be used to communicate between a server-side application and a client application running in a mobile device.

Consider this example message:

```
POST /push/receiver HTTP/1.1
Host: www.ppg1.unisys.com
X-Wap-Initiator-URI: http://www.cup.org/pushApp
Content-Type:  Multipart/Related;  boundary=oehfdslklkjasd;
               type="application/xml"
Content-Length: 634

--oehfdslklkjasd
Message body goes here…
```

Note the space between the HTTP header block and the body that begins with the multipart separator. This is an HTTP POST message directed to a URL at "www.ppg1.unisys.com/push/receiver." The host name appears on its own line (required by HTTP 1.1), and the first line contains the method (POST) and the path to the receiver of this request ("/push/receiver"). This URL path could identify a servlet that handles this push proxy gateway function. The first line also identifies the version of HTTP (1.1) to which this message conforms. The X-Wap-Initiator-URI is a WAP header defining the source of the request. The last two headers identify the body's content type and length. Note that the boundary attribute ("oehfdslklkjasd") is simply a unique string that will be used to separate sections of the message.

The body format may be a MIME multipart/related compound object (see sidebar "MIME and Multipart/Related Messages") or a simple application/XML entity when there is only one body entity (see "Push Access Protocol" later for more information on body entities).

Push messages are transmitted as multipart MIME messages (see sidebar) with Extensible Markup Language (XML) payloads containing one of the above message types. These messages are sent between the server application and the gateway using the Push Access Protocol (PAP).

MIME and Multipart/Related Messages

Multipurpose Internet Mail Extensions (MIME) define a standard representation for complex message bodies – that is, message bodies that are not simple human-readable ASCII text messages. Multipart/Related MIME messages are made up of a number of related MIME body parts (compound objects). Each body part is separated by a boundary string identified in the content type header. The type of information in the body must be identified by a type parameter (e.g., "application/xml"). The following MIME message contains two parts, both of which are XML documents. The second document is a service loading document (identified by <sl...>), which we discuss later. "example1" is a unique string used as a boundary between these parts:

```
Content-Type: Multipart/Related; boundary=example1;
type="application/xml"

--example1
Content-Type: application/xml

<?xml version="1.0"?>
    <!DOCTYPE pap PUBLIC "-//WAPFORUM//DTD PAP 1.0//EN"

  "http://www.wapforum.org/DTD/pap_1.0.dtd">
      <pap>
        . . .
      </pap>
--example1
Content-Type: application/xml

<?xml version="1.0"?>
<!DOCTYPE pap PUBLIC "-//WAPFORUM//DTD SL 1.0//EN"
                  "http://www.wapforum.org/DTD/sl.dtd">
<sl . . ./>
--example1  ▢
```

Push Access Protocol

The Push Access Protocol (PAP) defines a protocol for sending and receiving messages between a push initiator (server application) and a push proxy gateway. The protocol outlines a message body layout that may contain up to three separate entities or sections:

- Control
- Content
- Capabilities

The control entity defines what the type of message is and to whom it is addressed. It may also contain values that specify the quality of service required for this message. The content entity contains the information that is to be delivered to the mobile client. This might be a service indication or service loading message. The capabilities entity describes the capabilities that the push application expects to be supported by the mobile client. Typically, a message body contains a control entity and may contain a content entity. Service messages (see later) may contain content entities (in the third body part), and Client Capability Responses contain a content entity as the second body part.

PAP allows the following message pairs:

- Service message/response
- Cancel message/response
- Status Query message/response
- Client Capabilities Query message/response
- Result Notification message/response

PAP also describes a Bad Response message to handle messages that cannot be understood. All messages are sent from the push initiator to the push proxy gateway, except for the result notification message, which is initiated by the push proxy gateway.

Control

The control body part is an XML document that describes what type of
message is contained in the content body part as well as other information
about this message. The `<pap>` element may contain one of the message
request/response types mentioned earlier (e.g., `<push-message>` identifies a service indication or loading request message). These message elements contain other elements and attributes that may describe where a
message should be sent to (`<address>`), a desired 'quality of service', or
the status/progress of a request. The following control XML document
illustrates a confirmed push message control part. This part would be followed by a service indication or service loading message:

```
<?xml version="1.0"?>
<!DOCTYPE pap PUBLIC "-//WAPFORUM//DTD PAP 1.0//EN"
                    "http://www.wapforum.org/DTD/pap_1.0.dtd">
<pap>
  <push-message
        push-id="pid123@cup.org"
        ppg-notify-requested-to="http://www.cup.org/myPushApp"
        deliver-before-timestamp="2000-09-15T10:30:00Z">
    <address
      address-value="WAPPUSH=crb%40cup.org/TYPE=USER@ppg1.unisys.com">
    </address>
    <quality-of-service priority="low" delivery-method="confirmed"/>
  </push-message>
</pap>
```

The `push-id` attribute (`"pid123@cup.org"`) is a unique identifier
defined by the push application and can be used to later cancel or check
the status of this request. The `ppg-notify-requested-to` attribute
tells the gateway that we would like a notification of message outcome
and to where this notification message should be directed. The `deliver-
before-timestamp` attribute defines the latest time that the gateway
should deliver this message (in this case before 10:30 on the morning of
September 15, 2000 UTC). Note that this time must be formatted in
Coordinated Universal Time (UTC) because time zones are not supported
by push messages. The addressee is `"crb@cup.org"` and this address is of
type `"USER"`. We assume that the push proxy gateway can map this
to a mobile network address. Note that device addressing can also

be used, in which case a telephone number or IP address could replace the illustrated user-defined address (e.g., `address-value="WAPPUSH= 187.153.199.30/TYPE=IPv4@ppg1.unisys.com"` would define an IP address that might be used with a CDPD IP-based network). The `<quality-of-service>` element specifies this is a low-priority message and that the gateway should request confirmation from the client device (note that this confirmation is between the client and the gateway and should not be confused with the `ppg-notify-requested-to` confirmation between the gateway and push application).

The following control XML document illustrates a possible response to the previously described push message:

```
<?xml version="1.0"?>
<!DOCTYPE pap PUBLIC "-//WAPFORUM//DTD PAP 1.0//EN"
                    "http://www.wapforum.org/DTD/pap_1.0.dtd">
<pap>
  <push-response push-id="pid123@cup.org"
                 sender-address="http://www.ppg1.unisys.com"
                 reply-time="2000-09-15T10:12:00Z">
    <response-result code="1000"  desc="OK"/>
  </push-response>
</pap>
```

This response indicates that the push message was successfully received (but not necessarily successfully processed by the mobile client – this will be indicated in a later `resultnotification-response`).

We describe additional message control parts later, and for more information, take a look at the WAP Push Access Protocol specification. This WAP Forum document contains complete definitions (including XML DTDs) of all push control document types.

Service Loading

Service loading describes a method where a server application can cause a mobile client to load a specified resource immediately. For example, a telephone billing application might send a service loading request to a user's cellular phone, causing the phone to load a WML page automatically that displays a low account balance warning. The service loading message specifies a URL from which the WML content should be fetched and optionally suggests how the client should treat this message (i.e., low priority, high priority, or load in the background – cache). The following illustrates a possible service loading body:

```
<?xml version="1.0"?>
<!DOCTYPE pap PUBLIC "-//WAPFORUM//DTD SL 1.0//EN"
                     "http://www.wapforum.org/DTD/sl.dtd">
<sl  href="http://www.cup.org/myApp"  action="execute-high"/>
```

This tells the client to load `"myApp"` at `"www.cup.org"` with a high priority. Note that the push initiator and the server specified by `href` need not be the same. Other allowable `action` values are `"execute-low"` and `"cache."` Also note that no `<address>` element is contained in this document because this is specified separately in the `<pap>` document that would precede it. More information can be found in the WAP Service Loading specification.

Service Indication

Service indications provide a more indirect and subtle way of contacting a mobile client. When a typical service indication message is sent, it contains a text message that will be displayed to the user indicating that a server-side event has occurred (e.g., the arrival of new mail). The user may then choose to take a specified action or defer this to a later time. There are advantages to this approach over service loading. The users (rather than the push service) remain in control. Also this may improve network loading in cases where a push initiator broadcasts a message to many clients. Although the initial broadcast may consume a burst of bandwidth, the resulting pulled content will not occur at once, spreading the load on network and server depending on when each user decides to retrieve the referenced content.

Service indications are more complicated than service loading messages and allow the push application to specify:

 A unique identifier – required to distinguish pending service indications from one another.

◼ Creation date/time – used by a client to ensure that this message supersedes an existing message.

◼ Expiry date/time – used by a client to discard messages that have not been dealt with by the specified time.

◼ Action – specifies the action to be taken by a client on receipt of this message. This action can be to delete a previously sent service indication, to let the user know of this request (with low, medium, or high priority), or to inform the user of additional information as specified in the <info> element.

◼ Info – specifies a vendor-specific list of information items that can be used to pass additional information to the client.

The following example shows a service indication similar to our service loading message example:

```
<?xml version="1.0"?>
<!DOCTYPE pap PUBLIC "-//WAPFORUM//DTD SI 1.0//EN"
                     "http://www.wapforum.org/DTD/si.dtd">
<si>
   <indication  si-id="si_id123@cup.org"
                href="http://www.cup.org/myApp"
                created ="2000-09-15T10:12:00Z"
                si_expires ="2000-09-15T18:00:00Z"
                action="signal-high">
     Today's schedule has changed!
   </indication>
</si>
```

This service indication could be used to inform field workers that their schedule has been altered for today. Details of this will be displayed when users acknowledge this message and request `"myApp"` (which could map to a servlet) at `"www.cup.org."` The creation date was set to 10:12 a.m. on September 15 and this message expires at 6:00 p.m. on the same day. A high-priority action was specified because changes to a field worker's schedule should be acted on immediately. Another allowable action is `"signal-none,"` used when an <info> element should be acted on by the client. Actions `"signal-low,"` `"signal-medium,"` and `"signal-high"` tell the client that the indication text should be displayed (with varying degrees of urgency). An action of `"delete"` specifies that an existing message with `si-id` should be deleted from the client's message queue. More information can be found in the WAP Service Indication specification.

Cancel Messages

The cancel message provides a means to cancel a previously submitted push message. The following example cancels the push message described in the "Control" section:

```
<?xml version="1.0"?>
<!DOCTYPE pap PUBLIC "-//WAPFORUM//DTD PAP 1.0//EN"
                    "http://www.wapforum.org/DTD/pap_1.0.dtd">
<pap>
  <cancel-message push-id="pid123@cup.org">
    <address
      address-value="WAPPUSH=crb%40cup.org/TYPE=USER@ppg1.unisys.com">
    </address>
  </cancel-message>
</pap>
```

This would cancel message `"pid123@cup.org"` for the specified addressee. If no addresses are specified, the gateway will attempt to cancel the specified message for all associated addressees. Note that support for this message type within a push proxy gateway is optional; sending a cancel message to a gateway that does not support this function will result in a cancel response message with a result code that indicates this (e.g., code `"3001"`– `"Not Implemented"`).

The cancel response message informs the push application of the outcome of a cancel message. This message contains one or more results that may reference the address or addresses for which the result applies. For example:

```
<?xml version="1.0"?>
<!DOCTYPE pap PUBLIC "-//WAPFORUM//DTD PAP 1.0//EN"
                    "http://www.wapforum.org/DTD/pap_1.0.dtd">
<pap>
  <cancel-response push-id="pid123@cup.org">
```

```
      <cancel-result code="1000" desc="OK">
        <address
          address-value="WAPPUSH=crb%40cup.org/TYPE=USER@ppg1.unisys.com">
        </address>
      </cancel-result>
    </cancel-response>
  </pap>
```

This indicates that the cancel request was successful for the specified address.

Status Query Messages

The status query message is used by a server application to inquire about an outstanding push message submission. It is similar in structure to the cancel message, as the following example shows:

```
<?xml version="1.0"?>
<!DOCTYPE pap PUBLIC "-//WAPFORUM//DTD PAP 1.0//EN"
                     "http://www.wapforum.org/DTD/pap_1.0.dtd">
<pap>
  <statusquery-message push-id="pid123@cup.org">
    <address
        address-value="WAPPUSH=crb%40cup.org/TYPE=USER@ppg1.unisys.com">
    </address>
  </statusquery-message>
</pap>
```

The gateway responds with a result message specifying when the message reached its current state, what that state is (e.g., "delivered", "undeliverable", or "expired"), and a status code and description. The result message may also list the addresses to which this result applies and will include a quality of service element describing the delivery methods that were used, if the message was delivered successfully. Note that as with cancel messages, gateway support for this message type is optional, and sending a status query message to a gateway that does not support this function will result in a status query response message with a result code of "3001"– "Not Implemented."

Here is an example status query response:

```
<?xml version="1.0"?>
<!DOCTYPE pap PUBLIC "-//WAPFORUM//DTD PAP 1.0//EN"
                    "http://www.wapforum.org/DTD/pap_1.0.dtd">
<pap>
  <statusquery-response push-id="pid123@cup.org">
    <statusquery-result event-time="2000-09-15T10:12:16Z"
                        message-state="pending"
                        code="1001"
                        desc="Accepted For Processing">
      <address
        address-value="WAPPUSH=crb%40cup.org/TYPE=USER@ppg1.unisys.com">
      </address>
    </statusquery-result>
  </statusquery-response>
</pap>
```

This message indicates that the request has been validated and is still in progress. No `<quality-of-service>` element is specified because final delivery has not yet occurred.

Result Notifications

The result notification message is initiated by a proxy gateway following the final outcome of a push message submission. This message is sent only if the push application indicated within the push message that result notification was required. The following example shows a result notification for our original push message which indicates that it was successfully delivered to the client (at 10:12:28 a.m.) and also tells us which delivery method, network, and bearer were used for delivery (because we included a quality of service element in our original push message):

```
<?xml version="1.0"?>
<!DOCTYPE pap PUBLIC "-//WAPFORUM//DTD PAP 1.0//EN"
                    "http://www.wapforum.org/DTD/pap_1.0.dtd">
<pap>
  <resultnotification-message
                    push-id="pid123@cup.org"
                    sender-address="http://www.ppg1.unisys.com"
                    sender-name="MegaWAP1.1"
                    received-time="2000-09-15T10:12:07Z"
```

```
                      event-time="2000-09-15T10:12:28Z"
                      message-state="delivered"
                      code="1000" desc="OK">
      <address
       address-value="WAPPUSH=crb%40cup.org/TYPE=USER@ppg1.unisys.com">
      </address>
      <quality-of-service delivery-method="confirmed"
                          network="GSM"
                          bearer="CSD"/>

   </resultnotification-message>
</pap>
```

This notification will be sent to the application that was specified in the initial push message `ppg-notify-requested-to` attribute. This application should respond to the gateway with a result notification response as follows:

```
<?xml version="1.0"?>
<!DOCTYPE pap PUBLIC "-//WAPFORUM//DTD PAP 1.0//EN"
                     "http://www.wapforum.org/DTD/pap_1.0.dtd">
<pap>
   <resultnotification-response
                     push-id="pid123@cup.org"
                     code="1000" desc="OK">
      <address
       address-value="WAPPUSH=crb%40cup.org/TYPE=USER@ppg1.unisys.com">
      </address>
   </resultnotification-response>
</pap>
```

Client Capabilities Queries

Client capabilities query messages allow a server application to determine the capabilities of a specified mobile client. Responses to these queries are defined using Resource Description Frameworks (RDF) documents (see Chapter 9 for more information on RDF). The following message requests the client capabilities for the client addressed in the examples here:

```
<?xml version="1.0"?>
<!DOCTYPE pap PUBLIC "-//WAPFORUM//DTD PAP 1.0//EN"
                     "http://www.wapforum.org/DTD/pap_1.0.dtd">
<pap>
```

```
<ccq-message query-id="ccq123@cup.org">
  <address
    address-value="WAPPUSH=crb%40cup.org/TYPE=USER@ppg1.unisys.com">
  </address>
</ccq-message>
</pap>
```

A response to this query might be as follows:

```
<?xml version="1.0"?>
<!DOCTYPE pap PUBLIC "-//WAPFORUM//DTD PAP 1.0//EN"
                    "http://www.wapforum.org/DTD/pap_1.0.dtd">
<pap>
  <ccq-response query-id="ccq123@cup.org"
                code="1000" desc="OK">
    <address
      address-value="WAPPUSH=crb%40cup.org/TYPE=USER@ppg1.unisys.com">
    </address>
  </ccq-message>
</pap>
```

A separate MIME message body part would follow containing the actual client capabilities:

```
<?xml version="1.0"?>
<rdf:RDF xmlns:rdf="http://www.w3.org/1999/02/22-rdf-syntax-ns#"
         xmlns:prf="http://www.wapforum.org/UAPROF/ccppschema1.0#">
  <rdf:Description>
    <prf:WapVersion>1.2</prf:WapVersion>
    <prf:WmlDeckSize>3800 octets</prf:WmlDeckSize>
    <prf:WapDeviceClass>A </prf:WapDeviceClass>
    <prf:WapPushMsgSize>3800 octets</prf:WapPushMsgSize>
    <prf:WmlVersion>
      <rdf:Bag>
        <rdf:li>1.2</rdf:li>
      </rdf:Bag>
    </prf:WmlVersion>
  </rdf:Description>
</rdf:RDF>
```

This contains metadata for a device capable of receiving 3800 byte decks and push messages and supporting WAP version 1.2 and WML version 1.2.

Bad Message Response

A bad message response will be received when the gateway is unable to understand or process a message from a push initiator. This happens when the message is unintelligible or specifies a version of the push access protocol that the gateway does not support. The following response informs the push initiator that its request is not understood:

```
<?xml version="1.0"?>
<!DOCTYPE pap PUBLIC "-//WAPFORUM//DTD PAP 1.0//EN"
                     "http://www.wapforum.org/DTD/pap_1.0.dtd">
<pap>
  <badmessage-response code="2000" desc="Bad Request"/>
</pap>
```

Message Addressing

The push initiator deals with a number of addresses that specify the following:

- Push proxy gateway

- WAP application that will handle client requests

- Result notification handler

- Mobile device(s)

- User agent within a mobile device

The gateway is addressed by its URL (assuming PAP is running over HTTP). The WAP application is identified by the `href` URL in a service indication or loading message. This is typically the address of a servlet or CGI program that can satisfy a normal WAP pull request with WML content. The result notification handler is often the same as the push initiator because result notifications should correlate with the push requests. The mobile device address is the only address that is not simply a URL.

The mobile device address contains a client and gateway address formatted as follows:

```
WAPPUSH=ClientAddress/AddressType@GatewayAddress
```

Note that "/" separators may appear before the `ClientAddress` and after `AddressType`.

The client address may be either user defined (i.e., defined by a particular gateway provider) or a device address. User-defined addresses consist of a text string and are accompanied by an address type of `TYPE=USER`. Device addresses may be telephone numbers, IP addresses, or other bearer-specific address types. For example, `183.143.199.30/TYPE=IPv4` identifies a device-specific address for an IP version 4 compatible client. `TYPE=IPv6` and `TYPE=PLMN` are used for IP version 6 and public land mobile network telephone numbers, respectively.

The gateway address contained in the mobile device address can be a regular domain name or IP address (e.g., `ppg1.unisys.com`). A complete mobile device address might resemble one of the following:

- `WAPPUSH = chris.bennett@unisys.com/TYPE=USER@ppg1.unisys.com` (user-defined client address that uses an e-mail address as a device identifier).

- `WAPPUSH=+119024212345/TYPE=PLMN@ppg2.unisys.com` (device-dependent client address using a phone number to identify the client).

- `WAPPUSH=183.143.199.30/TYPE=IPv4@ppg3.unisys.com` (device-dependent client address using an IP address to identify the client).

Note that it is possible to address multiple clients with a single message simply by adding address elements for each addressee. The push access protocol specifies that each request will receive a single response regardless of how many addressees are included. This also applies to result notifications. In addition, certain addresses may be expanded by the gateway to accomplish a broadcast message. This broadcast is not visible to the push initiator, and a single response will be returned for this request.

Application-level addressing (i.e., addressing a specific user agent application in a mobile device) is done using a WAP header

(X-Application-Id) in the push message. This header can be set to a URI or a numeric value. Although this would probably not be used by a general push application, this would be required when pushing messages to a user agent other than the default WML browser (e.g., the wireless telephony application).

Responses and Status Codes

When a message response is returned, it often contains a code attribute that describes the status of the processed message. These status codes are divided into the following classes:

1. Success

2. Request message errors

3. Errors related to the push proxy gateway

4. Mobile client abort

Note that the Push Access Protocol specification differentiates between server and service errors, both of which are errors related to the push proxy gateway. For a complete list of error codes and descriptions, refer to the WAP Push Access Protocol specification.

Capabilities

Following a capabilities query, a capabilities body part will be included in a the Multipart/Related MIME capabilities query response. Refer to the "Client Capabilities Queries" section earlier for more information. Note that device capabilities can be dealt with in a number of ways:

 Capabilities query (as discussed earlier)

■ Capabilities selected during client subscription

■ Capabilities assumed and passed to the gateway with push message

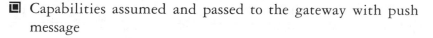

As we discuss later, a push application usually requires a client to sign up via some form of subscription service. This subscription application would obtain the client address and preferences and could note device capabilities during sign-up. Push proxy gateways may support capabilities information as part of a push message. A gateway that does will use this information to ensure that the target device(s) are capable of handling the pushed request. The push response result will indicate this.

PUSH DESIGN ISSUES

Following are some issues that should be considered when designing a push application:

- Selecting a message type
- Confirmation
- Addressing
- Security (authentication and encryption)

Selecting a Message Type

There are two choices when considering what type of message to use in an application: service loading and service indication. Service indication messages are preferred in general because they are less invasive (requiring user acceptance) and may be easily deferred by the user. Most service loading applications assume a privileged relationship with the user (e.g., that of a mobile provider).

Confirmation

Accepting confirmations provides an assurance that the end user(s) received (or failed to receive) a pushed message. However it has a price associated with it in that the push initiator (or its delegate) must be able to accept unsolicited HTTP messages and reconcile these messages with previous requests. This makes the initiator application more complex. Consider skipping this unless strictly necessary. Another way to determine if a request was successful is to use a service indication message and track when a client requests the content referenced in this message.

Addressing

How clients are addressed depends on network and/or WAP service. The client address must somehow be obtained prior to sending a push message, either through an online subscription process or a previously established relationship (such as that of an employee/employer or mobile subscriber/provider). User confidentiality is sure to become a significant issue as push applications become widespread.

Security

Security issues are very important when building a push service, and the following questions need to be answered:

- Will the message and resulting pulled content be secure? (Encryption)

- Will my push message be allowed through by the gateway? (Proxy authentication and trust)

- Will the client accept pushed messages from my URL? (Client authentication and content trust)

Add to this that the mobile device (i.e., the client) may or may not trust the push proxy gateway, and security begins to look quite complex! Encryption is probably the simplest part of this equation.

Encryption is usually achieved by a combination of TLS (between servers and gateway) and WTLS between the push proxy gateway and the client. However, not all gateways and mobile devices support encryption. Encryption over HTTP (via TLS) can be enforced for pulled content by specifying a secure URL (e.g., `https://. . .`) in the service indication or loading message. The mobile device may support encryption (via WTLS), but some current devices allow the user to override this (a security problem when the WAP service expects end-to-end security). It is also possible that the push application and mobile client could perform application-level encryption and authentication (using signed and/or encrypted content); how this would be achieved is not defined by the WAP standards.

In a push application, two entities must be authenticated – the push initiator and the resource referred to in the push message. This authentication must be established to the mobile client's satisfaction. Authentication of the push initiator is often left to the push proxy gateway, which can use session-level certificates that are part of TLS or perhaps some form of HTTP authentication (e.g., Basic authentication using user ID and password). As far as trusting the content referred to in a push message, the Over the Air protocol supports delegation of this to the gateway (assuming the mobile client trusts this gateway), or the client can maintain a list of trusted URIs and compare the URI in the message to this list.

One concern around authentication and access is that push proxy gateways can choose to disallow entry to any push application that does not have some form of previously established business agreement with the gateway owner. This is equivalent to the "walled garden" policy adopted by some mobile providers in an attempt to retain control of the mobile client's Internet access. Admittedly, some form of filtering is probably needed to prevent denial of service, spam, and other attacks on mobile devices.

ARCHITECTURE

Push applications require a slightly different architecture from pull applications due to the inclusion of a push initiator program. The push initiator plays a client role in that, like a Web browser, it initiates an HTTP request with a server. The initiator may be a polling application (or be invoked by a polling application) in the case of

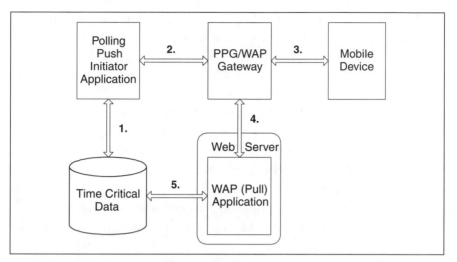

FIGURE 8-2. Separate Polling Initiator and Web-Server-Based WAP Application

time-sensitive notification services (e.g., stock price alerts or e-mail notifications). Alternatively, the initiator could be activated by a pull from a client (which would be one way to implement an instant messaging service). Java, with its inherent network support, makes a logical choice for the push initiator; a Java application could be used for a monitoring/polling service, and a servlet would work in the case of a client-initiated push service. Note that things get more complicated if a stand-alone initiator application requires result notification, because this requires the ability to accept HTTP requests (like a Web server).

In Figure 8-2, a separate application takes care of polling a data source (1) to determine when time-critical data should be sent to mobile clients. When data is ready to be sent, this application sends a message to the PPG (2), which passes it to the client (3). The client retrieves the specified resource (3) via the PPG, which sends the request to a standard WAP application accessed via a Web server (4). This application can access the time-critical data (5) to build its response.

Figure 8-3 shows an alternative to the stand-alone push application that separates the polling of time-critical data from the push initiation. This has the advantage of allowing the push initiator and WAP application to run inside a Web server (handy when receiving HTTP requests). These applications could even be combined. A monitor periodically checks time-critical data (1), and when data is available for a mobile client notifies an 'event-driven' push initiator by sending this application an HTTP request (2). The push initiator sends a message to the PPG (3), which passes it to the client (4.). The client retrieves the specified resource (4) via the PPG, which sends the request to a WAP 'pull' application accessed via the Web server (5). This application can access the time-critical data (6) to build its response.

The layout in Figure 8-3 could also be used when one client device needs to send information to another. This initiating client device would send a request (1a and 2a) to the event-driven push initiator, which would pass on the specified information via a push message to another mobile device client (3 and 4).

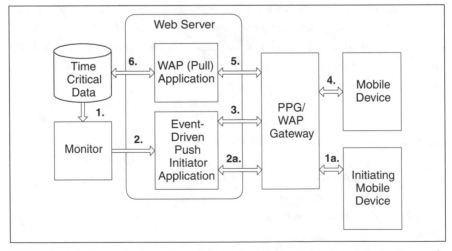

FIGURE 8-3. Event-Driven Push Initiator and WAP Application Co-Located

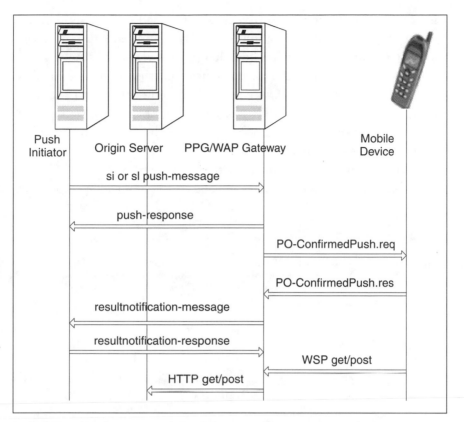

FIGURE 8-4. A Representative Push Messaging Scenario

AN EXAMPLE MESSAGING SCENARIO

We conclude this chapter with a push messaging scenario (illustrated in Figure 8-4) that shows a typical sequence of messages.

The push initiator begins things with a service loading or indication message to the gateway. The gateway parses and validates the message immediately, responding with a push response message. Assuming the push message request is validated, the gateway encodes the request including headers and content for over-the-air transmission and sends the message to the client. In this case a confirmed push has been requested by the initiator, so a confirmed push request is sent to the client. The client responds with a confirmed push response, and the gateway uses this information to construct and send a result notification to the initiator, which acknowledges this via a result notification response. In parallel to the result notification, the client does a WSP GET/POST request over the wireless session protocol, which the gateway transforms into an HTTP GET/POST to the appropriate server. Not shown is the HTTP and WSP response chain, passing requested WML content to the client device.

A complete service indication message (sent via an HTTP 1.1 POST) follows, containing two MIME body parts (control and content):

```
POST /push/receiver HTTP/1.1
Host: www.ppg1.unisys.com
Date: Sat, 15 Sep 2000 10:12:18 GMT
X-Wap-Initiator-URI: http://www.cup.org/myPushApp
Content-Type: Multipart/Related; boundary=gskdhaieuqoe;
              type="application/xml"
Content-Length: 997

--gskdhaieuqoe
Content-Type: application/xml

<?xml version="1.0"?>
<!DOCTYPE pap PUBLIC "-//WAPFORUM//DTD PAP 1.0//EN"
                   "http://www.wapforum.org/DTD/pap_1.0.dtd">
<pap>
  <push-message
        push-id="pid123@cup.org"
        ppg-notify-requested-to="http://www.cup.org/myPushApp"
        deliver-before-timestamp="2000-09-15T10:30:00Z">
    <address
      address-value="WAPPUSH=crb%40cup.org/TYPE=USER@ppg1.unisys.com">
    </address>
    <quality-of-service priority="high" delivery-method="confirmed"/>
  </push-message>
</pap>
--gskdhaieuqoe
Content-Type: application/xml

<?xml version="1.0"?>
<!DOCTYPE pap PUBLIC "-//WAPFORUM//DTD SI 1.0//EN"
                   "http://www.wapforum.org/DTD/si.dtd">
<si>
  <indication  si-id="si_id456@cup.org"
             href="http://www.cup.org/myApp"
             created ="2000-09-15T10:12:00Z"
```

```
            si_expires ="2000-09-15T18:00:00Z"
            action="signal-high">
   Today's schedule has changed!
  </indication>
</si>
--gskdhaieuqoe
```

The first message body contains a PAP push message specifying the client to send this to, where a result notification should be sent, and a high-priority, confirmed quality of service. The second message body contains a service indication which requests that the client 'execute' myApp at www.cup.org. The message "Today's schedule has changed!" will be displayed on the client's screen, and he or she will have the choice of acting on this alert or postponing. This service indication will expire and be removed from gateway or client by 6 p.m.

That wraps up our look at push applications. In the next section we look at WAP in practice covering design issues, architectures, usability, development, and testing of WAP applications.

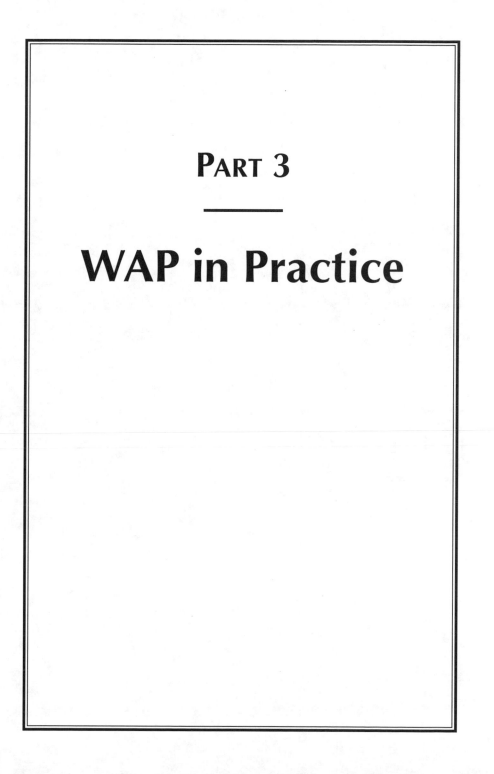

PART 3

WAP in Practice

9 Design Factors

Architectural and software selection decisions are critical to the success of a WAP development effort. These decisions are constrained by the answers to questions such as these:

- Is this an extension to an existing application? If so, is there already a Web interface to this application?

- Who will access the application (e.g., general public, registered users, employees)?

- Is personalization important?

- Are you targeting an international market where many languages must be supported?

- What types of devices will users employ to access the application?

- Is there a need to push information to these users?

- What is the expected load (total users, simultaneous sessions)?

- What are the sources of data, and is the security of this information important?

- What is the complexity/diversity of the data?

- Is knowledge of the user's location needed?

- Will this application be extended in the future to other interfaces (such as TV or voice)?

- Is the application highly complex?

We discuss these issues in detail in Part 3. Careful consideration of these issues is vital to selecting a long-lived architecture and third-party software to reduce development costs. It is usually a nontrivial task to extend an existing system to the wireless Web. The user interface flow is different from a Windows or Web interface, and existing systems rarely provide a clean separation of content from the view of that content. Unless you are lucky enough to inherit a well-designed n-tier system, you will need to refactor the system to separate the content so it is easily available to multiple interface channels.

We consider critical design success factors in this chapter and explore architectures suitable for WAP applications in Chapter 10. Usability is critical to mobile applications, and application testing is even more important in the WAP world because of the diversity of devices and the importance of usability. These topics are discussed in Chapter 11. Chapter 12 describes a development project that puts together much of what we have covered in earlier chapters. It follows a government inspection system, written using Java servlets and a relational database, from concept to deployment.

This chapter looks at a number of critical success factors in designing WAP applications. These factors include those that are important to any Internet application including scalability and security as well as those peculiar to mobile applications (e.g., target device dependencies).

SECURITY

Security can be defined as peace of mind or safety. Keep this in mind when analyzing the security requirements of your system. Obviously some systems require little protection because the information they deal with is public and may be read-only. However, financial systems, those that access or update personal data (e.g., driver's abstracts or credit histories), and mobile commerce applications require a careful analysis of security threats and countermeasures. If your application requires any degree of protection, consider creating a security policy.

A security policy defines the security issues that an application must face and how these should be dealt with. Security threats include the following:

- Compromised information (disclosure of confidential information)
- Violations of integrity (e.g., modification or destruction of data)
- Misuse of services

To avoid compromises to information, encrypt the data and limit access to authorized users. To deal with integrity problems, use message authentication codes. To prevent (or at least detect) abuses of a service, log transactions and/or employ digital signatures (the electronic equivalent of the written signature). We discuss security issues and some solutions from a functional perspective, covering:

- Authentication
- Encryption
- Authorization
- Data integrity
- Nonrepudiation

Wireless Web applications are little different from Web applications in their requirements for security, but there are a couple of additional factors to consider. On the downside, the WAP protocol requires a proxy (WAP gateway) between client and server. This introduces an extra link in the communications chain and, when combined with the protocols on either side of it, makes a secure solution more complicated. On the plus side, the typical mobile Internet client is a personal device. This creates an ideal opportunity to associate a device directly with its user, enabling the creation of personalized, highly secure mobile commerce solutions. We touch on these factors as we discuss the general security issues.

Authentication

Authentication is the ability to determine the identity of a user (or client device). This typically requires users to reveal a secret they share with the application (e.g., a password or PIN), but may also be based on a smart card containing the user's digital identity (e.g., their digital certificates and private keys). WAP uses the first type of authentication and may also provide digital certificate-based authentication (discussed later).

Simple authentication is usually based on a user ID and password scheme. WML supports entry of a nonechoing password to prevent onlookers from learning the secret. The WAE specification also states that client devices should support Basic authentication as per the HTTP specifications, and the WAP Forum's device test suite includes tests to verify this functionality. It is probably best not to rely on Basic authentication in all cases; authors of software-based WML browsers, gateways, and emulators have not been consistent in providing support for this. The Phone.com microbrowsers and gateways provide support for this (at least in versions 3.1 on). The Nokia 7110 also supports Basic authentication, although the Wapman Palm browser relies on the WAP gateway to provide this functionality.

For high-security applications, client digital certificates can authenticate the client device as part of the SSL protocol. A digital certificate is the electronic equivalent of a passport. It is issued by a trusted authority (a certificate authority) that certifies the holder of the certificate is who he or she claims to be. Certificates hold a public key that is used when sending encrypted information to the certificate holder. These certificates may be stored in the phone (and possibly downloaded from the Internet), or they may be located in a WAP Identity Module. The WAP Identity Module, or WIM, is usually implemented as a smart card – a miniature computer protected from tampering by software, electronic, and physical safeguards (refer to the WAP Forum's WAP Wireless Identity Module Specification for more information). As Table 9-1 illustrates, this approach provides the highest level of authentication that is usually implemented over HTTP. The table also makes reference to HTTPS, which indicates that SSL is used for encryption of information passing from the WAP gateway to the Web server. We discuss encryption in the next section.

TABLE 9-1. HTTP Authentication and Encryption

PROTOCOL AND SECURITY MECHANISM	SECURITY LEVEL
HTTP	None
HTTP with Basic Authentication	Low
HTTPS with Basic Authentication	High
HTTPS with SSL Client Certificates	Very high

For many applications, a user ID and password scheme is adequate. Note that if you use your own WML-based password scheme, the password value will remain in the browser context and hence will be accessible to other decks unless you deliberately clear out the context following password verification. Passwords will also be transmitted in an unprotected form unless your server specifies a secure URL (e.g., https:// . . .) and the mobile device and gateway support WTLS. LDAP directories can be used on the server side to store client authentication and access control information (see sidebar "LDAP").

LDAP

The Lightweight Directory Access Protocol (LDAP) is an open standard for directory services on the Internet. Directories store information such as e-mail addresses, telephone numbers, and user passwords in a hierarchical structure that can encompass everything from country, through organization and organizational units, to the individuals and resources that belong to an organization. The items stored in a directory are called entries, each of which contains information about some object (e.g., a person). Entries are composed of attributes, which have a type and one or more values. The syntax of an attribute determines the kinds of values allowed (e.g., ASCII strings, JPEGs, URLs, and PGP keys). LDAP enjoys widespread industry support from such disparate vendors as Microsoft, Sun, Oracle, Novell, and Netscape.

LDAP can be used for user authentication and access control, hosting information about user accounts and preferences. A login authentication service can query an LDAP directory each time a user attempts to log in. The results of the query are used to validate the user and, if authorized, to locate and load additional information such as access control data or preferences. LDAP provides a simple command set including directory search, add, modify, and delete operations. Because it functions over TCP/IP and is inherently distributable and scalable, LDAP is an ideal choice for write infrequently/access-a-lot-solutions such as access control. For more information, you can start with Linux World's articles on LDAP (see *http://www.linuxworld.com/linuxworld*).

Encryption

Encryption is used to ensure that meaningful information cannot be extracted from data while it is in transit. This is usually done at the communications protocol level, which, in the case of the WAP network protocols, is the WTLS layer. Encryption presents unique challenges in the mobile environment due to the limited number-crunching abilities and memory constraints of mobile devices. The algorithms used in WTLS reflect this, and elliptic curve cryptography is a popular choice because its processing demands and key sizes are lower than more traditional alternatives. However, RSA ciphers are also supported, and a WTLS implementation may choose either approach. There are a couple of well-publicized problems with WAP's approach to encryption. Because the WTLS protocol is used between the mobile device and gateway and SSL between the gateway and Web server, data must be decrypted and then reencrypted in the gateway. This presents a security hole (the so-called "white spot") if the gateway is not trusted or is vulnerable to hacking. In high-security applications, this may influence the location of the gateway (see sidebar "Physical Gateway Solution"). There are solutions to the white spot problem and the WAP Forum has proposed a solution where communications switch to a secure proxy gateway for the duration of the secure session (see Chapter 13 for more details).

The other major WAP security issue revolves around the client. It is possible for users to disable security between the device and

---

Physical Gateway Location

For those new to the wonderful world of WAP, the WAP gateway presents a bit of a puzzle. It is a necessary piece of the solution that is not present in the regular Web world and appears to have an inordinate amount of power over your applications. It enforces caching policies, security, access control, and even WML interpretation requirements. So why not install your own gateway and bypass the third party? The simple answer is cost – gateways are expensive. However, if your application requires the utmost security, then you are limited to using a trusted third party gateway or hosting your own. It is possible to host a gateway and not support dial-up connections. In this case, the gateway is simply a server with an IP address that accepts WAP traffic over an IP network, relying on a mobile provider or wireless Internet Service Provider to link the device with the Internet. Another option is to provide dial-up services via a toll-free or regular number in which case you have just become your own wireless Internet Service Provider! This option may make sense for large corporations that want to provide secure mobile access to the corporate intranet. ▣

---

the gateway, thus exposing data on the cellular network. This is not a big issue when the mobile networks themselves provide encryption (e.g., Cellular Digital Packet Data networks) but is a cause of concern in some networks. This issue will probably be addressed by additional security constraints in the Wireless Application Environ ment specifications.

Session IDs can be embedded in WML decks to implement server-side sessions where cookies are not supported. These IDs should be encrypted to prevent a user from altering an ID to gain access to another user's session data. This encryption will occur in the server application, and a number of publicly available libraries can be used for this purpose (e.g., the Cryptix toolkit for Java available at *www.cryptix.org*). Note that cookies are not consistently supported across WAP devices and gateways and you should not depend on cookies for state maintenance. Some gateways provide caching of cookies on behalf of WAP devices, but this cannot be relied upon unless you are building a solution where your users will use a specified gateway.

Authorization

Authorization is the process of restricting access to various functions of your application to certain users only. Although authorization is typically well thought out in major database systems, this is not always the case in the Web world. However, Java 2 Enterprise Edition (J2EE) application servers and recent Java servlet containers (e.g., Tomcat) provide an access control infrastructure that you should take advantage of if possible. If access control is retrofitted or implemented throughout an application's code, the results can be difficult to maintain, extend, and configure.

WAP provides access control support through the `<access>` element found in the head of a deck. A `domain` and `path` can be specified which determine the URLs that may request this deck. This access specifier is also supported in WMLScript. Another feature of WML is the `sendreferer` attribute in the `<go>` element (e.g., `<go sendreferer="true" ... >`) that instructs the WML browser to send an HTTP header (HTTP_REFERER) containing the invoking URL of the current request. If your service performs sensitive operations, it should check the HTTP Referer header to make sure the requests originate from friendly domains.

Nonrepudiation and Data Integrity

Nonrepudiation ensures that users cannot deny they performed a particular action (yes – you really did buy that life-size rubber crocodile!). This is accomplished in the electronic world using a digital equivalent of a written signature. Digital signatures use a private key (i.e., a secret electronic key that is known only to its owner) to sign an electronic document (e.g., a WAP request). This private key actually signs a computed hash of the message in question. This hash is a string computed from a message in such a way that it is effectively impossible for the same hash to have come from two different messages. The receiver of the message uses a corresponding public key (a publicly available electronic key associated with the sender's private key) to decrypt the signature. To verify the identity of the sender, the receiver compares this decrypted signature with a recomputed hash of the message. If they match, then the message must have been sent by the owner of the private key. This comparison has the added benefit of ensuring that the message has not been altered during transmission. SSL uses the same technology to compute MACs (message authentication codes), which are used for data integrity checks. The WMLScript `Crypto` library supports digital signing of user requests (see Chapter 7 for more details).

Consider a security policy even if your application seems to have minimal need for it. Having a good understanding of threats, issues, and potential weaknesses reduces the chance of damage or costly retrofits to patch security holes. Security impacts client, gateway, and server selection and deployment, all of which affect the cost and difficulty of creating a WAP service.

EXISTING WEB APPLICATIONS AND MULTIPLE CHANNELS

A WAP application is often an extension of an existing HTML-based Web service. Adding WAP to an existing Web service can be relatively simple if the existing service is well partitioned and, in effect, an API to access business logic can be used by the new interface channel. As we discuss in Chapter 10, an abstraction layer, surrounding the business logic and data, facilitates multiple interface channels. If the system in question is not layered in this way, there are a number of approaches to adding the new mobile channel:

- Refactor the application to extract business logic and data and repackage these so HTML and WML interfaces can use common logic and data.

- Develop a parallel system with its own business logic, data interfaces, and WML view.

- Filter the HTML produced by the existing system to build a WML interface.

The first option is probably the best in the long term, particularly if you anticipate a requirement to add new interface channels such as voice or TV. However, it is costly to perform major surgery on a live system and requires familiarity with the existing code.

The second option is similar to the first but requires development of a completely new application to access the same information as the existing application. This could be carried out as a pilot project to provide wireless access and prove a new architecture or technology infrastructure (e.g., an application server platform). The pilot could then be used as a springboard for the next generation HTML interface, reusing portions of the existing HTML system where possible (perhaps wrapped as components).

The third option is intuitively appealing and does not require major modifications to production code. To be effective, however, the filtering software must be able to extract appropriate content from the HTML and arrange it in a manner that is appropriate for mobile devices. A general algorithm to extract appropriate content is not trivial, and tags that single out content may need to be added to the HTML prior to filtering. To present this material in a way that fits the form factor of the mobile device is also difficult but is more feasible for devices such as PDAs, which are closer to a standard Web browser. We discuss HTML filters later.

Assuming we select option 1 or 2, we still must choose how to specify the user interface so it will support multiple channels. There are two main choices:

- Use a channel-independent language for specifying presentation. Transform this to the desired markup language before delivering to the client browser.

- Use native markup language presentation for each target markup family.

The first approach to interface specification reduces the effort required to maintain the system's user interface. Changes in functionality can be specified once, and when a new channel is added, a transformation method (such as a translating style sheet) is added to support this. There are a few difficulties with this approach. Performance is an issue when using a technology such as XSLT where parsers and processors place a heavy load on the server during page generation. Another downside is that the generated markup will probably not be ideal and the presentation developers will have to work with a 'logical' view, not having complete control over the final appearance. Yet another difficulty with this approach is that WML devices require special consideration due to their extremely limited capacity and display size. When defining a template that will support a WML target, care must be taken to ensure that tabular data is not more than a couple of columns wide and that logical pages are split up for delivery if they are too large. The latter must be done at run-time, and issues include where to cache the generated markup and how to split it up in a way that is easy for the user to navigate. These are significant problems. and creating a truly general-purpose solution is difficult.

Oracle's 'Portal-to-Go' takes the channel-independent language approach to supporting multiple channels. It specifies a common XML-based markup language that is transformed to WML, HTML, and other markup languages via XSLT. 'HawHaw', a multichannel PHP solution we discuss in Chapter 10, provides another alternative that uses an object-oriented API to build a user interface. This interface is then generated in a markup language appropriate to the client. XHTML may eventually form the basis of a single-source multichannel presentation. XHTML Basic has been developed with mobile devices in mind and forms a subset of XHTML that could be used for Web and wireless Web clients (see Chapter 13 for a brief discussion of XHTML).

The second approach to interface specification requires a parallel set of presentation templates or application code for each supported channel. This has the advantage of allowing developers to work directly with the target markup language. Developer familiarity and tool availability are big pluses here. In addition, the flow of WML presentation may be quite different from that which works well in the HTML world. The downside is the requirement for parallel maintenance and extension. This can be large when many channels are supported. With this approach, the dynamically created portions of the presentation should be factored out so that common code can be used for all channels. Regardless of which presentation approach you select, it pays to factor out common text (which, in the Java world, should be internationalized in properties files) as well as dynamic data. Let's look at a mechanism that can be used to support multiple channels using parallel sets of presentation templates.

XSL Generation

A technology that has received much attention in the last couple of years is Extensible Markup Language (XML) and a related standard, Extensible Style Language (XSL). Wireless Markup Language is an XML language (see the sidebar "An XML Primer" in Chapter 5). XML can also be used to define business data, and support for this is provided by major database and application server vendors including Oracle, Microsoft, Sybase, BEA, and Bluestone. What is useful about defining your business data in XML is that it provides a text-based human and machine readable format that can be used to interface with external systems and organizations. Business data in XML format can also be used to generate display markup output such as HTML, XHTML, and WML. The technology to do this is XSL and in particular, XSL Transformations (XSLT) – a subset of the XSL standard. XSLT style sheets can be defined that extract content from an XML document, format it, and generate a specified display markup document. These style sheets consist of a set of rules that locate or match content in an XML document and generate output markup based on this content. The XSLT specification is quite rich and provides procedural programming constructs including loops and condition statements. For more information on XSL and XSLT, refer to the OASIS home page (*www.oasis-open.org*) or XML.com (*www.xml.com*). It is possible to create style sheets by hand because they are, themselves, XML documents. In addition, style sheet editors that support HTML output are widely available, although support for WML is not yet common. The power of this approach is illustrated in Figure 9-1.

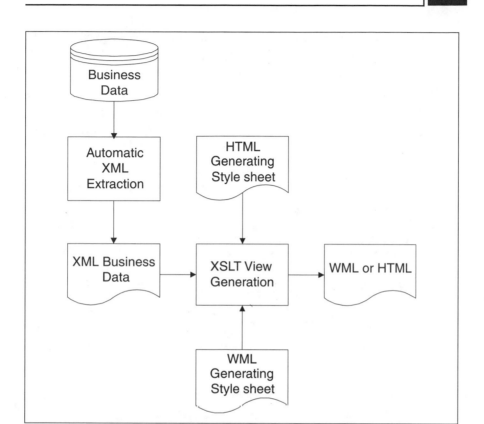

FIGURE 9-1. XSLT-Based Multichannel Support

XML business data is automatically extracted from a data source such as a relational database or CORBA object. The important point here is that this is something currently built in to many tools. Hence little actual coding is required to obtain an XML representation of the data. The XSLT view generation module is a general-purpose component that generates markup (e.g., WML or HTML) based on what is specified in the supplied style sheet. This component uses an XML parser and XSLT processor, both of which may be freely obtained (e.g., Apache's Xerces and Xalan are available at *xml.apache.org*). A real-world example of automatic XML document creation is provided by the eBASE framework, described in Chapter 10. View processing code in this framework performs automatic conversion between XML data documents and Java objects using Java's Reflection API.

To illustrate XML/XSLT generation, let's look at some simple data XML that describes a house from a home buyer's perspective. We primarily use separate tags for each item of interest, with the exception of a `style` attribute in the house element. The XML contains a query results structure with two house records that might be returned from a SQL query on a real estate database. The tags are self-explanatory, defining house age, number of bedrooms and bathrooms, heating method, price, and address (street and city).

```
<queryResults>
  <house style="Bungalow">
    <age>33</age>
    <bedrooms>4</bedrooms>
    <bathrooms>1.5</bathrooms>
    <heating>hot air</heating>
    <price>150000</price>
    <address>
      <street>45 Laurentide Dr.</street>
      <city>Halifax</city>
    </address>
  </house>
  <house style="Side Split">
    <age>18</age>
    <bedrooms>3</bedrooms>
    <bathrooms>2</bathrooms>
    <heating>electric</heating>
    <price>135000</price>
    <address>
      <street>18 Gateway Av.</street>
      <city>Halifax</city>
    </address>
  </house>
</queryResults>
```

An XSL style sheet can be used to extract information from this XML and display it in a simple single card deck. This style sheet defines the output type and an XML prologue (`<xsl:output...`), which will be the first thing generated when run through a processor. Then we specify two rules: a root rule and a `house` rule. The root rule is evaluated only once for the root of the input XML document to create a WML deck and card. The `house` rule will be applied once for each

house in the XML data (in our case, this second rule will be applied twice). The first rule states that for the root match (`<xsl:template match="/">`), generate a deck with a card entitled `"Results"` and then apply other template rules (`<xsl:apply-templates/>`). The house rule (`<xsl:template match="/queryResults/house">`) will apply whenever the house tag occurs within a queryResults tag in the XML data. This rule extracts the style, address, number of bedrooms and bathrooms, and the price of the house. Note that we do not extract heating method or age from the XML because we do not need to display this in our summary. The second rule produces the extracted information within a WML paragraph (`<p></p>`), italicizing the style of house and bolding the price. Refer to Chapter 5 for further explanation of WML. The style sheet follows:

```
<xsl:stylesheet xmlns:xsl="http://www.w3.org/1999/XSL/Transform"
                version="1.0">
  <xsl:output type="wml"
              media-type="text/x-wap.wml"
              doctype-public="-//WAPFORUM//DTD WML 1.1//EN"
              doctype-system="http://www.wapforum.org/DTD/wml_1_1.dtd"
              indent="yes" />
  <!-- Generate deck and card -->
  <xsl:template match="/">
    <wml>
      <card title="Results">
        <xsl:apply-templates/>
      </card>
    </wml>
  </xsl:template>

  <!-- Generate house paragraphs (one per house) -->
  <xsl:template match="/queryResults/house">
    <p>
      <i><xsl:value-of select="@style"/></i><br/>
      <xsl:value-of select="address/street"/><br/>
      <xsl:value-of select="address/city"/><br/>
      Bdrms: <xsl:value-of select="bedrooms"/><br/>
      Baths: <xsl:value-of select="bathrooms"/><br/>
      <b>Price: <xsl:value-of select="price"/></b>
    </p>
  </xsl:template>
</xsl:stylesheet>
```

Running this style sheet against the XML data using an XSLT processor such as Apache's Xalan will result in the following output WML:

```
<?xml version="1.0"?>
<!DOCTYPE wml PUBLIC "-//WAPFORUM//DTD WML 1.1//EN"
   "http://www.wapforum.org/DTD/wml_1_1.dtd">
<wml>
   <card title="Results">
     <p>
        <i>Bungalow</i><br/>
        45 Laurentide Dr.<br/>
        Halifax<br/>
        Bdrms: 4<br/>
        Baths: 1.5<br/>
        <b>Price: 150000</b>
     </p>
     <p>
        <i>Side Split</i><br/>
        18 Gateway Av.<br/>
        Halifax<br/>
        Bdrms: 3<br/>
        Baths: 2<br/>
        <b>Price: 135000</b>
     </p>
   </card>
</wml>
```

Figure 9-2 shows how this WML might appear (note that screen *b* is reached by scrolling from screen *a*).

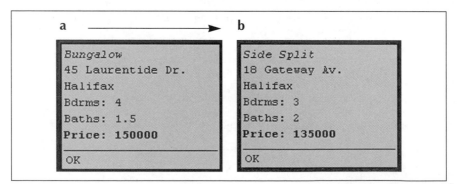

FIGURE 9-2. House Query Results

An HTML-generating style sheet could also be created. This could generate more information for display and reference images showing the house from the inside and outside. Technically, the only differences between this and the WML-generating style sheet would be the output type (HTML), which, because it is not XML, requires different handling by the XSLT processor and the generated markup itself, which would probably conform to HTML 4.x or XHTML 1.1.

HTML FILTERS

Software developers face a huge challenge. Their employers have heard about the wireless Web and want a piece of the action. However, the cost of building Web sites and applications is still fresh in their minds. Why can't we just convert the existing Web content to the new wireless Web format? After all, WML is just another markup language and it's even an XML one! We have talked about the "impedance mismatch" between HTML and WML in other chapters, but let's take a different tack now and assume we have been told that we must make HTML application *XYZ* available to our wireless Web audience and we are not allowed to rebuild the application to achieve this. Obviously there are ways to turn HTML into WML, and an entire class of "mobile middleware" has arisen that purports to do just that.

The types of conversion that we must consider include:

- Markup language conversion – converts HTML tags to WML equivalent (e.g., image maps are translated to links).

- Filtering – removes tags that are unsupported (e.g., objects).

- Image conversion (JPEG or GIF to WBMP).

- Content-specific filtering – uses templates to translate selected portions of the source document.

- Physical deck partitioning – reduces decks to an acceptable size.

The lower end filters take a simplistic approach and usually rely on you to add preprocessing tags to existing markup so the filter can extract appropriate information from the HTML. If the HTML you are filtering is simple to begin with (i.e., it was created with a wireless or voice channel in mind), then a simple approach can work. There are guidelines available from the W3C for writing HTML so it can be more easily rendered by mobile devices. These include the Web Content Accessibility Guidelines and the W3C Note (HTML 4.0 Guidelines for Mobile Access) available at *www.w3.org/TR/*. In the eBASE framework (discussed in Chapter 10), XSL style sheets and an XSLT transformation convert documents specified in an intermediary XML language (similar to HTML) into WML output. This works when the input does not do fancy things like nest tables or rely on frames or tables for layout. However, real-world HTML pages are often much too complex for a simple style sheet approach, and a combination of XSLT and programmatic transformation will be required. Using content filtering where preprocessor directives are embedded in the HTML to indicate wireless content can be very useful because wireless audiences rarely require the full scope of an HTML page.

Figure 9-3 shows a possible architecture for a general-purpose filter. This system could be run in batch mode to convert relatively static content on a daily basis or (with enough parallelism, CPU, and memory) could provide on-the-fly translation. Note that XSLT processors may place a heavy load on both memory and CPU, making a programmatic approach more feasible for very large loads.

The design outlined in Figure 9-3 assumes that content has been marked for use in a wireless application. If this is not so, content filtering would be omitted. The wireless bitmap conversion can take place in parallel with the markup filtering (a number of off-the-shelf tools are available to help with this – see Chapter 4). The content filter uses a parser to locate the preprocessing directives and remove extraneous markup as directed. The reduced HTML page is then translated to a logical markup. This could be done by an XSL transformation or using custom application code. Tags are mapped from HTML to WML, and tags that have no equivalent are removed. Here we use WML as the target logical markup, but an intermediate format (e.g., User Interface

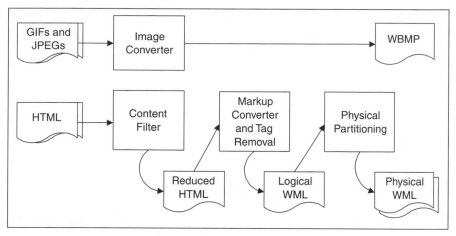

FIGURE 9-3. An HTML Filter Mechanism

Markup Language – *www.uiml.org*) that would facilitate translation to other markups (such as VoiceXML) could be used. The final step is to physically partition the logical view so that it can be sent to a real-world device. At this point, large tables can be split into master-detail relationships and multiple linked decks created from the single logical deck. This will keep the size of each deck below the maximum that can be accommodated by the target device. These decks could be cached at the 'view' level or created as physical files that the Web server would serve directly. These physical decks would be linked using dynamically generated names (perhaps based on the user's session ID). Note that relying on the Web server to serve generated WML decks requires careful consideration of security (in particular access control) to ensure that unauthorized users cannot obtain other users' result decks.

DEVICE DIFFERENCES

By the end of 2000, the Internet Alchemy Web site (*www.internetalchemy.org*) listed more than 940 WAP user agent identifiers. Closer examination of this list yields fewer than 100 distinct browser/device combinations, the majority of which are based on the Phone.com platform. In addition to the Phone.com (Unwired Planet) browser (used by Alcatel, Ericsson, Motorola, Panasonic, Philips, Siemens, Samsung, and others), Ericsson and Nokia both have their own browsers. Also in the handset market, Benefon and Sony have licensed Microsoft's Mobile Explorer. The situation is similar in the handheld computer space with at least four browsers for the Palm platform and a number for Symbian and PocketPC devices. How a browser renders the compiled WML, displays images, and processes WMLScript varies among vendors and even among versions of the browser. This is complicated by something that varies far less in the desktop world – device capabilities. The standard desktop PC can be counted on to have at least a 640 by 480 pixel color display, some sort of full-size keyboard, and a pointing device such as a mouse. In the wireless world, the size of screen and how user input is achieved varies widely.

The variety of devices that are different enough to require customization is evident in mobile portal sites such as that operated by mobileID. The mobileID wireless portal caters to more than 60 handheld devices ranging from RIM pagers and HP PocketPCs to Mitsubishi and Nokia handsets. Although the Phone.com browser may power many of these, different displays and keypad layouts result in a different look and feel for each device. Browsers for the Palm provide a much richer experience than handsets, displaying generous paragraphs of text and providing less painful entry of text fields. All this points to a need for a standard way to determine the capabilities of the device we are talking to. This will allow us to display an appropriate amount of information in a card, cope with the input limitations of handsets, and still be able to provide a reasonably rich experience for handheld or desktop browsers.

Here are some approaches to handling multiple mobile device form factors:

- Assume a lowest common denominator ('minimalist' WML).

- Create device-specific WML for all supported devices.

- Transform general-purpose WML presentation based on device profile.

The first approach is obviously the simplest. WML is itself a very simple markup language, but there is enough room for interpretation of the WML specifications that devices produce surprisingly different renderings of the same markup. Selecting a subset of WML that works adequately on all targeted devices is possible, but the results are not particularly exciting. Presentation is limited to simple text display, text inputs, selection lists, line breaks, and links for navigation.

Creating separate WML decks for every target device will produce a superior user experience, but at the cost of some supreme headaches as vendors churn out new wireless devices and business rules change. This approach has the advantage of simplifying the generation of markup because device capabilities have already been considered by the creator of the WML. In a real-world application that has to support general access, this is not a particularly economical alternative.

A two-stage process where a base presentation is either augmented or filtered (using device capabilities) is a reasonable compromise between multiple sets of WML presentations and a lowest common denominator approach (see Fig. 9-4). The data and text labels are referenced by a WML template and merged at run-time (note that the labels can be merged at compile time for increased efficiency). This produces a logical WML deck that can now be adjusted for the target

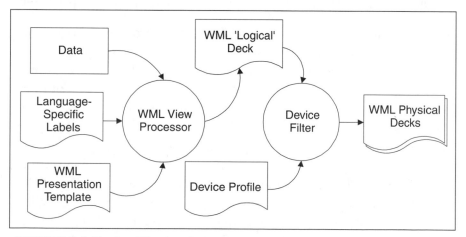

FIGURE 9-4. Device Filtering from Common WML

device. A device profile that specifies maximum deck size, support for images and tables, optimal navigation strategy (e.g., links vs. option lists), and other device characteristics is used by a device filter to produce a deck or decks that suit the target device. As discussed in the "HTML Filters" section, a caching mechanism can be used to cope with multiple physical decks.

Not surprisingly, the WAP Forum anticipated the need for determining device capabilities, and the Wireless Application Group User Agent Profile specification (WAG UAProf for short) addresses this issue. The user agent profile is a way of capturing device characteristics (Capability and Preference Information, or CPI) such that they can be used to format content to suit the client device. Device characteristics include hardware (screen size, image support), software (OS version, audio encoders), network (latency, reliability), browser (markup languages, scripting support), and WAP capabilities (version, WML versions). The UAProf specifications rely on a variety of supporting technologies including:

- ☐ CC/PP – Composite Capabilities/Preference Profiles

- ☐ RDF – Resource Description Framework

- ☐ XML – Extensible Markup Language and XML Namespaces

- ☐ CC/PP Exchange Protocol and HTTP Extension Framework

Composite Capabilities/Preference Profiles provide an extensible framework for describing device capabilities and user preferences. CC/PP relies in turn on the Resource Description Framework to provide an extensible mechanism for defining metadata (i.e., descriptions of things). At first glance, you would think we could use a simpler mechanism for describing the attributes of a mobile device that we would like to convey to a WAP application for use in presentation formatting. For instance, we could use a dictionary-style mechanism like an XML document type definition of schema. However, RDF provides a superior way for creating a more easily extended "dictionary," called an RDF schema. RDF schemas may seem a bit abstract on first acquaintance because they are actually documents that describe metadata (i.e., they contain meta metadata).

RDF, in turn, relies on XML and XML namespaces for the actual specification of RDF schemas and RDF documents. XML namespaces provide a way to work with separate vocabularies (i.e., sets of tags) within a single document without conflicts between names. CC/PP Exchange Protocol defines how capability and preference information is actually transmitted among clients, proxies, gateways, and servers. This must be done over WAP's WSP as well as the Internet's HTTP. When transmitting profiles over HTTP, the HTTP Extension Framework is used.

If that seems like a lot to take in just to understand user agent profiles, you are absolutely correct! This probably explains why there are few real-world applications of UAProf to date. However, a few examples and a bit more explanation, and the mist will begin to lift. For more reading (lots more reading), refer to the W3C Web site (*www.w3.org*), which has information on CC/PP, XML, XML Namespaces, RDF (and RDF schemas), and the HTTP Extension Framework.

Let's start with a picture. Figure 9-5 shows one interpretation of the user agent profile. A *user agent profile* contains a number of components. These *components* may be of various subclasses (e.g., 'SoftwarePlatform') and provide a way of grouping similar sets of core device characteristics. A component contains a *default profile*, which usually contains a *URI* reference to a default profile document but may directly contain the profile's attributes. A component also contains a number of overriding *attributes*, which may be simple (containing a single *value*) or a *group* (containing *list items*). To avoid confusion when reading about RDF, note that what UAProf refers to as attributes, RDF considers 'properties.' Similarly, a default profile or component in UAProf is equivalent to a 'resource' in RDF parlance. When reading through the text examples to follow, it may help to refer to this figure.

The following component describes the hardware characteristics of the Nokia 2160 cell phone. This example is from the WAP Forum's WAG UAProf specification (Version 10, Nov. 1999, pp. 38–39).

```
<?xml version="1.0"?>
<rdf:RDF xmlns:rdf="http://www.w3.org/1999/02/22-rdf-syntax-ns#"
         xmlns:prf="http://www.wapforum.org/UAPROF/ccppschema-
         19991014991014#">
<rdf:Description ID="MyProfile">

<prf:component>
  <rdf:Description ID="TerminalHardware">
    <rdf:type
        resource="http://www.wapforum.org/UAPROF/ccppschema-
                19991014/#HardwarePlatform" />
    <prf:Defaults rdf:resource="http://www.nokia.com/profiles/2160" />
    <!-- override the ImageCapable property, and add VoiceInputCapable
    and Keyboard properties -->
    <prf:Imagecapable>Yes</prf:Imagecapable>
    <prf:Keyboard>Disambiguating</prf:Keyboard>
    <prf:VoiceInputCapable>Yes</prf:VoiceInputCapable>
  </rdf:Description>
</prf:component>
...
```

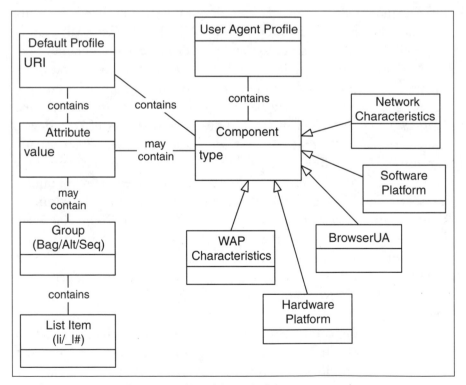

FIGURE 9-5. User Agent Profile Object Model

This profile is described using an RDF (XML version 1.0 compliant) document. Two namespaces are defined by the `xmlns:rdf` and `xmlns:prf` namespace attributes. The `rdf` namespace is used for tags that are part of the RDF standard (e.g., `RDF`, `Description`, and `type`). The `prf` namespace is used for user agent profile tags such as `component`, `Defaults`, and `Imagecapable`. Table 9-2 provides a description of some RDF and profile elements that will help you understand this and the following example. The component identified as `TerminalHardware` describes the hardware attributes of the Nokia 2160. The class of this component is uniquely described by the `type` element, which references a WAP Forum-controlled URL identifying the UAProf schema for hardware platforms. All hardware components of user agent profiles would reference this schema.

TABLE 9-2. RDF and Profile Tags

NAMESPACE	TAG	MEANING
`rdf`	`RDF`	Document tag for entire profile
	`Description`	Describes a resource in terms of its properties (or attributes)
	`type`	Uniquely identifies the type of a resource by referencing a URI
	`Bag`	An unordered list of resource properties
	`Seq`	An ordered list of resource properties
	`Alt`	A list of resource property alternatives
	`li or _1#`	An item in one of the above property lists. `li` is an unnumbered item, `_1#` (e.g., `_13`) is a numbered item, which in this example is the third item
`prf`	`component`	A set of related attributes (e.g., attributes that describe a device's hardware)
	`Defaults`	Points to a URI that describes the default attributes of this component

The `prf:Defaults` tag contains another URL, this time pointing at a default profile that contains the vendor-defined attributes of the specified device (or family of devices). We look at this default profile later. The next tags are specific to the UAProf profile namespace and describe hardware attributes that either override (e.g., prf:Imagecapable) or augment (e.g., prf:Keyboard) the default profile.

The following XML markup is a default profile for the Nokia 2160, which was referenced in the user agent profile earlier.

```
<?xml version="1.0"?>
<rdf:RDF xmlns:rdf="http://www.w3.org/1999/02/22-rdf-syntax-ns#"
        xmlns:prf="http://www.wapforum.org/UAPROF/ccppschema-19991014#">
  <-- Default description of properties -->
  <rdf:Description>
    <prf:Vendor>Nokia</prf:Vendor>
    <prf:Model>2160</prf:Model>
    <prf:CPU>PPC650</prf:CPU>
    <prf:TextInputCapable>Yes</prf:TextInputCapable>
    <prf:ImageCapable>No</prf:ImageCapable>
    <prf:SoftKeysCapable>Yes</prf:SoftKeysCapable>
    <prf:SoundOutputCapable>Yes</prf:SoundOutputCapable>
    <prf:PointingResolution>Pixel</prf:PointingResolution>
    <prf:ColorCapable>No</prf:ColorCapable>
    <prf:ScreenSize>600x400</prf:ScreenSize>
    <prf:ScreenSizeChar>12x4</prf:ScreenSizeChar>
    <prf:MaxScreenChar>48x32</prf:MaxScreenChar>
    <prf:InputCharSet>
      <rdf:Bag>
        <rdf:li>US-ASCII</rdf:li>
      </rdf:Bag>
    </prf:InputCharSet>
    <prf:BitsPerPixel>8</prf:BitsPerPixel>
    <prf:OutputCharSet>
      <rdf:Bag>
        <rdf:li>US-ASCII</rdf:li>
        <rdf:li>Shift_JIS</rdf:li>
      </rdf:Bag>
    </prf:OutputCharSet>
  </rdf:Description>
</rdf:RDF>
```

Again, this is an RDF document that defines the rdf and prf namespaces. The default profile contains most of the properties specified in the set of core hardware attributes including Vendor, Model, CPU, and so on. One element we have not seen yet is the rdf:Bag element, which is found in both InputCharSet and OutputCharSet. This element simply provides a way to group multiple items within a given attribute. These items are contained in list item elements (rdf:li). In our example, only one input character set is accepted by this device (US-ASCII), but both US-ASCII and Shift_JIS can be produced.

A complete listing of the components and attributes of the user agent profile schema is available as Appendix A.1 to the WAG UAProf specification. It is possible to extend this schema, adding new components and attributes, and the process for this is described in the same document.

We have not yet seen how to make use of all this information in a WAP service. To do this, let's look at some scenarios that use user agent

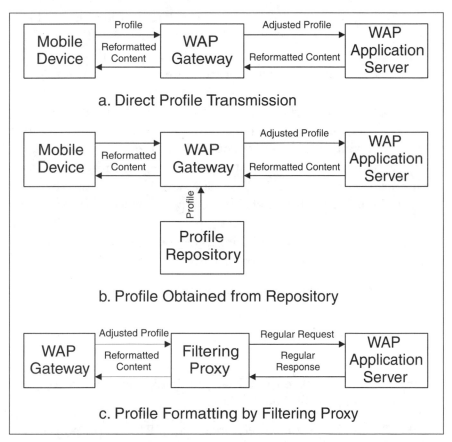

FIGURE 9-6. User Agent Profile Transmission Scenarios

profiles to convey capabilities to WAP applications servers. Figure 9-6 outlines a number of possible scenarios including direct transmission of capabilities, retrieval from a profile repository, and capability adjustment by a filtering proxy.

In scenario *a,* "Direct Profile Transmission," the mobile device sends the gateway a user agent profile (using the CC/PP Exchange Protocol over WSP). Note that the WAP gateway caches profile headers from the mobile device so this transmission needs to be performed only once per session. The gateway will look up the default device capabilities at the URL specified in the profile and adjust these, based on the overriding attributes in the profile as well as any additional capabilities provided by the gateway (e.g., image conversion from GIF to WBMP). This adjusted profile is passed to the WAP application via HTTP as `Profile` and `Profile-Diff` HTTP headers. The WAP application will parse these headers and using the extracted capabilities can reformat and filter the presentation prior to returning it to the gateway.

Scenario *b,* "Profile Obtained from Repository," differs from the first in that the user agent is unable to supply a profile (perhaps being an older device). In this case, the gateway consults a profile repository (perhaps querying on the User Agent identifier) to retrieve a profile.

In scenario *c,* "Profile Formatting by Filtering Proxy," the WAP application does not need to be UAProf aware. The URL that the client device requests is actually that of a filtering proxy, which is responsible for formatting responses based on the supplied profile. It is possible that there could be more than one filtering proxy between the WAP gateway, each carrying out a specific type of formatting or filtering.

In order for a WAP application to read and understand user agent profiles, the application must:

- Extract the HTTP Extension Framework headers, `Profile` and `Profile-Diff`.

- Parse and validate the URIs, profile difference references, and RDF contents of these headers.

- Obtain the profile(s) referenced by URI if applicable in the `Profile` header.

- Apply multiple profile differences to the original profile following overriding rules and using defaults where applicable.

- Validate and use the contents of the profile (e.g., hardware, software, and WAP attributes) to modify the presentation so it suits the target device and user. For example, the browser attribute `CcppAccept-Language` might be used to generate content in the user's language of choice.

- Generate an HTTP Response header `Profile-Warning` with a value of `"100"` if the profile was used and `"200"` if it was not (other values are defined in the CC/PP exchange protocol referenced later).

A complete discussion of the CC/PP Exchange Protocol is beyond the scope of this book, but the W3C note, "CC/PP Exchange Protocol Based on HTTP Extension Framework" (available at *www.w3.org/TR/ NOTE-CCPPexchange*), defines the formatting of request and response headers and provides some useful examples of how profiles are exchanged. RDF parsers and processing tools are available to assist in validating and extracting profile content.

Because UAProf specifications are not yet widely supported, we need some other way to define and cope with device differences. As an interim measure, it is possible for a WAP application to identify the device and browser that is making a request by examining the HTTP User Agent header. The HTTP Accept header can also be used to determine if this user agent accepts WMLScript and wireless bitmaps in addition to WML (see sidebar "HTML and WML User Agents").

HTML and WML User Agents

It is often useful to use a common URL for Web and WAP content. If the HTTP Accept header contains the string "WML" it is a pretty good bet that this browser accepts "text/vnd.wap.wml" or perhaps compiled WML. This allows you to differentiate between WML and HTML browsers, although "WML" will also be present in HTTP Accept headers from a dual mode browser such as Opera or MS Mobile Explorer. The keyword "Mozilla" can be used to detect these cases because this will usually be present in an HTML-capable user agent header.

An example of a user agent header is "R380 2.0 WAP1.1," which identifies the Ericsson R380, telling us that this browser supports version 1.1 of the WAP specs. If a user agent header contains "UP" (short for Unwired Planet), it is probably powered by a Phone.com microbrowser. If the header contains "Nokia," that microbrowser can be accommodated. Anywhereyougo.com (*www.anywhereyougo.com*) has collected a simple table of device capabilities that you can use as the basis for your own local capabilities profiling. The `Accept-Language` header is also useful in determining the user's language preferences. We discuss this in the section on internationalization later.

SCALABILITY

The most elegantly designed WAP application may be impractical because it does not scale to satisfy the demand placed on it by heavy use. Although this problem is not unique to wireless Web applications, the potentially steep increase in wireless Web access predicted by industry analysts means that we had better plan well ahead. Scalability can be defined in a number of ways:

- In terms of simultaneous sessions

- As a function of ultimate load (e.g., everyone pushing a button at same time)

- Based on throughput or response time

In an application that maintains session state on the server, the number of simultaneous sessions (both active and inactive) can be a major limiting factor on how may people can use the system. Once physical memory is exceeded and the system switches to virtual memory, performance can suffer to the point where response times become unacceptable. When designing a system, it pays to consider this issue early on. A system that works well with dedicated resources for each user session will probably not work so well with thousands of similar sessions. Some things that can help are:

- Prototyping and memory profiling – don't wait until system testing uncovers a problem (or worse still, feedback from users in production!)

- Share resources (e.g., templates, database connections, and view processing code) between sessions

- Use persistent state management (available in some application servers) where state is saved to disk periodically and probably cached to improve performance

- Be careful how much state you store per user (e.g., some information that is not often used can be retrieved from an LDAP directory or database when needed)

- Use the client to store state (e.g., cookies, WML variables, postfields, or URL rewriting)

- When using Java, check the size of the virtual machine process(es) and if too large, investigate alternative run-time environments. Java 1.3 claims to have improved memory usage per virtual machine over version 1.2

Processing performance (both peak load and average response time) can be a problem, in particular in systems that are highly template driven or those that query large databases. In our experience, XSLT processing of XML data can be CPU and memory intensive. Poorly written database queries (e.g., those that make indiscriminate use of outer joins) may be another performance culprit. Some methods to cope with performance issues include the following:

- Benchmarking hot spots such as presentation generation, legacy system access, and complex back-end queries. Prototyping can be used to remove bottlenecks.

- Early and continued use of load testing tools to simulate realistic usage. WAP load testing tools are available to help with the HTTP side of requests and responses (refer to Chapters 4 and 11 for more information on testing).

- ▣ Have experienced developers perform code walkthroughs of identified hot spots.

- ▣ Consider partitioning the application so that load is distributed across multiple servers (e.g., use separate physical servers for the Web server and legacy system or database access).

- ▣ Build caching into the design to reduce fetching and recalculating values (e.g., a cache of parsed user interface templates needs to be updated only when the user interface is changed).

Caching can improve performance and is usually provided by Web servers, gateways, and WAP clients. The variety of places where caching can occur can make this a double-edged sword, and much traffic on WML developers lists is directly or indirectly related to problems associated with "stale" information. Caching is usually enabled in WAP unless you explicitly turn it off using an HTTP header or the `cache-control` attribute of the WML `<go>` element. See Chapter 6 for more details.

There is not space to do the subject of scalability justice, but giving early consideration to scalability issues can save unwelcome attention once your application is in production!

LOCATION-BASED SERVICES

Location-based services manually (through user input) or automatically determine the user's whereabouts and use this to produce location-related content. These applications range from safety and emergency response, through traffic, navigation, and mobile yellow pages, to fleet management and asset tracking. Applications can be broadly classified as those where mobile users request information and supply their location with the request (e.g., mobile yellow pages) and applications that determine users' positions without an explicit user request (e.g., push services such as asset tracking). Demand for these applications is driving standardization of automated positioning in mobile devices. In the United States, emergency response requirements (the 'E911' initiative) mandate that cellular devices will provide positioning information to assist in locating people in an emergency. The first phase of this (slated for the end of 2001) requires accuracy that can be supplied by existing networks with minor modification (cell of origin technology). Options for determining a user's location include:

- Manual entry of a postal code or address
- Cell of origin
- E-OTD
- TOA
- A-GPS

Manual entry of postal codes or address (e.g., city name) is used in most current location-based services. Cell of origin uses the mobile network base station cell area to locate the caller. This method allows positions to be fixed to about a 150-meter accuracy in urban areas but is significantly less accurate in rural locations where cells are much larger. The Enhanced Observation Time Difference (E-OTD) system overlays reference beacons that generate time stamps on an existing cellular network. An E-OTD equipped handset uses the time differences and beacon locations to perform triangulation. An accuracy of 50 meters is possible, but response times are slower than with cell of origin (approximately five seconds vs. three seconds for cell of origin). Time of Arrival (TOA) uses direct synchronization of base stations to carry out similar computations to E-OTD but without the need for handset modifications. Response time is slower (around ten seconds), and this mechanism is currently only available in networks that synchronize their base stations (e.g., cdmaOne in the United States). The Global Positioning System (GPS) is based on satellite-supplied signals and has a superior accuracy to the land-based techniques. However it requires that the handset be equipped with a GPS unit. Benefon has produced such a unit (the 'ESC!' GSM/GPS mapping phone) that provides an integrated mapping function in addition to GPS and digital voice features.

Design issues surrounding location-aware services include the following:

- ◙ The accuracy of positioning mechanism

- ◙ How position information is defined and transmitted in push or standard architectures

- ◙ How information is retrieved for use by an application

- ◙ Privacy of mobile device users in the push (unsolicited) scenario

Obviously, WAP applications have little control over the accuracy of the user's position, but this should be taken into account (if accuracy information is available) when providing a response or making a decision related to position. The definition of standard formats for position data within WAP has been underway since 1999. It is likely that information will be encoded using an RDF-based scheme, similar to the user agent profile (see earlier) and transmitted in a similar fashion (using WSP and HTTP headers). Because positional information may not be available to the device, it could be added as HTTP headers by a location server or location-aware WAP gateway. The WAP application would simply read these extended HTTP headers and process an XML structure containing geographic information. Privacy of the end user will need to be considered (e.g., the user could disable positioning features), and it may not be possible for general WAP applications to obtain positional data without some sort of prior approval or agreement with the mobile network provider.

PERSONALIZATION

It has been suggested that each extra button press halves the likelihood of a Web user completing a transaction. This is even more likely in the wireless Web where quality of navigation can make or break an application. Personalizing the user interface is one way to improve the likelihood that the user is only a click or two away from his or her most desired information. The goal here is much like that of a good restaurant – to encourage customer loyalty by providing a meal that caters to its clients' tastes in pleasant surroundings without any long waits! Mobile portals, like their wired counterparts (e.g., 'My Yahoo'), make a point of personalizing the user experience, and you should consider some form of personalization for any but the simplest general wireless Web service. Issues surrounding personalization include how to:

- Adjust the user interface to minimize the steps users must take to get to their most frequently accessed information.

- Anticipate user needs and proactively recommend options (the application functions as a friendly adviser).

- Adjust content or allow the user to select content (e.g., the personal home page) so that only what is desired is displayed.

- Ensure that content is prioritized on a given page so that scrolling is reduced.

- Track user usage and actions and solicit user feedback in a way that allows an accurate profile to be constructed.

Commercial wireless personalization products are beginning to appear including products from Oracle, IBM, and BroadVision. It probably makes sense to use these products rather than building a complete solution from scratch. If you have simple requirements and want to go ahead on your own, here are a few suggestions:

- To make the user interface configurable, specify menu lists and navigation options using metadata (e.g., configuration files). By uniquely identifying navigation options, users can dynamically alter their user interface, their choices being stored in a server-side personal profile.

- Personal home pages can be constructed by a user if the application uses standard templates that can display any combination of user-specified content channels. The content channels must be clearly separated from the interface.

- Anticipating user needs is more complex than the items just listed, requiring that you track the user's interactions with the site and draw conclusions. This is probably one area where it makes sense to buy rather than build your own (as even large e-business Web sites like Bid.com have found).

One aspect of personalization is tailoring the user interface for the language and nationality of the user. This is important and complicated enough to warrant its own section.

INTERNATIONAL ISSUES

Making your WAP applications work for clients of different nationalities and languages is known as internationalization, and it is a great deal more complex than translating the text of your application into an appropriate language. In addition to language translation, issues include:

- Character sets

- Date, time, and time zone formatting

- Numeric (e.g., currency) formatting

- Text organization (e.g., what constitutes a word, sentence, and paragraph)

- Text classification (e.g., finding the set of lowercase letters for a specified language)

With the rise of the Internet, the need for a common way to express the characters and symbols of all languages drove the creation of Unicode. WAP supports this universal character set and the encodings that form this standard including UCS-2, ISO-8859-1 (an extended ASCII encoding), and US-ASCII. Because the Wireless Session Protocol is based on HTTP 1.1, the `Accept-charset` and `Content-Type` HTTP headers are supported. The `Accept-charset` header specifies the character set(s) that a user agent supports. The UAProf Specification, described earlier, also provides a way for user agents to specify what character sets they are capable of working with. The `charset` attribute of the `Content-Type` header defines the character set actually used for application content. The `go` element in WML can also be used to specify a list of character sets that the WAP application will accept from the user agent. These character sets are specified in a space or comma delimited field in the `accept-charset` attribute. If present, this value determines how the user agent will transcode postfields. If not specified, the user agent will use the same character set as the last server response. The `go` element also supports an `enctype` attribute that can be used to tell the user agent how to encode posted parameters from a WAP form. If these parameters contain characters other than US-ASCII characters, the WAP specifications recommend that you use an encoding type of `"multipart/form-data"`.

WAP benefits from using XML as the basis for message payloads and WML markup. XML was designed specifically to facilitate communication across boundaries and allows the creator of an XML document to specify the character set in the prologue. When creating WML markup in a character set other than UTF-8 or UTF-16, be sure to include a character set specification in the XML declaration (e.g., `<?xml version="1.0" encoding="US-ASCII" ?>`).

WAP includes support for multiple languages via the `xml:lang` attribute in WML elements and the `Accept-language` WSP/HTTP header (language preferences are also specified in the browser profile of UAProf, covered earlier). The `xml:lang` attribute is an XML standard mechanism for defining the language of content found within the declaring element. This attribute uses language codes defined by RFC1766 (*www.ietf.org/rfc/rfc1766.txt*) and if specified, will be used by a mobile browser to render this content appropriately. The `Accept-language` header will specify the user's locale as either a language or language/country combination as defined in ISO-639 (see *www.w3.org/WAI/ER/IG/ert/iso639.htm*) (e.g., `en` for English or `fr-CA` for French Canadian). You can use this in your applications to tailor their content to the user's language and nationality. In Java, this is facilitated by resource bundles and property files that can be used to specify application labels and messages for all supported languages. Resource bundles provide automatic look-up facilities, removing some of the drudgery of multilanguage support.

The last area we look at is support in WML for formatting user-entered data via the `format` attribute of the `input` element. Because date, time, and currency formatting varies from locale to locale, use a format mask that conforms to the user's locale. For example, the position of the currency indicator (e.g., "$") is before a dollar value in English, but after a franc value in French. Once again, if Java is your application language, you can use properties files to store WML format masks.

That concludes our look at design issues affecting WAP applications. Chapter 10 proposes some architectures that are appropriate for a range of applications.

 **Architectures**

This chapter explores architectures that can help us build WAP applications. By *architecture* we mean a distinct style of building systems (we generalize these into lightweight and enterprise-scale solutions). Within these architectures, we look at specific technologies including CGI, Perl, PHP, servlets, and application servers. Where possible, we illustrate our discussion with real-world case studies.

GENERAL PRINCIPLES

Which architecture you choose for your WAP application depends on the answers to the questions that we posed at the beginning of Chapter 9. Table 10-1 provides some very subjective rules of thumb. In addition, the languages and tool with which your team is familiar should play a significant role in determining your architecture.

If there is a golden rule for thin client architectures, it is that you will benefit (in the long term, anyway) from a clean separation of content from view and control (the Model/View/Controller [MVC] paradigm). Although interpretations of MVC vary, the model portion is concerned with business logic and data, the view portion is concerned with how the user interacts with the system, and the controller provides the glue that interfaces the view and model. It is particularly important to keep this separation in mind when designing wireless Web applications because they are often called on to support multiple access channels (i.e., different physical views), disparate data sources (which makes for a complex model), and integration with existing systems (which makes the controlling software that much more complicated).

TABLE 10-1. Issues to Consider When Selecting an Architectural Approach

QUESTION	LIGHTWEIGHT SOLUTION (E.G., TWO-TIER SCRIPTING OR SERVER PAGE SOLUTION)	ENTERPRISE SOLUTION (E.G., N-TIER APPLICATION SERVER SOLUTION)
What is your time to market?	< 4 months	Typical application server learning curve and additional configuration may make rapid solutions difficult (unless developers are already familiar with tools and methods)
Is this an extension to an existing application? If so, is there already a Web interface to this application?	OK if existing solution is light	A port to a more scalable and extensible architecture may make sense if current system cannot easily be extended
Who will access the application (e.g., general public, registered users, employees)?	Best for smaller groups of users, although can scale through addition of Web servers	Suitable for larger client bases (for example, applications that must sustain tens of thousands of simultaneous users)
Is personalization important?	May require custom solution	Component architectures should integrate with third party personalization products
Are you targeting an international market where many languages must be supported?	Internationalization is possible but should be designed up front	Typically better support for multiple languages due to view separation
What types of devices will user employ to access the application?	Multiple devices can be accommodated in any solution but add significant complexity	If many channels must be supported and/or device customization is needed, the complexity may be easier to handle in a well-partitioned framework
Is there a need to push information to these users?	See Chapter 8	See Chapter 8
What is the expected load (total users, simultaneous sessions)?		Better able to deal with very high loads
What are the sources of data, and is the security of this information important?	Fine for single data sources (no distributed transactions required)	Multiple disparate data sources are handled by data layer abstraction and integration modules. Support for transactions is usually built in to framework or available as an add-on
What is the complexity/diversity of the data?	Great for simple data requirements	Overkill for simple data requirements
Is knowledge of the user's location needed?		Geographic search may require large resources (big databases and hefty computation)
Will this application be extended in the future to other interfaces (such as TV or voice)?		If yes, this approach may provide easier expansion
Is the application highly complex?		Easier to develop complex applications due to the natural partitioning imposed by an n-tier framework

Separation of view from content and control makes it easier to:

- ▣ Support device tweaking.

- ▣ Add new devices.

- ▣ Add new channels and handle changes in WML specs.

- ▣ Handle new content and adapt to changes in content structure.

- ▣ Change the flow of control within a site and extend functionality.

Figure 10-1 illustrates a hypothetical architecture that partitions a system based on this separation. From left to right, the *Web server* and *firewalls* provide client access to the system (we assume an external WAP gateway or integration of this with the Web server). An *interaction controller* accepts requests from the Web server and determines which business logic will handle the request. The *business logic* implements business rules and work flow, providing the bridge between content and view.

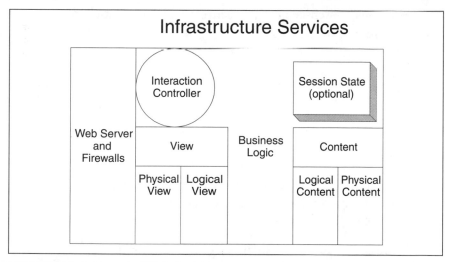

FIGURE 10-1. Generic WAP Architecture

View may be divided between *logical* (independent of device and channel) and *physical* (tailored to interface and possible device). In many solutions, this distinction will not exist, but this separation is invaluable where multiple interface channels are supported. Ideally, *content* is similarly divided so it can be dealt with in a source-independent way (*logical content*), which is derived from *physical content* (e.g., a SQL result set). This separation facilitates integration with legacy data and external systems. In-progress sessions are maintained by *session state* (optional). Infrastructure services may include security, logging, metadata (e.g., configurations), state management, and directory services. Although the actual layout of a WAP system contains most of these building blocks, the location (and existence) of each block depends on the selected architecture. For instance, in an object-oriented approach, business logic and content may be encapsulated within business objects or components. In later sections, we look at how these building blocks can be created within real-world architectures.

Although static WML decks are great for prototyping, they are usually not sufficient for a complete wireless application. However they can be part of a well-designed solution where they provide the framework for accessing selected dynamic content. The following sections focus on two broad categories of WAP architecture: lightweight systems (i.e., systems with minimal infrastructure) and enterprise-scale solutions, which typically execute within a scalable component-based distributed framework.

LIGHTWEIGHT SYSTEMS

As with any attempt to classify software, the term *lightweight* is open to interpretation. We assume that a solution which fits into this category:

- has minimal off-the-shelf infrastructure (e.g., simple or nonexistent support for transactions, access control, load balancing and distribution).

- employs a language (such as Perl, Java, or PHP) that integrates directly with popular Web servers.

◻ takes either a presentation-centric approach (e.g., 'server pages' where business logic is embedded in presentation) or a procedural approach (e.g., a request handler that dynamically builds presentation).

Many variations meet these requirements, so let's take a look at ways to build the components described earlier in our generic WAP architecture.

The lightweight system probably relies on Web server(s) for dispatch and load balancing, running multiple processes or threads on one or more machines. A container or plug-in integrated with the Web server will locate and run business logic contained in a Common Gateway Interface (CGI) program (e.g., PHP, Perl, or C++), a servlet or a server page (e.g., an Active Server Page [ASP] or Java Server Page [JSP]). The view may be provided by server pages with embedded markup, generated programmatically (e.g., by library calls or string operations), or created using an object model such as XML's Document Object Model (DOM). User interface templates or style sheets provide another way to define the presentation. Content acquisition (e.g., database calls) may be embedded in the business/control logic or separately contained in a Java bean, ActiveX control, or Java class (perhaps accessed remotely via RMI). Infrastructure is integrated with the Web server/container, custom built, or supplied by integrated third party products (e.g., Lightweight Directory Access Protocol [LDAP] for directory services).

Figure 10-2 illustrates some options for a lightweight WAP application. Option *a* shows how a server page dynamically adds content to presentation (WML markup) via direct database queries. Advantages of this approach are speed of development (in particular if one person is doing both presentation and business logic) and the intuitive way that presentation can be laid out. Disadvantages include the tight coupling between presentation, business logic, and data that can make changes difficult and a challenge when you have separate people developing the user interface and business logic. Option *b* goes a step beyond option *a,* providing a wrapper around the data, perhaps via a Java bean or tag library. This removes inline database calls and permits changes to the data without necessarily requiring modifications to the server page. It can also make the server page more readable.

Option *c* is a simple procedural approach analogous to options *a* and *b* except that stored procedures provide a wrapper around raw query language. The application uses the outputs from these stored procedures to generate the presentation markup programmatically. This might be done via simple print statements (e.g., `out.println("<card id=" + cardID + ">")` or via calls to an API that supports WML deck creation (e.g., `WMLDeck myDeck = new WMLDeck(); ... myDeck.addCard(cardID, "Main");`). The advantages of this are that stored procedures can be more efficient than discrete database calls and the business logic in the server can be cleaner without embedded data access/update statements. Also, if an object-oriented API is used, the code can be fairly readable

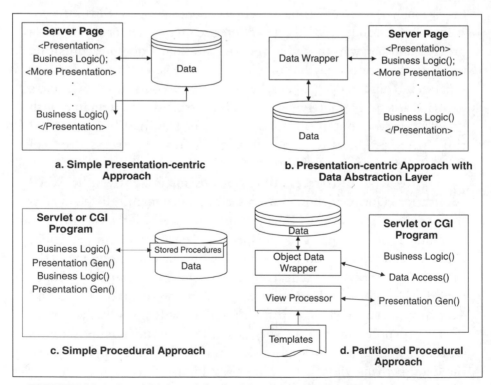

FIGURE 10-2. Some Lightweight Architectural Alternatives

and easy to update. However, this approach suffers from the same problem we encountered earlier where the coupling of view and logic makes it difficult for multiperson teams to partition the work of developing user interface and business logic. In addition, the programmatic creation of presentation markup is rarely as readable as static markup and is certainly less useful where nonprogrammers have the task of creating the user interface.

Option *d* addresses some of these concerns by separating business logic from presentation and data. An object wrapper provides an intuitive interface to the data. This could take the form of a data server or a set of classes that represents abstractions in the problem domain. Note that these classes could also implement business logic, leaving the Java servlet or CGI program (these technologies are discussed later) to orchestrate the flow of control. The servlet or CGI program is the coordinator and may correspond to a single business function (probably with multiple request/response steps). This program obtains data via calls to an object or objects and passes this to a view processor, which merges this data with markup specified in presentation templates. This approach is obviously a great deal heavier than the previous alternatives, and there is an overhead incurred by the template processor (although caching reduces this). However, this architecture provides a more easily maintained and extensible system. It also facilitates partitioning of development roles, allowing user interface designers to focus on template creation and programmers to write business logic. One major benefit of this option is that it makes migration to an application server architecture fairly simple. The view processor may become a component that can be distributed to balance load, and the object data wrappers could be mapped to entity and/or session Enterprise Java Beans.

Which approach you adopt for your project will depend on team size, time frame, and requirements for scalability and maintainability as well as familiarity with both the architectural approach and the technology. Familiarity is critical – experience has shown that biting off an ambitious architecture in addition to a new technology and nebulous requirements can jeopardize even the most promising project!

In the next section we look at technologies that can be used to create a lightweight WAP solution.

Technologies

CGI programs offer a simple way to process HTTP requests. Almost any language (e.g., Perl, Python, and C/C++) can be used for this, although some offer more or less support for Web-oriented processing. Traditional CGI programs are executed as stand-alone processes, although it is common for Web servers to support lighter weight mechanisms that improve scalability (e.g., Apache's FastCGI and mod_perl support). Perl is a highly popular language for server-side content generation. It is extensible through modules and has well-developed support for forms processing, database access (with persistent connections), XML parsing, and other Web-centric tasks. Because Perl was one of the original lightweight solutions for dynamic server-side applications, it boasts a huge base of third party modules that support every imaginable Internet application task (available through the Comprehensive Perl Archive Network, or CPAN) (see *www.perl.com*).

Presentation-centric architectures can be created in Active Server Pages, Java Server Pages, PHP, and more proprietary technologies such as Cold Fusion. Any type of server page technology that permits XML-compliant markup is a candidate for WML generation, and all of the above allow you to lay out WML decks. They also support setting the WML content type header and generation of the required XML prologue. In addition, both ASPs and JSPs support XML processing and document creation, opening up an alternative to static markup. An XML document can be built from retrieved data and translated into WML or HTML markup using an XSL style sheet. This is a much heavier approach than inline presentation (style-sheet-based transformation is an intense exercise in parsing!) but has the advantage of supporting multiple output formats from a single application. We discuss XML-based mechanisms in more detail in Chapter 9.

PHP ('Professional Home Page' – *www.php.net*) is a popular language for Web development that has found an early following in the WAP world, partly because of excellent database support, the ease with which markup can be laid out, and tight integration with the Apache Web server. PHP is extensible via modules and uses a syntax that will be immediately intelligible to those familiar with C or Perl.

WML can be laid out inline just like HTML, but an interesting option is a programmatic API with a great name. HawHaw ('HTML and WML Hybrid Adapted Webserver' [*www.hawhaw.de*]) is freely available under the GNU license. This PHP class library supports HTML, HDML, and WML generation from the same function calls. To create a presentation, you define a 'HAW_deck' as the base unit of display and then add text, images, tables, forms, or links to the page before invoking the 'create_page()' method. The HAW_deck constructor determines which language will be generated based on the HTTP User Agent and Accept headers.

ColdFusion from Allaire (*www.allaire.com*) is a Web application development and deployment environment that takes a page-centric approach. Developers specify the presentation using Cold Fusion Markup Language (CFML), which can then be rendered in the desired output format (e.g., as HTML or WML). Embedded scripting provides business logic, and visual editors simplify the process of building markup, scripting, and data access. At deployment time, a request is satisfied by processing a Cold Fusion page, embedding the results of script execution and data access and transforming the whole into WML. Integration with file systems, CORBA components, and e-mail services adds to the appeal of this solution.

Java has come into its own as a platform-independent language well suited to developing server-side Web applications. Servlets are the Java platform technology of choice for extending Web servers. They provide a platform-independent method for building Web applications, without the limitations of CGI programs (e.g., poor scalability due to a separate per user session). When first introduced, the Java Servlet API was relatively simple, analogous to proprietary Web server extensions such as Netscape Server API or Apache modules. Later versions of this API have improved the infrastructure provided by the servlet container to the point where servlet-based applications straddle the boundary between lightweight and enterprise-scale applications. Java servlets run in servlet containers, which provide services including security and configuration. Servlet containers are available for Apache Web Server, iPlanet Web Server, Microsoft IIS, and other servers. As part of an enterprise solution, these containers can also be

integrated with application servers including BEA WebLogic, iPlanet Application Server, and IBM WebSphere. Java Server Pages, mentioned earlier, are Sun's answer to Microsoft's Active Server Pages. They run in the same container as servlets (and in fact the embedded Java code is converted to servlets prior to execution).

Java supports WAP application development through:

- ▣ WML libraries (e.g., Ericsson's JAWAP).
- ▣ XML APIs and tools.
- ▣ JSP's support for direct WML layout.
- ▣ Easy access to HTTP request and response data.
- ▣ Strong network libraries.

Java (and servlets, in particular) is used in the development case study described in Chapter 12.

Case Studies

To illustrate the lightweight approach, let's look at a real-world WAP application that uses C++, PHP, and MySQL, running on inexpensive hardware to provide a location-based search service. Somewherenear was the brainchild of Mike Banahan and his friends at GB direct (*www.gbdirect.co.uk*), a UK firm that helps businesses take advantage of Internet and intranet technologies. The WAP service is an extension to an existing HTML service that provides assistance to business and recreational travelers. Users of this service can locate restaurants (e.g., curry houses), pubs, and other locations of interest by specifying a nearby town or postal code. An interesting feature is a facility to rate an establishment that you visit on its quality of service (e.g., food, drink, etc.).

WAP users can access the site through any open WAP gateway (the site does not contain its own gateway). Two servers are involved, the application server that runs a mixture of C++ CGI scripts, filling the role of controller, plus the database server that resides behind a

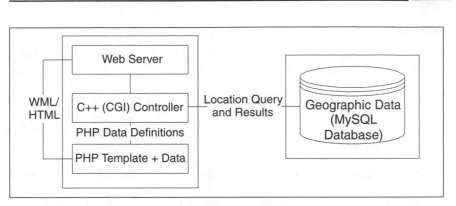

FIGURE 10-3. Somewherenear Architecture

firewall for protection. Templates, built from PHP3, format the output of the CGI scripts, allowing the same controller logic to be used unchanged for the HTML, WAP/WML, and I-Mode versions. The database is a relational model built with the freely available MySQL database. Security is provided by server-side username/passwords and sessions that time out. Encryption is not required.

Figure 10-3 illustrates the architecture of Somewherenear.com. The physical layout consist of two Linux servers, one for the Web server and application and the other hosting the data. The Web server uses simple CGI requests to a C++ controller, which performs the location query on the MySQL database. The controller selects the correct PHP template to display the results and appends the data to this template embedded in a series of PHP data definitions. The complete PHP output is run through a PHP interpreter to produce the merged markup, which is returned to the user via the Web server. In the case of HTML generation, this output is simultaneously validated (for debug purposes) by piping it through 'weblint'. Multichannel access is easy because the presentation is completely encapsulated in the PHP templates. This separation also makes it easier for developers to collaborate when updating the service.

The design is currently device independent, although hooks are in place for client discovery and tailoring if appropriate. The development of the complete service (HTML and WML) took experienced developers less than three months from concept to completion with only two days devoted to adding a WML channel. Challenges encountered in adding the WAP channel include:

- On-the-fly validation of generated WML not as well supported as HTML validation.

- WML's less-than-intuitive event model.

- Deck size limitations of prevalent WAP phones (<1400 bytes).

- WML layout limitations (when compared to HTML).

- Limited support for cookies by WAP gateways.

- Inconsistent rendering of WML between different phone browsers.

The URL for the WML service is *http://www.somewherenear.com/wap/index.cgi* and for the HTML site is *http://www.somewherenear.com*. Figure 10-4 displays a sequence of screens from Somewherenear.com.

In this example, we want to find some pubs (screen *a*) in the vicinity of Norwich (a city north of London, England) and specify the category of service in which we are interested (other options include cinemas, curry houses, accommodation, and mobile phone shops) as well as the geographic area (screen *b*). The search returns five items at a time (screen *c*), including name and phone number and a link to a detail screen. On the detail screen (screen *d*), you can see the address and who submitted this service for inclusion in Somewherenear. It also shows how patrons have rated this service, and a WTA URL link allows direct voice dialing from a WAP phone (where supported by the device and infrastructure). The HTML version is more feature rich, providing a visual search (using maps) and allowing you to vote on the quality of the service.

When asked to comment on his experience building a pioneer WAP service, Mike Banahan of GB direct had the following suggestions:

- Separate common view code into delivery-specific libraries.

- Consider using off-the-shelf lightweight tools with a shallow

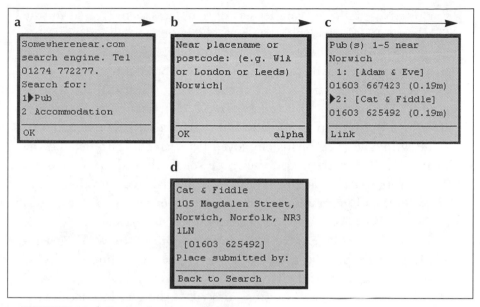

FIGURE 10-4. Somewherenear in Action

learning curve rather than having to gear up for the expense of XML/Java/XSLT (however, the latter is probably the long-run win).

■ Do not expect your first attempt to be tidy, polished, or pretty, but use this to validate your preconceptions.

■ Test early and often on real users.

BAWAG (Bank für Arbeit und Wirtschaft AG) is the first Austrian bank to deploy a WAP financial solution. This is an extension of an existing e-banking solution that allows clients to bank from home using the Internet. The wireless channel uses the same process employed in the Web banking solution, and bank functions include money transfer and account balances. In addition, mobile brokerage functions include stock accounts, stock orders, and near real-time quotes.

The BAWAG system uses Microsoft's Active Server Pages (ASP) and ISAPI extensions running within a Microsoft IIS Web server on a

Windows NT platform. Parallel sets of templates were created for the HTML and WML channels. The business logic is accessed through a transactional protocol converter that implements standard banking and brokerage functions, mapping these to a bank-proprietary inter-face (see Fig. 10-5). The security of this system is critical, and a dedi-cated WAP gateway (hosted by BAWAG partner, max.mobil) provides a WTLS (up to 48 bit) link between client and gateway. HTTP with TLS (128 bit) is employed between the gateway and the Web server. The system also uses a personal identification number (PIN) and transaction number (TAN) scheme that requires the user to enter a PIN and generates unique transaction numbers for future ref-erence. The BAWAG solution is also discussed in Chapter 3.

The project took a device-independent approach to WML genera-tion, targeting a popular subset of WAP phones including the Nokia 7110, Siemens x35, and Ericsson 320 models. Harald Lakatha of Unisys, the architect of this system, described the user interface as the primary technical challenge. It was challenging to produce a design that was clear and usable yet still corresponded closely to the existing Web interface. Other issues dealt with, included differences and defi-

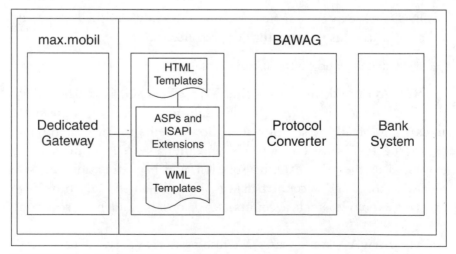

FIGURE 10-5. BAWAG Financial System Architecture

ciencies in gateway and client software. Despite these obstacles, the entire project took under four months to complete, six weeks for the banking interface and another six for the mobile brokerage.

That concludes our look at the lighter side of WAP systems. In the next section we examine some heavier architectures suitable for larger scale deployments.

ENTERPRISE-SCALE SYSTEMS

Whereas a lightweight architecture emphasizes time to market and typically uses a simple page-based or procedural approach, enterprise architectures place more importance on issues such as scalability, security, transactions, and support for multiple channels and disparate data sources. The challenges posed by high-volume services such as Internet portals point toward a more complex and well-partitioned solution. We assume that an enterprise solution exhibits most of the following characteristics:

- Employs a well-designed infrastructure such as that laid out in the Java 2 Enterprise Edition (J2EE) specification or the CORBA service specifications (e.g., integrated support for security, transactions, load balancing, etc.). This infrastructure is usually provided by a commercial application server such as BEA's WebLogic or IBM's WebSphere.

- Takes a distributed approach, taking advantage of the power of the network to produce scalable, fault-tolerant systems.

- Is implemented in a full-featured language (such as Java or C++) usually wrapped as components to encapsulate business logic and mid-tier business objects.

- Uses a scalable approach to interfacing with the Web server (e.g., NSAPI, ISAPI, or servlet containers).

- Sessions and state are carefully managed and persistence mechanisms may be used to handle the failure of individual servers.

As with the lightweight solutions, the system relies on Web servers for front-end load balancing. A dispatcher can be used to spread the load between these servers. Requests are directed to the appropriate application server, and multiple application servers can be spread across separate physical servers to provide load balancing and fault tolerance. These application servers execute within a services infrastructure that may transparently take care of naming, state management, access control, and persistence. As in the lighter approach, view processing may be provided by server pages, generated programmatically, template based, or created using an object model such as XML's DOM. Content acquisition is usually accomplished by invoking methods on business components (e.g., Entity EJBs). These in turn may use a "connector" approach to legacy integration (where this is required) so that disparate data sources are accommodated in a consistent manner. Figure 10-6 illustrates some options for an enterprise WAP application.

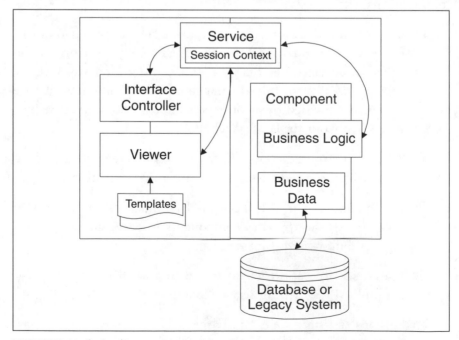

FIGURE 10-6. An Enterprise Architecture

This figure broadly partitions the system into a front-end interface subsystem and a business model subsystem. An *interface controller* would accept requests from a Web server (not shown). This HTTP interface controller could have siblings in the form of controllers for other interfaces (e.g., a Common Object Request Broker Architecture [CORBA] Internet Inter-ORB Protocol [IIOP] interface). These could inherit common functionality from a parent 'interface controller' class. The controller would extract information from the HTTP request and package this in a generic request format to be sent to a *service.* The service performs the role of work-flow controller as well as encapsulating the user's session context (state). It determines user interaction flows for an application, calling appropriate business components to satisfy user requests. The *component* would expose an interface to its functionality (*business logic*) and would work with business data. *Business data* provides a mid-tier abstraction (i.e., a logical data model) hiding the details of physical representation in *databases* or *legacy systems.*

One important feature of the proposed architecture is the use of a stateful *service* object containing a *session context* that is shared between subsystems. How this context is maintained (e.g., persistence, creation, and destruction) and how it is accessed or passed between components will impact performance and robustness of the system. The service and session context objects would be created by the interface subsystem when a user starts a session and then updated by interactions with business components throughout the life of the user's session. The *viewer* (view processor) accesses the session context to obtain dynamic content that it will merge with the appropriate template (logical view). The resulting markup (physical view – e.g., WML or HTML) is returned to the Web server. This entire process is orchestrated by the interface controller, although the service and/or business logic may dictate which view template should be used in each response.

Technologies

Although a number of technologies can be used to build enterprise-scale applications (e.g., CORBA, EJBs, and Microsoft's .NET), we look at the Java 2 Enterprise Edition (J2EE) platform because it illus-

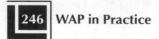

trates most of the functionality and services required for such systems. J2EE includes a set of APIs that support enterprise application development including:

- RMI – Remote Method Invocation

- JNDI – Java Naming and Directory Interface

- Servlets – Server-side Java applications

- EJB – Enterprise Java Beans

- JDBC – Java Database Connectivity

- JMS – Java Message Service

- JTA – Java Transaction API

RMI allows Java clients to invoke methods on remote objects without the hassle of explicit network communication. RMI uses Java's serialization (the ability to convert objects to and from strings) to implement distributed computing with all its advantages of improved scalability and fault tolerance. RMI can be implemented over standard internetworking protocols such as CORBA's IIOP.

JNDI provides a way for Java programs to look up objects and data by name and to search for objects or data by specifying target attribute values. JNDI can be implemented over Lightweight Directory Access Protocol (LDAP) and is useful when locating components (e.g., EJBs) in a distributed system and for tasks such as access control and client authentication.

We discussed servlets in the previous section on lightweight architectures. In an enterprise context, they usually provide interface processing linking the HTTP world with distributed components.

Enterprise Java Beans provide a server-side component framework that reduces the drudgery and complexity of writing middleware business logic. The EJB model defines a container within which beans execute. Containers live inside EJB servers, and the server and container take care of housekeeping tasks such as configuration, name services, component lifecycle, security, and transactions. EJBs can also provide automatic container managed persistence, relieving the programmer of this time-consuming task.

Java Database Connectivity (JDBC) provides a vendor-neutral standard for relational database access, allowing a Java program to send SQL statements to a database server and work with the returned results. JDBC drivers are available for popular databases on most platforms. JDBC specifies (optional) support for database connection pooling – which allows multiple sessions to share a database connection. This is a very necessary feature in high-volume database access situations.

The Java Message Service (JMS) can be used to implement message-oriented middleware in support of either a message queuing or publish-and-subscribe architecture. This is very useful in an environment where immediate request/responses are not realistic and/or information needs to be distributed to a large number of clients (e.g., paging or e-mail services). Business-to-business integration projects can also benefit from the loosely coupled message-based architecture made possible by JMS. This loose coupling means that such systems do not have to be available at the same time, yet can still guarantee the delivery of information between systems.

The Java Transaction API supports distributed transactions, necessary when updating disparate but related data. JTA supports two-phase commit (a facility whereby distributed transactions are coordinated to ensure that all transactions successfully complete or roll back). This facility is used by EJBs when they participate in a transaction.

The advantage of J2EE for enterprise development lies in its relatively complete treatment of the issues of enterprise computing coupled with Java's platform independence. Whereas CORBA's services also deal with these issues, J2EE provides a real-world, readily available language-specific equivalent to these specifications. Vendors have embraced the Java Enterprise specifications, and competition in the J2EE application server market is intense. There are some disadvantages to selecting a J2EE framework for your system. Developers are confined to writing in Java (although Java programs can call CORBA servers written in other languages). Java also has lower performance than compiled languages such as C++ (although native Java compilers reduce this gap). Finally, most application servers that implement the J2EE specifications carry a hefty price tag and learning curve, making them suitable only for larger scale efforts.

Case Studies

We look at two real-world systems that illustrate enterprise-scale architectures. The Integrated Personalization Platform is a carrier grade wireless portal platform that supports application service provision. The second case study is the eBASE framework, developed in Canada to provide electronic delivery of government services.

The Integrated Personalization Platform is a product of mobileID, a Silicon Valley company specializing in wireless Web content and services. It is a portal solution (used by application service providers) that supports personalization, e-mail messaging, and content delivery. The system is aimed at both enterprises and carriers and uses JSPs, BEA's WebLogic Server, Oracle 8i, and Apache Web servers to provide a scalable n-tier solution (see Fig. 10-7). mobileID provides a publicly available portal that uses this infrastructure as well as the WAPlite gateway. The user interface is tailored to specific devices, and support is provided for an impressive array of WAP devices, a list of which is available at mobileID's site (*www.mobileID.com*). These include more than sixty mobile phones, hand-helds, and hybrids. The architecture also supports HTML and HDML channels, and rolling out the WAP service took less than three months. Encryption and a password sign-on provide security.

The second case study is a framework developed in Canada in support of electronic delivery of government services. The eBASE framework provides access through multiple interface channels (including the Web and WAP) to a variety of government programs. Developed by Unisys Canada, it uses Java servlets, CORBA components (written in Java and C++), and an integrated back office data-

Usability and Testing

USABILITY

Everyone understands usability, but few can define it in a sentence or two (rather like defining "quality" or "happiness"). I am no exception to that rule, so we start with a simpler definition. *Use* (in our context) means to interact with an application to achieve a purpose (e.g., she used the Travel Assistance application to pick a good restaurant for tonight's meal). When an application helps users achieve their purpose in an effective (i.e., enjoyable, rapid, and easy) way, then that application is *usable* (e.g., she found the application usable because in a short time, she was able to find exactly what she was looking for – a nearby vegetarian Thai restaurant). Building on these concepts, *usability* is the quality of an application that permits its effective use (e.g., the Travel Assistance application has usability). By this definition, *good usability* is redundant (we can simply say *usability*) and the term *poor usability* can be restated as "a lack of" usability. Nokia's WAP Service Designer's Guide to Nokia Handsets provides a good definition of what we should aim for: WAP services "must be simple to use, easy to learn, pleasant to view, and meet user's need for useful information in a mobile context." Note that other vendors (e.g., Phone.com and Ericsson) also offer designer's guides for their WAP microbrowser products. These can be freely downloaded from the vendor's Web sites. A usability-related guide is also available from the WAP Forum site (see sidebar "Generic vs. Tailored User Interfaces").

> ## *Generic vs. Tailored User Interfaces*
>
> Usability is hotly debated on developer news groups and mailing lists. One school of thought proposes that usable applications can created in a generic way (i.e., a WML deck can be deployed that will be usable on all client devices). Others believe that only through device-tailored code can a workable user interface be accomplished. An informal note on the WAP Forum site, titled "Generic Content Authoring Guide for WML 1.1," attempts to outline a generic approach to WML development, This document is an excellent place to start learning about generic vs. device-tailored issues. ▣

So what can be done to help ensure that our applications have usability? There is no black and white prescription for this, but most problems in application usability (and life in general) stem from an inability to communicate.

Communication

Communication is at the heart of every application. An application must communicate its purpose, content, current state, and possible options to users. It must also allow users to communicate their needs easily. The purpose of an application must be clear, or users will have little incentive to learn it and use it. Users should be able to under-stand the content conveyed by an application. It should be obvious to users where they currently are, within an application, and what their navigation choices are at this point. Users should feel in control at all times and be able to express what they need in an intuitive way.

Let's take the Travel Assistance application. The main card of this application should clearly explain that this is an application to help trav-elers find services, perhaps through a title or maybe an 'About' link. When a list of restaurant addresses is displayed, it should be clear that the addresses belong to restaurants. It may be overkill to state that the street address is a street address (this is usually apparent without a label), and similarly, the phone number may not require a label. If users are looking at a restaurant details card, it would be good if it is clear that they can return to a list of restaurants or exit to the main menu at this point.

To achieve the goal of communication, we need to follow these basic principles:

- Simplicity

- Small is beautiful

- Clarity

- Feedback

- Balance

The next few sections look at these principles and list some rules of thumb that can help to achieve them. You may find it useful to extract your own list of rules from the following sections. Use this to guide your development, and add to it during the life of your application.

Simplicity

Simplicity is not simple. To craft a simple interface to a real-world application requires thought, feedback from real users, and many iterations. It also requires a genuine understanding of the problem (or challenge, depending on your philosophy and how much coffee you've had today) that the application is designed to solve. KISS (keep it simple, stupid) is often difficult advice to follow.

Rules of thumb to achieve simplicity:

- **Important information first:** Put the most critical, frequently accessed content first. This reduces the need to scroll off the screen.

- **Keep only the essentials:** Strive for essential cards and a simple navigation structure. If you lay out your navigation structure on paper, it may be possible to simplify the hierarchy to remove layers. Perhaps you can sequence some flows rather than nesting them. Similarly, examine each card to ensure it is really necessary.

■ **One topic per page:** Cover one topic per card or provide a clear separation of each topic via a linked table of contents.

■ **Use select lists:** Limit the amount of data entry by coding fields as selection lists and using previously entered information where possible. This is absolutely necessary when writing for handsets, but less critical for handheld computers.

■ **Pre-enter common data:** Save the user the pain of entering repetitive or assumed information (e.g., supply `"http://www."` as a default start for a URL and allow the user to overwrite this).

■ **Use shortcuts:** Use, but do not rely on, keypad shortcuts (access keys are optional from WML 1.2 on).

■ **Use numeric passwords:** Consider using numeric passwords to ease user entry on handsets.

■ **Build simplest interface first:** Design for the simplest device you will support. This interface should work all right on other devices. You can always tweak the interface for other devices if time allows.

■ **Build a complementary Web site:** To reduce the complexity of a wireless Web interface, build a complementary Web site for difficult items like preference setting and complex text entry. Do not try to duplicate all Web functionality in a wireless interface. A complementary Web interface to your mobile service can allow users to register for the service itself, enter information such as credit card details and their address, and enter personal preferences. An example drawn from personal information management applications would be the contact list that could be entered on the Web and searched using WAP.

Small Is Beautiful

Small is beautiful and, in the current WAP world, mandatory! Why not make a virtue out of necessity and think small for a change? Some ways to do this include the following:

◪ **Keep pages brief:** Use links to break up long pages into a linear set of linked pages.

◪ **Pick short URLs:** If a user has to enter your URL, it should be short and meaningful to make entry as easy as possible.

◪ **Remember the number seven:** Bear in mind the famous "seven plus or minus two" rule. Try not to present the user with more than seven options at any one time.

◪ **Keep menus short:** When handling large numbers of options or menu items, split these into multiple select lists or groups of links with a More option that links the lists. Phone.com recommends nine options per card maximum to allow use of access keys.

◪ **Use small decks and images:** Images should be less than 1400 bytes. Encoding normally reduces code size, but it is best not to rely on this and to keep noncompiled decks below 1000 bytes when writing for handsets. When displaying large quantities of text, use multiple decks if the total text size is larger than about 1000 characters (note that non-ASCII character sets may require more than one byte per character). Make use of a `"More"` do-go event handler or link to navigate from deck to deck.

◪ **No wide tables:** Do not use wide tables (stick to two or three columns) and do not use tables for physical layout because they are not supported by all devices.

◪ **Limit scrolling:** Limit text blocks to a few sentences (especially for handset applications) because more than this requires a lot of scrolling. Keep text lines short and assume they will wrap.

◪ **Use short meaningful labels:** Do not use uncommon acronyms or longer words for links (in particular), fields, and selection lists. Six characters is often quoted as a reasonable limit for handset displays. Long names and abbreviations are harder to follow.

■ **No deeper than three levels:** Keep hierarchies to three levels or less to prevent users from getting lost.

Clarity

Clarity is the rare quality that allows us to see directly the true meaning of something. The limits imposed by tiny handset screens can actually aid clarity: If you have the space for only one word, it had better be the right word! Here are some ways to improve clarity:

■ **Ensure content is essential:** Be ruthless in only displaying required content. As William Strunk, Jr., writes in *The Elements of Style,* "A sentence should contain no unnecessary words, a paragraph no unnecessary sentences . . . " and the same applies to WML cards and text!

■ **Group common options:** Group the most often used options together and make them accessible from the main menu. .

■ **Use consistent terminology:** Keep terminology consistent from page to page.

■ **Avoid too much white space:** Avoid using too much white space because it reduces the information available per card and increases the need to scroll or link.

■ **Use format masks:** When accepting text, use the `format` attribute of `<input>` to limit text length and type (e.g., use `'*x'` for e-mail addresses and `'20M'` to limit mixed case entry to 20 characters). Using format masks reduces user frustration as well as simplifying server-side validation.

■ **Don't optimize early:** Avoid the temptation of optimizing while developing for a particular device unless this is really the only client who will use your application. What looks great on one handset may not work at all on another. Optimization can occur after the core application is in place.

Feedback

Accepting and providing feedback is a critical facet of a usable WAP application. This ensures that users feel in control and retain an understanding of where they are, what they have done to date, and where they can go next. Consider the following rules of thumb for improving feedback:

- **Provide help:** If required, create help text for a specific page or function. Use a consistent approach to help (e.g., always use a Help link or soft key; use the same access key number).

- **Allow user customization:** Allow the user to customize the order of information on a preferences screen (perhaps via an associated Web application).

- **Provide a way home:** Ensure users can return to the main card easily – remember EXIT navigation.

- **Build in an escape hatch:** Ensure users can back up or cancel an operation. Do not assume that all devices provide a Back button. Users need an escape hatch, particularly when exploring or learning a new service.

- **Use formatting:** Make judicious use of the formatting tags (e.g., `<big>`, `<strong>`) to let users know the relative importance of text items. Do not assume they will always be implemented by a WML browser.

- **Handle errors:** Ensure that error conditions result in a clear way ahead. Users should not be left at a dead end!

- **Use titles:** Title each card to provide context, but do not rely on the `title` attribute being displayed by a given device. Some devices may use the title attribute of the first card when bookmarking a deck. Also, consider using the `title` attribute where available in other elements (e.g., tables). The browser may use this to provide users with additional information about a display element.

■ **Use consistent layout:** Familiar pages are easier to navigate. Use a consistent layout for all pages in a mobile service and try to match this to the layout of an associated Web site if applicable.

■ **Use a consistent navigation method:** WML lets you navigate in a number of ways. You can use links, embed `<go>` elements in select lists, and use `accept` or `options` event handlers. Not all techniques work equally well on all devices (links are the common denominator). Whatever you pick, be consistent.

Balance

■ **Balance page length with navigation:** Ensure pages are not too long, but balance the depth of page hierarchy with the amount of content per page.

■ **Don't overlabel:** Use labels where required, but do not label fields whose content is self-explanatory (e.g., when displaying an e-mail address on an electronic business card).

■ **Balance fields per card:** When creating cards for user input, remember that some WML browsers only display one entry field at a time (e.g., Phone.com's UP Browser). Make sure you consider this when putting multiple input fields on a card so you strike a balance between too many separate cards and too many fields in a row.

■ **Make judicious use of images:** Use graphics sparingly and only where they improve clarity (e.g., company logo or where an image takes up less space than the corresponding text (e.g., a copyright notice). Always use the `alt` attribute and test the appearance of this on real devices.

If that list of rules seems overwhelming, don't fret! The most important thing to remember when building a usable WAP application is that your intuition is still your best guide. If it doesn't seem quite right to you, then it probably needs fixing. Sometimes, however, it's hard to see the flaws in our own work and to ensure that an application lives up to its billing and meets a user's requirements. That's where testing come in.

TESTING

Unit testing is usually carried out by developers using device emulators (and possibly real devices). System testing is ideally performed by an independent test team using an environment similar to the production environment. System testing should use actual devices and is improved by involving end users. This testing ensures that the system meets externally observable requirements including:

- Functional requirements (e.g., "The system shall allow users to view their e-mail messages.").
- Derived requirements such as performance, robustness, and scalability.
- Usability requirements.

Functional, Regression, and Load Testing

Functional tests are captured in test cases and are usually derived from a requirements document and carried out by independent testers (at least on larger projects). Functional test cases consist of:

1. An assumed start state and preconditions (conditions that must be fulfilled before this test can be executed).
2. A sequence of steps to be carried out by the tester.
3. A well-defined test goal, possibly including a correct set of outputs (e.g., a screen capture or list of values).

Functional and derived requirements can be tested manually, but this may not be the correct approach with a large or long-lived system. In such a system, frequent changes can make running a complete test suite before every new release an expensive proposition. Fortunately there are ways to automate functional testing using tools such as e-TEST suite from Empirix (*www.empirix.com*), formerly RSW Software. This product lets you record a test case by interacting with a WAP simulator (the UP.Browser simulator from Phone.com).

Using a component called the 'HTTP Spy', it captures your interactions, timing information, delays, and cookies used in the interaction as well as the response returned by your WAP application. These interactions are recorded as "visual scripts" that you can view and update in a graphical editing environment (including full WML markup). e-TEST Scripts can be played back individually to duplicate a functional test and can also be used for regression testing (where a complete set of tests is rerun, following changes to your application, to verify that everything still works as it should). For load testing, e-TEST suite uses a specified number of "virtual users" to simulate real-world users working with your application. If you are on a shoestring budget, Apache Jmeter is a free load tester available from *www.apache.org*.

With all load testers, beware of misleading results arising from repeatedly requesting a single card or a small subset of cards due to potential caching in the Web server, WAP gateway, and browser/simulator. Although automated test tools have a cost and learning curve that may be difficult to justify for small projects, they can help improve quality of, and bring an element of control to, medium to large applications. Most of these products also work with HTML, a blessing for applications that support multiple interface channels.

Usability Testing

Usability testing is critical given the limited user interfaces offered by WAP phones and hand-helds. Requirements for usability can be based on mobile user interface design principles such as those discussed earlier (e.g., "All on-screen labels shall be between 4 and 8 characters" and "Menus shall not be nested more than 3 levels"). It is a good idea to lay out explicit guidelines for developers that will later be verified by testers.

You can also improve the usability of an application by recruiting end users to perform realistic usage scenarios. These can be laid out in a test plan with each test having a description, step-by-step instructions, and expected results. Tests should cover normal execution of functions, scenarios where the user aborts an operation, and various error conditions. Error conditions can be simulated by a test application server or brought about by entering parameters that are outside the bounds of a given function. Assume that end users will not have read documentation prior to using your application (a realistic assumption!).

Usability test results should note:

◫ Difficulties the user experiences carrying out each function.

◫ Comments on how the interface could be improved.

◫ Actual results (e.g., success, qualified success, or failure).

Usability tests are most effective if carried out early in the development process and can even make use of a static WML prototype. The feedback from these tests can be used to improve the flow through the application and correct inadequacies that if allowed into a production system would result in low user acceptance.

A survey of 300 WAP industry experts carried out by the ARC Group found that handset interoperability was seen as the biggest technical challenge they faced in developing WAP services (see *www.wap-resources.net/wapsurvey.shtml*). Obviously, a major factor in testing is the set of mobile devices on which the application will run. Ideally the system test suite should be carried out on each target device. Emulators can be used, but vary in the degree to which they are faithful to the physical device. There are dozens of WAP phones based on at least five flavors of WAP browser. Adding handheld and desktop browsers to this mix presents an almost overwhelming challenge to your testers. Testing with a subset that is popular in the area where you will deploy your application is a manageable alternative to complete coverage. For example, the Phone.com browser for mobile phones is popular in North America, and it may be adequate to test the application on a representative sample of Phone.com-based handsets. Adding tests with the Nokia and Ericsson emulators plus a Palm Pilot browser (e.g., the MobileID browser) will help to ensure that the application is usable on most devices.

The WAP gateways that will be used by the target audience should also factor into your testing. The gateway plays a central role in WAP communications, and there are differences between vendors' products (e.g., encoding/decoding performance, support for cookies, support for HTTP authentication, caching, and security). The online gateways provided by Ericsson and Phone.com provide an excellent way to test your application using production gateways. Developer gateways that may be downloaded and installed on a local network are another alternative, although considerably more effort is needed to set up and configure a local gateway.

An alternative to putting together a complete, realistic testing environment is to outsource this to a WAP testing lab. One such service is provided by Anywhereyougo.com (*http://www.anywhereyougo.com*) based in the United Kingdom.

An informal survey of WAP applications reveals that more than 25 percent fail to meet even basic requirements for usability and functionality. If users have to turn off their phone or exit their browser to cope with shortcomings in your application they will probably not come back. In an enterprise application, feedback from irate users will probably filter back rather more rapidly than you would like, making careful testing all the more appealing!

Application Development Case Study

WAP application development has much in common with thin client (HTML-based) Web application development. Both rely on servers and a server-side language to generate display markup and script. Both also typically use Web servers and access legacy systems or other sources of dynamic content. However, WAP application projects have unique requirements. WAP projects are often integration efforts that extend an existing Web or legacy system to wireless clients. This requires careful attention to a design that cleanly supports multichannel access to the same information. Also, the wide diversity of mobile devices combined with the varied behavior of different WAP gateways may dictate a more intense testing process, especially when an application is targeted to a general Internet audience.

THE APPLICATION

In this chapter we work through a development case study for a Java servlet-based WAP application describing each stage of the process that was used to build the application. This is illustrated with some of the artifacts (e.g., designs, code, and test results) that were created along the way. The aim of this exercise is to illustrate a realistic approach to a small-scale WAP development effort. Familiarity with Unified Modeling Language (UML), Java, Java servlets, and JDBC will be helpful when exploring the design and code. There is not space to provide a tutorial on these technologies, but many excellent books, Web sites, and articles are available that serve this purpose. The Rational Web site at *www.rational.com* is a good source of information on UML (the Rational Rose case tool was used to produce the UML diagrams in this chapter). Java is covered well by Sun's Java Web site (*java.sun.com*), and this is also a good starting point to learn about servlets and JDBC.

The application we look at is a scheduling and inspection system for a fictitious government department responsible for controlling the lucrative areas of alcohol and gambling (see sidebar "Application Background"). The current work flow in our imaginary government department uses printed schedules updated once every two weeks and paper forms to enter inspection information. The inspection forms are entered into a mainframe system by a data entry clerk whenever the inspector returns them to the office (e.g., by fax or courier). Schedules are currently printed from a central scheduling system using a Windows-based Visual Basic front-end. Inefficiencies in this system result from duplicate entry of data and extra time spent manually sending in inspection forms. The data is also out of date because a delay of days can occur between an inspection and the actual update to the central system. Changes to inspectors' schedules can occur as a result of sickness or special events that require impromptu licenses and inspections. These changes require human intervention and are usually done by phone calls (the inspectors currently carry cell phones). The scope of our application is limited to schedules and inspections of establishments that serve alcoholic refreshments (e.g., bars, cabarets, and lounges).

Application Background

Although the application presented here has been modified for use as a case study, it is based on a real-world pilot project developed at Unisys Canada. I am indebted to my friends at Unisys, in particular David Morash, who built the majority of this case study. ∎

THE PROCESS

A typical wireless Web application development process may include most of the following tasks:

- ▣ Opportunity assessment

- ▣ Requirements gathering and analysis

- ▣ Architecture and off-the-shelf software selection

- ▣ Setup development environment

- ▣ Prototyping

- ▣ Design (high level to detailed)

- ▣ Coding and developer testing

- ▣ System (usability and functionality) testing

- ▣ Release and/or deployment

These tasks may be arranged in a sequence (the now infamous waterfall method) or more likely in some sort of iterative spiral. All too often, the first few tasks and the independent testing items are skipped or hurried through with predictably disastrous results. WAP applications can benefit from a special emphasis on the opportunity assessment, architecture, and testing steps.

OPPORTUNITY ASSESSMENT

Part of an opportunity assessment should ensure your application is appropriate for the mobile world:

- ▣ User workflow can be broken into a series of simple steps.

- ▣ Minimal text entry is required.

- ◧ The application takes advantage of time, location, or personalization.

- ◧ The application has a sustainable business model (i.e., how will this be paid for?).

- ◧ The application satisfies a genuine user need or desire.

The Alcohol Inspection System satisfies these requirements as follows.

Simple Workflow

In our application, the inspection can be carried out using brief check lists, numeric entry, and optional entry of textual comments. The user's workflow consists of the following:

- ◧ Login

- ◧ Select schedule query (by date, location, or next)

- ◧ Select inspection

- ◧ Enter inspection details (approximately six fields)

- ◧ Enter comment (optional)

- ◧ Repeat with next

Minimal Text Entry

In our simple application, only numeric text is required and this is limited to a single field. An optional comment can be entered. Login requires a user ID and password, but these can be selected for ease of entry. Target devices include palmtops so that entry of brief text comments will not be too painful.

Time, Location, and Personalization

This application improves the timeliness of inspection information through a real-time interface with a central server. Up-to-the-minute schedules can also be accessed, and schedule data will be specific to the logged-in user. Although there is no personalization in our example application, since each inspector can be identified at logon, we could enhance the system to allow inspectors to customize their interface (e.g., by bringing up their most used function first or limiting searches to their territory).

Sustainable Business Model

This service will be paid for using an Application Service Provider (ASP) model. The government department will outsource this service to a third party ASP and pay a monthly charge based on the number of users. A cost/benefit analysis showed that the department should be able to realize cost savings of roughly 20 percent of their operational budget due to improved efficiencies in data entry and scheduling. Half of these savings will be used to pay for the new service.

Satisfies a Genuine Need

The manual process was cumbersome, and although some inspectors are not happy about the new approach, most understand the benefits and are willing to try out a service that should reduce their paper workload.

There are additional criteria that we could use to judge whether this makes sense as a wireless Web application. However, it is obvious that technological alternatives to WAP such as a laptop-based solution or a palmtop stand-alone application would either be more expensive or would not provide the benefits of real-time updates. Refer to Chapter 3 for more information on what makes an appropriate mobile application.

REQUIREMENTS GATHERING AND ANALYSIS

Our application has the requirements defined for functional capabilities, usability, and performance.

Functional

Functional requirements are:

1. Inspectors shall identify themselves to the system using a user name and password.

2. Inspectors shall be able to view their personal inspection schedule by:

   ■ Date

   ■ Location

   ■ Next schedule

3. Inspectors shall be able to enter inspection details for selected alcohol-serving establishments including:

   ■ Eating establishments

   ■ Cabarets

   ■ Lounges

   ■ Special occasion license (SOL)

4. Inspection information to be entered shall include the following Pass/Fail checks:

   ■ Tax stamps (do bottles have valid excise tax stamps?)

   ■ Stock (do bottles contain what their labels say they do?)

   ■ Measures (are legal-sized measures used in mixing drinks?)

   ■ Underage (are there underage clients drinking on premises?)

5. Inspection information shall include entry of a number indicating how many IDs were checked at the door while the inspector is present.

6. The inspection information shall include a comment field allowing free-form entry. The comment field shall be at least 50 characters long.

7. The inspection information shall include an overall status field allowing the following options:

- Pass
- Fail
- Reinspect

8. The inspection data shall use codes for each inspection item.

Usability

Usability requirements are defined in a checklist included in the testing section. These are generic usability requirements that could be applied to any wireless Web application that is to be accessed from handsets and palmtop devices. The only special requirement is that the application shall be usable in dimly lit conditions typical of the establishments described in the functional requirements.

Performance

Initial performance requirements are simple:

1. The system shall be capable of supporting fifty concurrent users.

2. Once entered, the submission of an inspection shall take no more than 30 seconds.

ARCHITECTURE AND OFF-THE-SHELF SOFTWARE SELECTION

We selected a Java servlet-based architecture with a relational database for storage of schedules and inspections. This solution requires these items:

- Java development kit (JDK)

- Java servlet engine

- Web server that can interface with the selected servlet engine

- A relational database that supports Structured Query Language (SQL) and JDBC

- A Unix server to host all of the above

- Target client devices (e.g., handsets and palmtops)

- A firewall to limit access to the server

Because of widespread support and inexpensive software (as well as certain biases), we selected open source software as follows. Open source products have the advantage of allowing you to become familiar with an architecture without a major initial outlay:

- Sun Java Development Kit (JDK) 1.2.2 provides a standard Java development and execution environment.

- Sun Servlet API 2.2 defines the objects and methods available to servlets.

- Apache Web server (version 1.3.12) provides HTTP access to our application, and the Tomcat Servlet engine (version 3.2) provides a container for our Java servlets.

- Java objects and static pages are used to produce a WML interface (view).

- A Java servlet is used as a controller for server-side processing.

- The model (business data) is created using Java objects that access a relational database via database wrapper objects. These objects could be wrapped as Enterprise Java Beans but are currently directly based on Java classes for simplicity.

- PostgreSQL relational database (version 7.02) accessed via class

4 (pure Java) JDBC driver provides storage for inspection data and schedules.

◨ A Linux Server running Caldera Linux version 2.2 on a Pentium PC provides the operating system and server hardware.

◨ These are the target client devices:

  ◨ Ericsson R280 CDPD phone with UP.Browser using a Phone.com gateway to access the Internet.

  ◨ Palm Pilot or compatible with wireless (RF) modem and AU-System browser using a WAPLite gateway to access the Internet.

◨ A firewall to limit access to the Linux server to HTTP or HTTPS traffic only. Note that for a more secure implementation we can add a firewall between the Web server/servlet environment and the database.

For simplicity, we build a user interface that is as device independent as possible so as to support Palm Pilots and the Ericsson R280 phones with no WML changes. We also make an effort to ensure that the application works on Nokia browsers in case we want to deploy this to a wider audience. This simple interface should also allow us to use different WAP gateways because we make few assumptions about gateway support.

Figure 12-1 illustrates the physical architecture of this system.

SETUP DEVELOPMENT ENVIRONMENT

The development environment consists of two machines (a Linux Server and Windows development client) on a local network. A terse installation sequence follows:

Install the following on the Linux server:

◨ Sun JDK (*www.javasoft.com*) and set initial CLASSPATH to include source directories

◼ Apache Web server and Tomcat servlet engine (*www.apache.org*)

◼ PostgreSQL relational database and JDBC driver (*www. postgresql.org*) and set CLASSPATH for the location of JDBC driver jar file

◼ gvim (optional), which is a cross-platform Vi editor with a plug-in for WML syntax (*www.vim.org*)

Install the following test and development tools on a networked Windows PC (refer to Chapter 4 for URL references):

◼ Phone.com UP 4.0 SDK

◼ Nokia WAP Toolkit Version 2.0

◼ M3Gate emulator (provides a palmtop simulator)

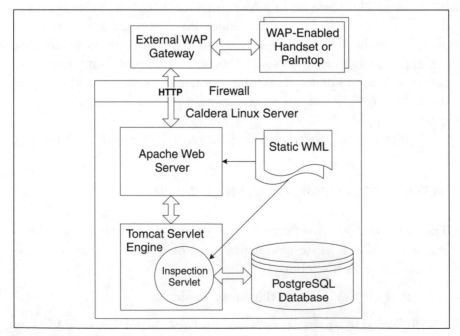

FIGURE 12-1. Physical Architecture

Set up the servlet and Web configuration including access control directives and files for HTTP Basic authentication (refer to Apache and Tomcat documentation for more information).

To serve WAP content, you will need to configure your Web server for the WAP MIME types. These include:

1. `text/vnd.wap.wml` (wireless markup language decks)

2. `text/vnd.wap.wmlscript` (WMLScript source files)

3. `image/vnd.wap.wbmp` (WAP bitmaps)

Note that, while not required for our application, to directly serve compiled WML and WMLScript files, you will need to add the following to your Web server configuration:

4. `application/vnd.wap.wmlc` (compiled wireless markup language decks)

5. `application/vnd.wap.wmlsscriptc` (compiled WMLScript)

When using an Apache Web server, these MIME types can be added to the .htaccess file in the directory in which the WAP files are defined using entries like the following:

```
AddType text/vnd.wap.wml wml
AddType text/vnd.wap.wmlscript wmls
AddType image/vnd.wap.wbmp wbmp
AddType application/vnd.wap.wmlc wmlc
AddType application/vnd.wap.wmlscriptc wmlsc
```

PROTOTYPING

To prototype our application we created a series of static WML decks containing mock data. The dynamically generated and static WML used in production was directly based on static prototypes because these ensured that what was generated was usable. We used the Phone.com simulator to test the prototype because this is the most limited target environment in terms of screen size and user interface.

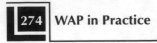

See the "Coding and Developer Testing" section later for sample screens.

DESIGN

A simple Unified Modeling Language (UML) model was developed to describe the alcohol inspection system's logical architecture. The classes in this model are conceptual and should not be confused with the actual Java classes and physical database tables created to implement this design (see Figure 12-7 for the physical class model). Figure 12-2 shows a class diagram containing the following classes:

- Controller – a controlling class that hands off requests to the Inspections business object and views the results using Inspection Display.

- Inspections – this provides the business logic and data for both schedules (lists of inspections) and each inspection. Inspections contain zero or more Inspection instances.

- Inspection – a single inspection that applies to an establishment.

- Establishment – the location for an inspection.

- Inspection Display – a class completely concerned with visualizing schedules and inspections.

- DB Wrapper – an encapsulation of the database access methods used to isolate these details from the inspection business logic.

- DB Connection Manager – a helper class whose purpose is to manage connections to the database efficiently.

The Controller, Inspections, and Inspection Display classes use HTTP servlet requests and responses to access the WAP client's requests and produce responses. The request and response classes are not shown in Figure12-2 and attributes are not modeled because these are dealt with during database creation. The methods illustrated in this figure are diagrammed in the following scenarios, which take place within a single inspection use case.

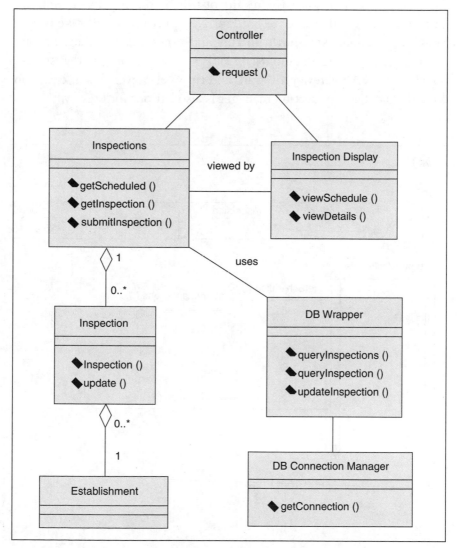

FIGURE 12-2. Logical Class Diagram

The scenario (UML sequence) diagram in Figure 12-3 shows how a WAP Client can interact with the system to request a schedule. The WAP Client makes a request of the controller specifying what operation should be performed (in this case, a schedule retrieval). The controller sends a getScheduled message to an Inspections object that uses a DB Wrapper object to get the schedule for the specified user. The controller displays the results of this by passing a viewScheduled message to an Inspection Display object that will take care of WML generation. Not shown in this and other scenario diagrams are interactions with the standard HTTP servlet request and response objects, the WAP gateway, firewall, and the Web server. The interaction with the database connection manager is also left out for brevity.

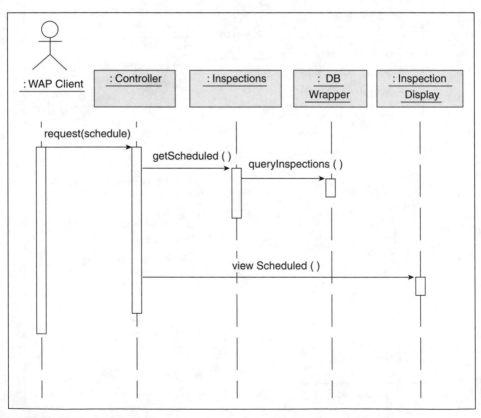

FIGURE 12-3. WAP Client Requests a Schedule Sequence Diagram

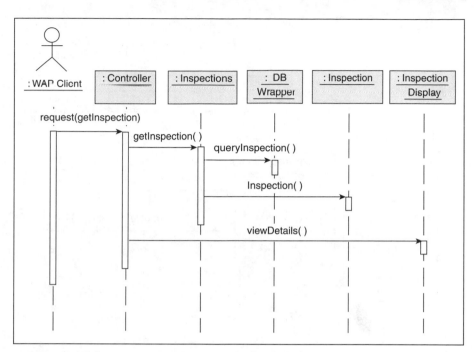

FIGURE 12-4. WAP Client Views Inspection Details Sequence Diagram

Figure 12-4 shows another sequence diagram in which the WAP Client (who has already viewed the schedule) selects an establishment to inspect and gets the details for this inspection (address, checklists, etc.). A getInspection request message is sent by the controller to the Inspections object that gets the requested inspection details from the database via a queryInspection message to the DB Wrapper. The Inspections object uses this information to create a new Inspection and this Inspection is visualized by the Inspection Display object (viewDetails).

The next scenario (Fig. 12-5) illustrates an inspection submission where the WAP Client's "submit" request is passed to the Inspections object by the Controller. The Inspections object updates its contained Inspection instance and uses this in a call to the DB Wrapper object to update the database with the submitted values.

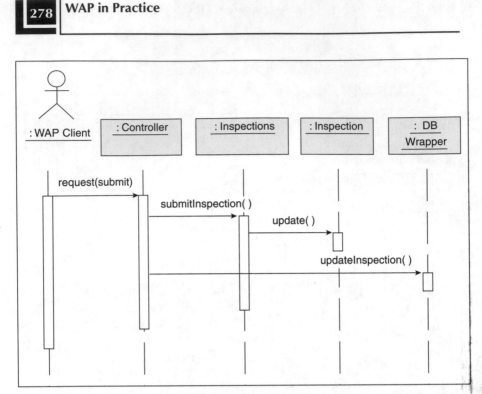

FIGURE 12-5. WAP Client Submits Inspection Results Sequence Diagram

The database entities behind this system are modeled in Figure 12-6. Fields will be added in the physical model (discussed later). An `Inspector` is assigned to a number of `Pending Inspections`. Each of these inspections is of a particular `Establishment` (note that an `Establishment` can have more than one `Pending Inspection` because these inspections are typically periodic – e.g., once a month). An `Establishment` is found within a `Territory` (e.g., a physical area within a given city). An `Establishment` has an associated set of `Inspection Results`, each of which has an `Inspection Status` and contains a number of `Inspection Checks`. `Inspection Checks` are assigned an inspection `Check Code`.

The actual database tables are created by a set of Structured Query Language (SQL) scripts. Two types of scripts were created: one to create the tables and relationships and the other to populate these tables with an initial dataset. The following script creates the inspection sta-

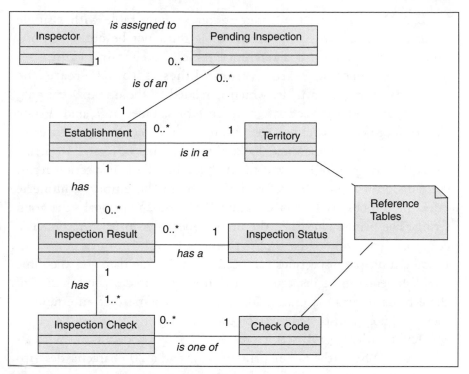

FIGURE 12-6. Entity Relationship Diagram for Inspection Database

tus and results tables and would be executed after the scripts that create inspectors and establishment tables. The line numbers are not part
of the script and have been added for ease of reference:

```
1.  CREATE TABLE inspection_status (
2.  status varchar(12) NOT NULL PRIMARY KEY CHECK (status <> '')
3.  );

4.  CREATE TABLE inspection_results (
5.  establishment varchar(20) REFERENCES establishment(id),
6.  inspectiondate DATE NOT NULL,
7.  inspector varchar(20) REFERENCES inspectors(inspector),
8.  idcount int2,
9.  status varchar(12) REFERENCES inspection_status(status),
10. comments varchar(50),
11. PRIMARY KEY(establishment, inspectiondate)
12. );
```

Lines 1 to 3 create the inspection_status table with a single status field. The status field in this table must not be null or empty. inspection_status is a reference table and contains a finite set of valid inspection status values. Lines 4 to 12 create the inspection_results table, which is related to the establishment, inspector, and inspection_status tables. Lines 5, 7, and 9 state that the records in inspection_results must contain references to existing records in these three 'lookup' tables. Lines 6, 8, and 10 define fields that are part of each record in this table: Each inspection result contains an inspectiondate that must not be empty, a numeric idcount (an observed count of liquor IDs), and an optional comments string. The primary key (i.e., the unique identifier for each record) is a composite of two fields: establishment and inspectiondate. Because multiple inspections can occur on the same date and the same establishment can be inspected many times, we need a combination of these fields to create a unique identifier (we assume that an establishment will not be inspected twice on the same day!).

The following SQL script creates a resultcodes table with 2-character ID field (the table's primary key) and a 20-character description field:

```
CREATE TABLE resultcodes (
   id char(2) NOT NULL PRIMARY KEY,
   description varchar(20) NOT NULL
);
```

The following SQL script populates the resultcodes table with a set of valid inspection check codes:

```
1. BEGIN;
2. INSERT INTO resultcodes VALUES ('10', 'Tax Stamps');
3. INSERT INTO resultcodes VALUES ('02', 'Stock');
4. INSERT INTO resultcodes VALUES ('05', 'Measures');
5. INSERT INTO resultcodes VALUES ('06', 'Underage');
6. COMMIT;
```

Line 1 begins a database transaction and line 6 commits this transaction. Lines 2 to 5 insert individual records into the resultcodes table placing the first value in id and the second in the description field.

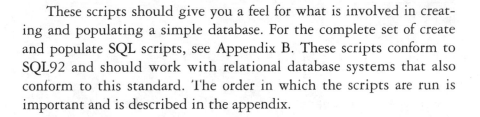

These scripts should give you a feel for what is involved in creating and populating a simple database. For the complete set of create and populate SQL scripts, see Appendix B. These scripts conform to SQL92 and should work with relational database systems that also conform to this standard. The order in which the scripts are run is important and is described in the appendix.

CODING AND DEVELOPER TESTING

The coding and developer testing of this application involved the following:

- Creating a database by running the SQL scripts just described.

- Developing Java classes and deploying these in Tomcat

- Building a user interface based on the prototyped WML decks and additional dynamically generated WML

- Unit testing the Java code

- Debugging

We look at each of these areas in the following sections.

Data

The following section documents the database contents used to test this system. These tables were created using the create and populate scripts described earlier. The first four tables are reference tables that constrain records in other tables. In the case of the resultcodes and territory tables, they also provide descriptions for other tables.

The inspectors reference table contains two records for Inspector Poirot and Inspector Marple:

INSPECTOR
poirot
marple

The `inspection_status` reference table defines the valid inspection status types:

STATUS
pass
reinspect
fail

The `resultcodes` reference table defines the valid inspection result code types:

ID	DESCRIPTION
10	Tax Stamps
02	Stock
05	Measures
06	Underage

The `territory` reference table lists all valid inspection territories. Note that our inspection test data covers only the Halifax area:

SHORTNAME	LONGNAME
hal	Halifax
dart	Dartmouth
bedford	Bedford
truro	Truro
other	Other

The `establishment` table describes all the establishments that can be inspected:

ID	LISTITEM	NAME	ADDRESS	LICENSETYPE	EXPIRYDATE	TERRITORY
attic	Attic	The Attic	1741 Grafton St.	Cabaret	2001-12-31	hal
bearlys	Bearly's	Bearly's House of Blues and Ribs	1269 Grafton St.	Eat Est	2003-01-31	hal
boomers	Boomers	Boomers Lounge	1725 Grafton St.	Lounge	2001-02-28	hal
cheers	Cheer's	Cheer's Lounge	1743 Grafton St.	Lounge	2001-09-30	hal
copper	Copper Penny	The Copper Penny	278 Lacewood Dr.	Cabaret	2001-12-31	hal
ess	Economy Shoe Shop	The Economy Shoe Shop	1663 Argyle St.	Cabaret	2001-12-31	hal
gatsby	Gatsby's	Gatsby's Bar and Eatery Ltd.	5675 Spring Garden Rd.	Eat Est	2000-09-30	hal
mafia	Ma'Fias	Ma'Fias Ristorante and Bar	5472 Spring Garden Rd.	Eat Est	2001-12-31	hal
marquee	Marquee	The Marquee Club	2041 Gottingen St.	Cabaret	2001-12-31	hal
oasis	Oasis	Oasis Bar and Grill	5675 Spring Garden Rd.	Eat Est	2000-02-29	hal
tickle	Tickle Trunk	The Tickle Trunk	5680 Spring Garden Rd.	SOL	2000-12-31	hal
volive	Velvet Olive	Velvet Olive Cocktail Lounge	1770 Market St.	Lounge	2001-12-31	hal

The `pending_inspections` table contains all outstanding inspections for all inspectors and establishments:

INSPECTOR	SCHEDULED	ESTABLISHMENT
poirot	2000-07-13	ess
marple	2000-08-25	attic
poirot	2000-09-01	cheers
poirot	2000-12-08	marquee
poirot	2000-01-09	volive
poirot	2000-08-13	gatsby
poirot	2001-12-01	mafia
poirot	2001-12-03	tickle
poirot	2001-07-04	copper
poirot	2001-12-01	bearlys
marple	2001-07-07	boomers
marple	2001-09-10	attic

The `inspection_results` table contains the results of all recent inspections (in this case only on record). Inspector Marple witnessed 24 liquor ID door checks on her inspection of The Attic cabaret on August 25, 2000. She passed this establishment, although her comments indicated that she may have had a rough time!

ESTABLISHMENT	INSPECTIONDATE	INSPECTOR	IDCOUNT	STATUS	COMMENTS
attic	2000-08-25	marple	24	pass	Nice place. Shame about the clients.

The `inspection_checks` table contains a record for each inspection check, for each inspection. The two checks in this table are associated with the record in `inspection_results` and refer to Tax Stamps and Stock checks (see the `resultcodes` table):

ESTABLISHMENT	INSPECTIONDATE	ITEM
attic	2000-08-25	02
attic	2000-08-25	10

Java Code and User Interface

Figure 12-7 shows a UML class diagram displaying the actual classes created during development of the application. Although these classes are similar to those described in the logical model we presented earlier (see Fig. 12-2), names have changed and many methods have been added. These classes are explained in the following section. Skim this diagram now and refer to it as you review the source code and detailed scenarios presented later.

Figure 12-8 displays a best case flow through the application (i.e., no errors are encountered). Screens are represented by boxes with a curved bottom (e.g., `"Splash & Login"`), server processing is portrayed using circles (e.g., `"Get Schedule"`), and the `"Inspection Data"` is represented by a database (can) symbol. The session begins at a splash screen that leads into a login deck (via HTTP Basic authentication).

Following login, a schedule selection deck is displayed and the

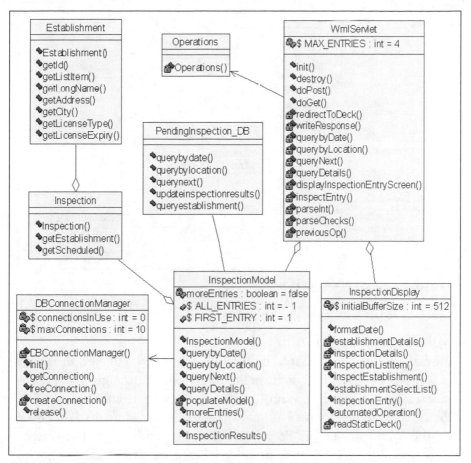

FIGURE 12-7. Inspection System Implementation Classes

inspector can select a schedule selection query to perform (Next, by Dates, or by Location). The list of establishments matching the query that require an inspection is displayed on the Establishments deck. The inspector selects one of these and its details are shown. Note that establishment data is pulled from the database. The inspector selects an inspection function that shows an initial inspection form. The inspector fills in the checks on this form and submits this information, which is used to update the inspection database. Finally a Continue deck is displayed that leads to an updated schedule of establishments. Each item in this diagram is explored in the following sections.

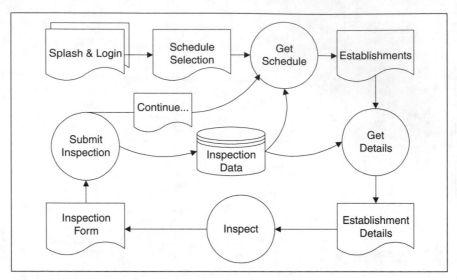

FIGURE 12-8. Application Flow

Splash and Login

Figure 12-9 shows the splash and login screens. The splash screen (screen *a*) is a static deck and the login screens (*b* through *d*) are automatically produced to handle HTTP Basic authentication. The Phone.com simulator uses a Windows dialogue box, similar to that used by the Web browsers, to do HTTP Basic authentication. The screens shown in Figure 12-9 were produced based on the Ericsson phone's actual display. The following static WML deck provides the splash screen. Because our target devices are compatible with WML version 1.1, we specify this in the DOCTYPE prologue. Note that an explicit back navigation soft key is coded so that this application will work with devices that do not have a built-in Back button. This will not cause a problem with the Phone.com microbrowser, which ignores the do element of type "prev." Also note the 30-second timer that results in the schedule selection deck being loaded automatically (if the inspectors do not select anything themselves). Although we specify a WAP bitmap (.wbmp) checkmark logo, the Phone.com microbrowser in our Ericsson target phone does not support wireless bitmaps. We use an alternative deck (not shown) and separate URL for this target device.

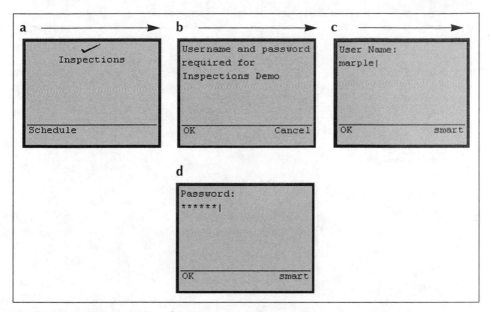

FIGURE 12-9. Splash and Login Screens

```
<?xml version="1.0"?>
<!DOCTYPE wml PUBLIC "-//WAPFORUM//DTD WML 1.1//EN"
                     "http://www.wapforum.org/DTD/wml_1_1.dtd">
<wml>
  <card id="Welcome" title="Inspections">

    <onevent type="ontimer">
      <go href="scheduleselection.wml"/>
    </onevent>
    <timer name="splashtimeout" value="300"/>

    <do type="accept" label="Schedule">
      <go href="scheduleselection.wml"/>
    </do>
    <do type="prev" label="Back">
      <prev/>
    </do>

    <p align="center">
      <img alt="Check " src="images/check.wbmp" align="middle"/><br/>
      Inspections
    </p>
  </card>
</wml>
```

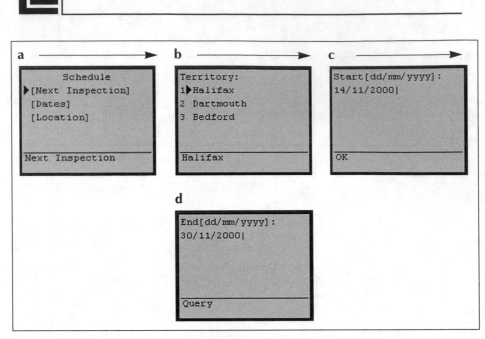

FIGURE 12-10. Schedule Selection Cards

Schedule Selection

Schedule selection is carried out using another static deck. This deck contains four cards: one for the main schedule query choice list, one for the location query entry, one for the date query entry, and a help card. Figure 12-10 shows these cards, minus the help card. Following is the WML for this deck. For illustration, we use links to select the type of schedule query and a select list when choosing a territory. Note that `"servlet/wmlservlet"` is mapped to `WmlServlet.class` in a Web server configuration file.

```
<?xml version="1.0"?>
<!DOCTYPE wml PUBLIC "-//WAPFORUM//DTD WML 1.1//EN"
                   "http://www.wapforum.org/DTD/wml1_1.dtd">
<wml>
<template>
  <do type="prev" label="Back">
    <prev/>
  </do>
</template>
```

```
<card id="selection" title="Schedule">
  <do type="help" label="Help">
    <go href="#selecthelp"/>
  </do>
  <p align="center">Schedule</p>
  <p align="left">
    <anchor title="Next Inspection">
      <go method="post" href="servlet/wmlservlet">
        <postfield name="op" value="next"/>
      </go>Next Inspection</anchor><br/>
    <a title="By Date" href="#bydate">Dates</a><br/>
    <a title="By Location" href="#bylocation">Location</a><br/>
  </p>
</card>

<card id="bylocation" title="Location">
  <do type="accept">
    <go method="post" href="servlet/wmlservlet">
      <postfield name="op" value="byloc"/>
      <postfield name="territory" value="$territory"/>
    </go>
  </do>
  <p align="left">
    Territory:
    <select name="territory" value="hal">
      <option title="Halifax" value="hal">Halifax</option>
      <option title="Dartmouth" value="dart">Dartmouth</option>
      <option title="Bedford" value="bed">Bedford</option>
    </select>
  </p>
</card>

<card id="bydate" title="By Dates">
  <do type="accept" label="Query">
    <go method="post" href="servlet/wmlservlet">
      <postfield name="op" value="bydate"/>
      <postfield name="datestart" value="$startdate"/>
      <postfield name="dateend" value="$enddate"/>
    </go>
  </do>
  <p align="left">
    Start[dd/mm/yyyy]:
    <input name="startdate" title="Start" format="NN/NN/NNNN"/>
    <br/>
    End[dd/mm/yyyy]:
    <input name="enddate" title="End" format="NN/NN/NNNN"/>
  </p>
</card>
```

```
<card id="selecthelp">
  <p>
    <strong>Dates:</strong>
    Select inspections scheduled between user entered dates.<br/>
    <strong>Location:</strong>
    Select inspections scheduled for selected areas.<br/>
    <strong>Next:</strong>
    Select the next scheduled inspection.
  </p>
</card>
</wml>
```

Get Schedule

Figure 12-11 shows a scenario where the inspector has selected the "Next" inspection option. Many operations have been omitted from this (and later scenarios) for clarity. Figure 12-13 shows the screen that would result from this query.

The inspector's request is submitted as a POST to the WMLServlet, which looks at the operation ("next") and calls the queryNext method of the InspectionModel object. The following code is the doGet method of WmlServlet (this method is called internally by doPost). Note the redirect to a static error deck if an unknown operation is encountered. Also note the way that the operation processing is carried out (see the code for comments that explain this). The complete source code for this class can be found in Appendix B:

```
/**
   * Parse out the operation and call the appropriate
   * method.
   * @param request the Http request from the user agent
   * @param response where the response is to be written
   */
  public void doGet(HttpServletRequest request,
    HttpServletResponse response) throws IOException, ServletException {
    String operation = null;
    String user = null;

    /* ensure we have an authenticated user */
    user = request.getRemoteUser();
    if (null == user) {
      /* encode a redirect to the "unauthorized access" deck,
         n.b. this could be caused by the authentication header not
         being passed to us, or incorrect webserver - servlet engine
         integration  */
      redirectToDeck(request, response, InspectionDisplay.UNAUTHORIZED_DECK);
```

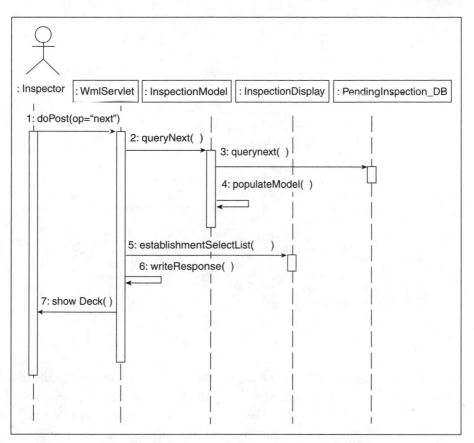

FIGURE 12-11. Get Schedule Scenario Sequence Diagram

```
        return;
    }

    /* extract the requested operation and call the corresponding private
       method for that operation.

       The operation is simply a parameter in the Http GET or POST request.
       Each operation will have corresponding parameters which are parsed
       from the request by the private method which corresponds to the
       operation. e.g. when op=bydate is found, querybyDate() is called
       to process the operation. It is responsible for extracting the
       datestart and dateend parameters, querying the database and
       generating a response.
    */
    operation = request.getParameter(Operations.OPERATION);
```

```
/* if an operation was found, trim any whitespace and
   convert it to lowercase to make string comparisons
   simple */
if (null != operation) {
  operation = operation.trim().toLowerCase();

  if (operation.equals(Operations.OP_INSPECTENTRY)) {
    inspectEntry(request, response, user);
  } else if (operation.equals(Operations.OP_INSPECT)) {
    displayInspectionEntryScreen(request, response, user);
  } else if (operation.equals(Operations.OP_DETAILS)) {
    queryDetails(request, response, user);
  } else if (operation.equals(Operations.OP_QUERYBYDATE)) {
    querybyDate(request, response, user);
  } else if (operation.equals(Operations.OP_QUERYBYLOCATION)) {
    querybyLocation(request, response, user);
  } else if (operation.equals(Operations.OP_QUERYNEXT)) {
    queryNext(request, response, user);
  } else {
    /* unknown operation (this should never happen) */
    redirectToDeck(request, response,
      InspectionDisplay.INTERNALERROR_DECK);
  }
}
}
```

The `queryNext` method of the `WmlServlet` handles the details of the "next" query and calls the `queryNext` method of the `InspectionModel` object (`model`). The following source code is from the `WmlServlet`'s `queryNext` method and includes view processing code (discussed later). Note the update performed to the `HttpSession` object, which saves the type of query that the inspector has selected. This information will be used when carrying out the next schedule query. See the code for additional comments:

```
model = new InspectionModel();
if (true == model.queryNext(inspector, startNdx, MAX_ENTRIES)) {
  /* at this point we have a model which may or may not have
     any entries, but we can at least display a deck from it */

  /* here we've made a design tradeoff in favour of simplicity
     If there are more inspections than can be displayed
     at one time (MAX_ENTRIES), we will use these to add an entry
     to the generated WML deck that executes the same query but
     results in the next MAX_ENTRIES being displayed.
     This is done by building a model which holds
     the number of entries we are willing to display. The
```

```
    start parameter is used to pick the starting query results
    entry from which the model is built.

    N.B. this is fine for a small example application but doesn't
    address scalability issues. Ideally query results should be
    cached and cached results returned instead of executing
    the same query again.
*/

params = new java.util.Vector();
values = new java.util.Vector();
params.add(Operations.START_NDX);
values.add(Integer.toString(startNdx + MAX_ENTRIES));

/* generate a WML deck containing a single card which will display
   the names of each establishment contained in the model,
   selecting an establishment will result in the establishment
   details being displayed

   by using getContextPath() and getServletPath() we don't need to
   'hard code' our servlet path when we generate href's, we simply
   parse it from the incoming request here and pass it to the routines
   which generate WML

   the operation, parameters and values are supplied so we can
   construct an entry that will display the next set of results
*/
deck = new StringBuffer();
view = new InspectionDisplay();
view.establishmentSelectList(deck,
  model,
  "",
  inspector,
  request.getContextPath() + request.getServletPath(),
  Operations.OP_QUERYNEXT,
  params,
  values);

/* attempt to add the parameters for this request to the HttpSession
   if it exists. Other operation processing routines will use this to
   return to this previous operation.

   Once inspection results have been submitted (and accepted) we
   allow the user to return to the list of "query" results by
   executing the latest query operation with the same parameters.

   To accomplish this, we store operation and parameters in the
   user's session and retrieve these once in inspectEntry() which
   processes the inspection results submission.
*/
HttpSession theSession = request.getSession(true);
```

```
        theSession.setAttribute(Operations.OPERATION, Operations.OP_QUERYNEXT);
        writeResponse(response, deck.toString());
    } else {
        redirectToDeck(request, response, InspectionDisplay.INTERNALERROR_DECK);
    }
}
```

The model uses the `PendingInspection_DB` class to carry out the actual SQL query (the call to the database is not shown in Fig. 12-11). The `InspectionModel` updates itself by creating a list of inspections from the result set (`populateModel`). The following source code is from this class and also shows how the `DBConnectionManager` class is used for efficient connections with the PostgreSQL database. Figure 12-12 shows a scenario where the `DBConnectionManager` is used to do a query by date.

```
public boolean queryNext(String inspector,
                         int startingIndex,
                         int numberOfEntries) {
  boolean success = true;

  java.sql.Connection connection = null;
  java.sql.ResultSet rs = null;

  connection = DBConnectionManager.getConnection();
  if (null == connection) {
    System.err.println(
      "InspectionModel.queryNext():failed getting connection");
    success = false;
  } else {
    rs = pendinginspection_db.querynext(connection,
      inspector);
    if (null == rs) {
      success = false;
    } else {
      populateModel(rs, startingIndex, numberOfEntries);
    }
    DBConnectionManager.freeConnection(connection);
  }
  return success;
}
```

The `WMLServlet` passes the `InspectionModel` object to an `InspectionDisplay` object, which visualizes the list of establish-

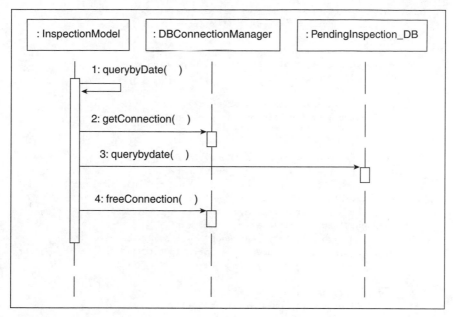

FIGURE 12-12. Database Connection Details Sequence Diagram

ments (establishmentSelectList) as a WML deck containing a list of links (anchor elements). The following source code shows the InspectionDisplay object's processing:

```
...
iterator = inspectionModel.iterator();

deck.append(prologue);
deck.append("<wml>\n");
deck.append("<card>\n");
deck.append("<do type=\"prev\" label=\"Back\">\n");
deck.append("<prev/>\n");
deck.append("</do>\n");
deck.append("<p>\n");

/* do we have entries or should we display a no entries message ? */
if (false == iterator.hasNext()) {
  deck.append("No entries.");
} else {
  /* use the title attribute if supplied */
```

```
if ((null != title ) && (false == title.equals(""))) {
  deck.append("<strong>" + title + "</strong><br/>");
}


/* iterate through each element of the inspection model */
while (iterator.hasNext()) {
  ndx++;
  inspection = (Inspection)iterator.next();
  inspectionListItem(deck, inspection, encodedURL, inspector);
}


/* determine if we need to add a "More..." entry to
   the list. Do this by adding an operation request
   consisting of the original source operation and parameters */
if (inspectionModel.moreEntries()) {
  /* generate a link that retrieves the next numberOfEntries entries */
  deck.append("<anchor title=\"More\">More\n");
  deck.append("<go href=\"" + encodedURL + "\" method=\"post\">\n");
  deck.append("<postfield name=\"" + Operations.OPERATION + "\" value=\""
    + sourceOperation + "\"/>\n");

  /* add each parameter and value */
  java.util.Iterator p = opParams.iterator();
  java.util.Iterator pValue = paramValues.iterator();
  while (p.hasNext()) {
    deck.append("<postfield name=\"" + (String)p.next() + "\" value=\""
      + (String)pValue.next() + "\"/>\n");
  }
  deck.append("</go>\n");
  deck.append("</anchor><br/>\n");
}
}
deck.append("</p>\n");
deck.append("</card>\n");
deck.append("</wml>\n");
}
```

Initialization code has been omitted. Processing begins by obtaining an iterator of inspections from the inspection model that was passed to this method. Our output deck is named `"deck,"` and we start by appending the standard WML prologue (a previously defined constant). Following the usual deck, card, and paragraph tags, a check is performed to see whether there are any pending inspections in the inspector's schedule. Assuming there are inspections, a list of links will be generated. Not shown here is code to check for more inspections than will fit on a card and to display these inspections on separate decks (see Appendix B for details). Each link is generated by a call to `inspectionListItem`, which is listed below. This method creates an `anchor` element that does a POST to the servlet passing enough information to retrieve schedule details. Note the generation of a name value pair of `op` and `"details,"` which is highlighted in the following source code. When the user picks an establishment to inspect, this is how the servlet determines what action the inspector wants to perform.

```java
/**
 * Add an item (link) for the inspection to the supplied StringBuffer.
 * Links are used because current Nokia phones don't work well
 * with select lists.
 * @param deck the StringBuffer to add output to, must not be null
 * @param inspection the inspection instance containing the establishment
 * instance to display
 * @param encodedURL the URL resulting the display of details for the
 * establishment, must have been encoded in order to be properly
 * processed by servlets
 * @param String inspector the inspector
 */
private void inspectionListItem(StringBuffer deck,
    Inspection inspection,
    String encodedURL,
    String inspector) {
  Establishment establishment = inspection.getEstablishment();
  deck.append("<anchor title=\"Details\">");
  deck.append(establishment.getListItem());
  deck.append("\n");
  deck.append("<go href=\"" + encodedURL + "\" method=\"post\">\n");
  deck.append("<postfield name=\"" + Operations.OPERATION + "\" value=\""
    + Operations.OP_DETAILS + "\"/>\n");
  deck.append("<postfield name=\"" + Operations.INSPECTOR + "\" value=\""
    + inspector +"\"/>\n");
  deck.append("<postfield name=\"" + Operations.ESTABLISHMENT
    + "\" value=\"" + establishment.getId() + "\"/>\n");
  deck.append("<postfield name=\"" + Operations.SCHEDULED + "\" value=\""
    + formatDate(inspection.getScheduled()) + "\"/>\n");
  deck.append("</go>\n");
  deck.append("</anchor><br/>\n");
}
```

Finally, the `WMLServlet` writes the generated WML into the HTTP servlet response (`writeResponse` in Fig. 12-11) and the list of establishments is displayed to the inspector.

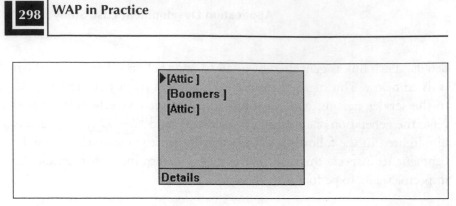

FIGURE 12-13. Schedule of Establishments

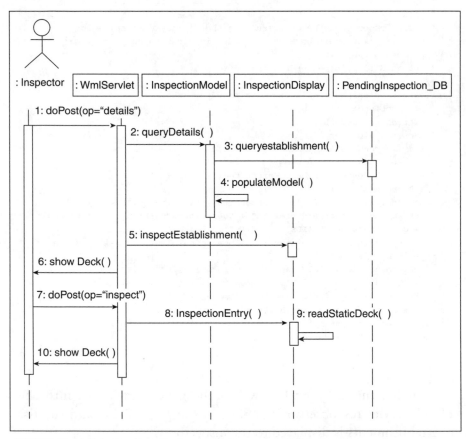

FIGURE 12-14. Get Details Scenario Sequence Diagram

Establishments

The establishments list for Inspector Marple is shown in Figure 12-13. She has three inspections lined up (a rather relaxed schedule!) with The Attic cabaret scheduled for two inspections (on different dates).

Get Details

When the inspector selects an establishment to inspect, the details of that establishment including its full address are displayed. Figure 12-14 shows a scenario in which the inspector has selected a schedule item. This figure also contains a second operation (inspect) that is discussed in the "Inspect" section later.

As in the previous scenario, a POST is sent to the WMLServlet. This time, the queryDetails method of the model is used to populate the model with the details of an establishment. An InspectionDisplay object is called on to render these details as WML. The inspectEstablishment method produces an Inspect event handler and establishment details, which are displayed by calling the inspectionDetails method (highlighted).

```
/**
 * Generate a single card deck with a full description of the supplied
 * inspection along with an accept Inspect action (via a
 * post action and a supplied URL).
   ...
 */
    ...
   Inspection inspection = (Inspection)iterator.next();
   Establishment establishment = inspection.getEstablishment();

   deck.append("<do type=\"accept\" label=\"Inspect\">\n");
   deck.append("<go href=\"" + encodedURL + "\" method=\"post\">\n");
   deck.append("<postfield name=\"" + Operations.OPERATION + "\" value=\""
      + Operations.OP_INSPECT + "\"/>\n");
   deck.append("<postfield name=\"" + Operations.INSPECTOR + "\" value=\""
      + inspector + "\"/>\n");
   deck.append("<postfield name=\"" + Operations.ESTABLISHMENT
      + "\" value=\"" + establishment.getId() + "\"/>\n");
   deck.append("<postfield name=\"" + Operations.SCHEDULED + "\" value=\""
      + formatDate(inspection.getScheduled()) + "\"/>\n");
```

```
    deck.append("</go>\n");
    deck.append("</do>\n");
    deck.append("<p>\n");
    inspectionDetails(deck, inspection);
    deck.append("</p>\n");
  } else {
    deck.append("<p>\n");
    deck.append("Could not retrieve details on selected establishment.");
    deck.append("</p>\n");
  }
  deck.append("</card>\n");
  deck.append("</wml>\n");
}
```

The actual establishment information is generated by retrieving information from the `establishment` object, which is aggregated by the `inspection`:

```
private void inspectionDetails(StringBuffer deck,
      Inspection inspection) {
    establishmentDetails(deck, inspection.getEstablishment());
    deck.append("Sched: " + inspection.getScheduled().toString());
    deck.append("<br/>\n");
}
...

  private void establishmentDetails(StringBuffer deck,
      Establishment establishment) {
    /* simply retrieve each attribute and append to the deck
       with appropriate (minimal) formatting tags */
    deck.append(establishment.getLongName());
    deck.append("<br/>\n");
    deck.append(establishment.getAddress());
    deck.append("<br/>\n");
    deck.append(establishment.getCity());
    deck.append("<br/>\n");
    deck.append(establishment.getLicenseType());
    deck.append("<br/>\n");
    deck.append("Expires: ");
    deck.append(establishment.getLicenseExpiry().toString());
    deck.append("<br/>\n");
  }
```

Establishment Details
The establishment details are displayed as shown in Figure 12-15.

> The Attic
> 1741 Grafton St.
> Halifax
> Cabaret
> Expires: 2001-12-31
> Sched: 2000-08-25
>
> Inspect

FIGURE 12-15. Establishment Details

Inspect

When the user selects the "inspect" option from the establishment details, the scenario illustrated in the second half of Figure 12-14 occurs. The operation is processed by WMLServlet, which calls the inspectionEntry method of an InspectionDisplay object. Unlike the previously discussed methods, no database or model are involved. Instead, the InspectionDisplay object reads two static WML files and appends these, inserting some dynamic data in between to produce the Inspection form deck. The following source code from InspectionDisplay shows this:

```
public void inspectionEntry(StringBuffer deck,
     String URLBase,
     String encodedURL,
     java.util.Vector opParams,
     java.util.Vector paramValues) {
  /* the static inspection results entry screen is in two parts,
     these are "joined" by the opParams and paramValues output as
     postfields */
  String inspectionEntryPart1 = null;
  String inspectionEntryPart2 = null;
  String inspectionEntryPart3 = null;

  deck.append(readStaticDeck(URLBase + INSPECTIONENTRYP1_DECK));
  deck.append("<go href=\"" + encodedURL + "\" method=\"post\">");

  /* add each parameter and value */
  java.util.Iterator p = opParams.iterator();
  java.util.Iterator pValue = paramValues.iterator();
  while (p.hasNext()) {
```

```
    deck.append("<postfield name=\"" + (String)p.next() + "\" value=\""
        + (String)pValue.next() + "\"/>\n");
}
deck.append(readStaticDeck(URLBase + INSPECTIONENTRYP2_DECK));
}
```

In Appendix B, you can find the static WML files, `inspectionen-tryp1.wml` and `inspectionentryp2.wml`, which are processed by this code.

Inspection Form

The inspection form is shown in Figure 12-16 as a series of screens. Screen *a* and *b* contain a checklist (filled out in screen *b*). Screen *c* allows the inspector to enter a numeric value for the number of liquor ID door checks that were witnessed (24 on this occasion). Screen *d* provides a select list containing valid values for the inspection status, and screen *e* can be used to enter comments.

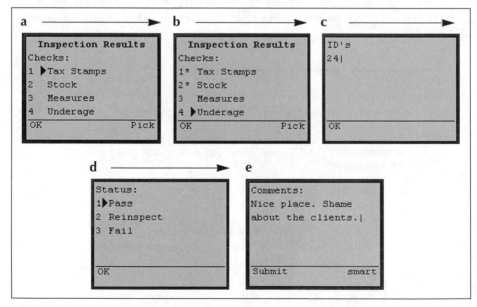

FIGURE 12-16. Inspection Form Screens

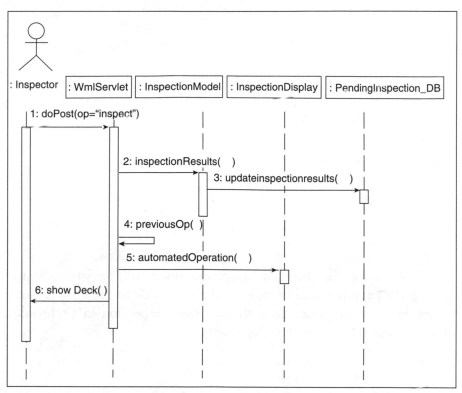

FIGURE 12-17. Inspection Submission Sequence Diagram

Submit Inspection

After the inspectors have entered the details of their inspection, they press the "Submit" button and the scenario depicted in Figure 12-17 occurs. The inspector's submission is processed as a POST by the WMLServlet, which extracts the "inspect" operation and calls the inspectionresults method of an InspectionModel instance, which in turn uses the DBConnectionManager and PendingInspection_DB classes to commit the inspection data to the database:

```
...
boolean success = false;
...
java.sql.Connection connection = null;
connection = DBConnectionManager.getConnection();
```

```
if (null == connection) {
  System.err.println(
    "InspectionModel.inspectionResults():failed getting"
    + " connection");
} else {
  success = PendingInspection_DB.updateinspectionresults(
      connection,
      inspector,
      establishment,
      scheduled,
      inspected,
      inspectionchecks,
      ids,
      status,
      comments);
}
DBConnectionManager.freeConnection(connection);
return success;
```

The WmlServlet then calls the private operation, `previousOp`, to set up the parameters to be used on the next deck in such a way that inspectors will be presented with their next inspection in a schedule that is ordered based on their last query:

```
private void previousOp(HttpSession theSession,
    java.util.Vector opParams,
    java.util.Vector paramValues) {
  String operation = (String)theSession.getAttribute(Operations.OPERATION);

    if (null != operation) {
    operation = operation.trim().toLowerCase();
      opParams.add(Operations.OPERATION);
      paramValues.add(operation);
    } else if (operation.equals(Operations.OP_QUERYBYDATE)) {
      opParams.add(Operations.DATE_START);
      paramValues.add((String)theSession.getAttribute(
        Operations.DATE_START));
      opParams.add(Operations.DATE_END);
      paramValues.add((String)theSession.getAttribute(Operations.DATE_END));
    } else if (operation.equals(Operations.OP_QUERYBYLOCATION)) {
      opParams.add(Operations.TERRITORY);
      paramValues.add((String)theSession.getAttribute(Operations.TERRITORY));
    } else if (operation.equals(Operations.OP_QUERYNEXT)) {
      /* only need the operation */
    } else {
      /* this isn't an operation that should have been found
         in the session. */
    }
  }
```

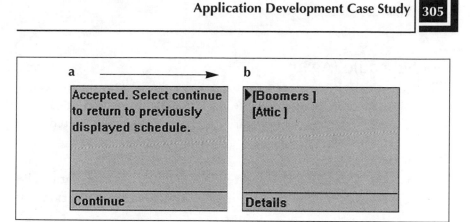

FIGURE 12-18. Continue Deck and Schedule Redisplay

The `automatedOperation` method produces a simple deck (see Fig. 12-18 screen *a*) with a "Submit" button, behind which are the operation parameters set by `previousOp`:

```
public void automatedOperation(StringBuffer deck,
    String message,
    String encodedURL,
    java.util.Vector opParams,
    java.util.Vector paramValues) {
    deck.append(prologue);
    deck.append("<wml>\n");
    deck.append("<card>\n");
    deck.append("<do type=\"prev\" label=\"Back\">\n");
    deck.append("<prev/>\n");
    deck.append("</do>\n");
    deck.append("<do type=\"accept\" label=\"Continue\">\n");
    deck.append("<go href=\"" + encodedURL + "\" method=\"post\">");

    /* add each parameter and value */
    java.util.Iterator p = opParams.iterator();
    java.util.Iterator pValue = paramValues.iterator();
    while (p.hasNext()) {
        deck.append("<postfield name=\"" + (String)p.next() + "\" value=\""
            + (String)pValue.next() + "\"/>\n");
    }
    deck.append("</go>\n");
    deck.append("</do>\n");
    deck.append("<p>" + message + "</p>\n");
    deck.append("</card>\n");
    deck.append("</wml>\n");
}
```

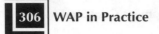

Get Schedule (Again)

When the `GetSchedule` processing recurs, the previously inspected establishment is no longer visible on the schedule (see Fig. 12-18 screen *b*) and the sequence of operations just described is repeated.

Inspection Data

The inspection database is updated with the following data. The `inspection_results` table contains the results of the inspection:

ESTABLISHMENT	INSPECTIONDATE	INSPECTOR	IDCOUNT	STATUS	COMMENTS
attic	2000-08-25	marple	24	pass	Nice place. Shame about the clients.

The `inspection_checks` table contains a record for each inspection check. The two checks in this table refer to Tax Stamps and Stock checks:

ESTABLISHMENT	INSPECTIONDATE	ITEM
attic	2000-08-25	02
attic	2001-08-25	10

See the "Data" section earlier for more information.

Error Handling

Errors are handled in a consistent fashion using a static WML error deck as shown in Figure 12-19. The explanation text must be scrolled through, and screens *a* and *b* show the first part of this.

Unit Test

Formal automated unit testing was not carried out, but unit test drivers were created for some parts of the system including the database layer. Here is an example:

```
/**
 * Test driver for DBConnectionManager class.
 */
public class testDBConnection {
```

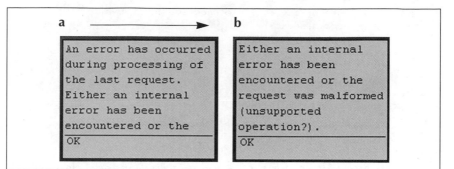

FIGURE 12-19. Error Screens

```
/* DBConnectionManager initialization parameters */
final static String j = "org.postgresql.Driver";
final static String d = "jdbc:postgresql:inspections";
final static String u = "dmorash";
final static String p = "";
final static int maxConnections = 10;

public static void main(String[] args) {
  boolean success = false;
  java.util.Vector connections = new java.util.Vector();

  /* initialization success */
  System.out.println("Initializing DBConnectionManager");
  System.out.println("Expect success (i.e. true)");
  success = DBConnectionManager.init(j, d, u, p, maxConnections);
  System.out.println(success);

  /* allocate connections */
  System.out.println("Allocating connections. Expect failure on " +
                     "the last 2 allocations.");
  java.sql.Connection connection = null;
  for (int index=0; index < maxConnections + 2; index++) {
    connection = DBConnectionManager.getConnection();
    if (null != connection) {
      System.out.println("success allocating " +
                         Integer.toString(index));
      connections.add(connection);
    } else {
      System.out.println("failed allocating " +
                         Integer.toString(index));
    }
  }

  System.out.println("Freeing all allocated connections. " +
                     "Expect no error messages.");
```

```
    java.util.Iterator iterator = connections.iterator();
    while (iterator.hasNext()) {
      connection = (java.sql.Connection)iterator.next();
      DBConnectionManager.freeConnection(connection);
      iterator.remove();
    }
    /* release all drivers */
    DBConnectionManager.release();
  }
}
```

This is a test driver for the DBConnectionManager class, which performs a bounds test on this class. It instantiates a DBConnection-Manager specifying database connection parameters and a maximum number of connections. It then attempts to obtain two connections beyond the maximum number allowed, expecting these to fail. If, at some later point, we decided that the system should cope with more database connections, we could update this procedure to use more than the specified ten-connection maximum to ensure that our code still functioned correctly.

Debug

We used System.out.println for debug and exception printing and redirected Tomcat's stdout and stderr to logs. Tomcat automatically does a stack trace dump, which can be very useful in tracking down Java problems. The following is an example log entry created when we were unable to establish a connection to the inspections database:

```
...
Starting tomcat. Check logs/tomcat.log for error messages
2000-09-27 07:49:21 - ContextManager: Adding context Ctx(
  /inspections )
2000-09-27 07:49:22 - ContextManager: Adding context Ctx(  )
2000-09-27 07:49:22 - ContextManager: Adding context Ctx( /test )
2000-09-27 07:49:32 - PoolTcpConnector: Starting
  Ajp12ConnectionHandler on 8007
Couldn't establish connection to db: database:jdbc:postgresql:
  yaminspections user:dmorash password:
WmlServlet.queryNext():using default startndx
Couldn't establish connection to db:
  database:jdbc:postgresql:yaminspections user:dmorash password:
```

```
InspectionModel.queryNext():failed getting connection
2000-09-27 07:52:02 - Ctx( /inspections ): 302 R( /inspections +
  /servlet/WmlServlet + null) http://stooges.detroit.ns.ca/usr/
  local/apache/htdocs/inspections/error.wml
...
```

The majority of problems were traced by checking what operation was being executed at the time of the problem and examining the parameters sent from the Web browser to the servlet. This allowed us to trace the problem to an error, typically in the generated WML or the Java code. Another way to trace problems is to use the debugger provided by an Integrated Development Environment (IDE) such as Borland's JBuilder. A free "Foundation" version of this toolkit which integrates with Tomcat is available from *www.inprise.com.*

Challenges

An appropriate cliché for WAP development is that "the devil is in the details." The WAP development mailing lists and developer forums at Nokia and Phone.com are full of postings where the developer has a good basic understanding of WAP but runs into problems with HTTP, Web servers, caching, and similar sordid details. Some of the challenges we encountered include the following:

- URL redirection to use static pages: When testing with an alternative Palm WAP browser from 4th Pass (the Kbrowser), HTTP Basic authentication was not supported by the browser gateway combination. The MobileID Palm Pilot browser had problems with the redirect message (believing the content type to be HTML) when redirecting from the servlet to static pages. This is a commonly reported problem on development newsgroups and mailing lists.

- Bitmap support (Phone.com vs. Nokia): The Phone.com microbrowser in the Ericsson R280 phone expects bitmaps (.bmp files), not wireless bitmaps as per the WAP standards. In fact, this phone's microbrowser is not fully WAP 1.1 compliant, relying on a Phone.com gateway to translate WML into HDML.

- The Phone.com microbrowser does not use the deck title, whereas the MobileID (Ericsson-derived) browser and Nokia browsers do.

- Because we were not writing for a Nokia browser, we did not have to cope with this problem, but during tests with the Nokia simulator, we noted that when a select list is displayed, only the default option is initially shown. This differs from the Phone.com SDK browser, which displays an entire select list. Hence it is better (unless doing device tailoring) to use lists of links for navigation choice lists. A general rule of thumb (if all browsers must be supported) is to start with the Nokia 7110 simulator because this is less forgiving than the Phone.com simulator.

- Formatting of dates for display and unformatting for storage posed problems. This problem is not limited to WAP, but is a general issue with thin client interfaces.

- POST/GET parameter names must be synchronized with the Java code that processes them. Any information embedded in static and dynamically created WML must be synchronized with the Java processing code. We used the Operations class to encapsulate valid operations, which partially deals with this.

System Testing

We carried out system testing using:

- The UP 4.0 SDK simulator from Phone.com.

- A Palm Pilot equipped with a MobileID (AU Systems) WAP browser (talking to a WAPlite gateway).

- An Ericsson R280 handset equipped with Phone.com micro-brower (talking to a Phone.com gateway).

Functional Testing

The following shows a sample functional test case results sheet used during system testing:

TEST CASE 5	
Functional Requirements Tested	4. Inspection information to be entered shall include the following Pass/Fail checks: ▣ Tax stamps (do bottles have valid excise tax stamps?) ▣ Stock (do bottles contain what their labels say they do?) ▣ Measures (are legal-sized measures used in mixing drinks?) ▣ Underage (are there underage clients drinking on premises?) 5. Inspection information shall include entry of a number indicating how many IDs were checked at the door while the inspector is present. 6. The inspection information shall include a comment field allowing free-form entry. The comment field shall be at least 50 characters long. 7. The inspection information shall include an overall status field allowing the following options: ▣ Pass ▣ Fail ▣ Reinspect
Preconditions	The tester has logged on to the application. An establishment has been selected for inspection.

INSTRUCTIONS	EXPECTED RESULTS	DEVIATIONS	PASS/FAIL
1. Verify that Tax Stamps, Stock, Measures, Underage items can be selected and deselected.	All items should be available for selection or deselection.	*Noted deviations from expected results go here.*	Check this.
2. Verify that the number of observed liquor ID door checks can be entered.	Only numeric values should be allowed. These should be limited to a range of 0 to 1000.		
3. Verify that a comment field can be entered.	The comment should allow alphanumeric entry of up to 50 characters		
4. Verify that an inspection status can be input.	The inspection status should be limited to Pass, Fail, and Reinspect		
5. Check the database (using a SQL query on `inspectiondate` and `establishment` on the `inspection_results` and `inspection_checks` tables) to ensure that the inspection data are updated.	The `inspection_results` and `inspection_checks` tables should be updated with the inspection data that was entered. One record should exist in the `inspection_results` table, and one record for each acknowledged check should be found in the `inspection_checks` table.		

PASS/FAIL	INDICATE PASS OR FAIL HERE
Comments	Tester's comments here

Note that this test case would be repeated with variations of entered parameters. For example, the first time through, the tester might check off all checks, enter a positive number for IDs observed, select "Pass," and enter a brief textual comment. Additional passes would be carried out using the same basic procedure, but entering no checks, failing the inspected establishment, and so on.

Usability Testing

The following check list was derived from Chapter 11. It contains items to check arranged by category (e.g., layout considerations, navigation, and input). Checking a box indicates that this area is satisfactory, whereas an X can be used to fail a test. Usability testing may require several passes through the application focusing on layout in one pass, error handling and help in a second pass, and so on. Some of the numbers used in these tests should be revised depending on the target client devices and personal opinion (e.g., nine fields per screen may be considered too many for applications targeted only at a handset).

We could improve the usability of this application by adding help functions as well as some additional navigation that would let an inspector back out of an inspection in progress. The latter would be of much greater concern if there were a large number of entry fields for each inspection or if our device was not equipped with a Back button. Fortunately, both the phone and the Palm Pilot offer backlighting, making them usable in dimly lit establishments (our single special usability requirement).

Layout
☐ Is the layout of screens consistent across the application?
☐ Is content arranged in a logical way (e.g., important information placed first)?
☐ Is all information that is displayed necessary?
☐ Is each screen a reasonable size?

☐ Are titles provided for each screen?
☐ Are labels short and meaningful (between 5 and 10 characters)?
☐ Are all labels necessary?
☐ Is terminology consistent?
☐ Is information formatted logically (e.g., use of italics, bold, caps)?

Input

☐ Does each deck contain less than 10 fields?
☐ Are format masks used to limit type and length of input fields?
☐ Are select lists used where sensible?

Navigation

☐ Are menus less than 10 items long?
☐ Is the navigation hierarchy less than 4 levels deep?
☐ Is the navigation between screens consistent?
☐ Is it possible to return home from anywhere in the application?
☐ Is the amount of scrolling required reasonable?

Error Handling and Help

☐ Is help provided?
☐ Are errors handled consistently?
☐ When an error occurs, can I recover gracefully?

Special

☐ Is the application usable in low light conditions?

RELEASE AND DEPLOYMENT

The inspection application was deployed on a Linux Server running in a "demilitarized zone," or DMZ. This server is protected by packet filtering router hardware and a freely available packet filtering firewall called "ipchains." Packet filtering rules allow outside access only on the HTTP port where Apache listens. In a production system, a proxying firewall would probably be added to better validate the contents of requests to this server. In the demo system, the database is co-located with the Web server and application. The database would normally be located in a secure application area behind another firewall that would only allow traffic on the port on which PostgreSQL listens. The servlet source code was packaged as a '.war' file. This is a standard Web application archive used for servlet deployment.

That concludes the application development case study. Full SQL and Java source code for this can be found in Appendix B. In Chapter 13 we look at where WAP is going and related trends in the wireless Web.

Future of WAP

The future of WAP and the wireless Web are popular topics in the media today with critics labeling WAP as a short-term solution and others equating WAP with the second coming. In this chapter, we look at the direction in which wireless Web technology and applications are moving. We try to provide a relatively unbiased overview of evolving technologies that will influence the course of WAP. These include WAP technology, complementary technologies, as well as potential competition. A realistic assessment sees WAP as an evolutionary suite of standards that deals with current wireless Web issues and will continue to do so, even as new issues arise.

Although the technology is compelling (to those of us who work with it, anyway), it is the future applications that are of interest to the general public. WAP and related technologies enable completely new classes of application, most of which are in their infancy. We look at the types of applications that are poised to take off as the wireless Web becomes an accepted part of people's lives.

FUTURE WAP TECHNOLOGY

WAP does not stand still. The WAP Forum is driven by its 500-plus members via a number of internal special interest groups and through liaisons with external standards bodies such as the World Wide Web Consortium (W3C). Revised and new standards are officially added to the WAP suite every six months, and work is underway in dozens of areas including improved security, voice interfaces, multimedia, and location-aware technologies. Some of these initiatives are viable on today's infrastructure, and others do not make sense until we have improved devices and higher bandwidth networks.

Voice

Voice recognition and synthesis technologies have made their way out of the research lab and promise to supplement more traditional Web interfaces. VoiceXML is an XML-based language for specifying voice interfaces. Currently the processing requirements for general-purpose speech recognition and synthesis are beyond the capabilities of mobile devices. Applications are available that use a server-based voice gateway to provide interactive voice response (IVR) capabilities, and IBM has a voice browser product available on its Alphaworks site (*www.alphaworks.ibm.com*) that will run on a PC equipped with its ViaVoice application. Client-side speech processing is probably a few years off, but an integrated data (WAP) and voice (VoiceXML) product has the potential to overcome the weaknesses of both types of interface. The WAP Forum has indicated that an integrated speech interface will make its way into the WAP specifications.

Multimedia

Multimedia support including streaming multimedia, music downloads, color graphics, and animation are on the horizon for WAP. Applications that support streaming multimedia are already available for wireless devices. PacketVideo (*www.packetvideo.com*) has a Moving Picture Expert Group (MPEG-4) compliant product that supports multimedia transmission over current, 2.5G, and 3G networks such as GSM, CDMA, GPRS, and WCDMA. PacketVideo claims that its technology supports streaming video at transfer rates as low as 14.4 kilobaud. Texas Instruments (*www.ti.com*) produces digital signal processing hardware (its Open Multimedia Application Platform) for use in wireless handsets. This hardware is specifically designed to support processing and display of streaming video and audio media and will be installed in products from Ericsson and Nokia. With multimedia capable devices, efficient multimedia transmission technology, and the proliferation of broadband networks, the stage is set for mobile multimedia. It is only logical that the WAP standards will evolve to support device and network neutral mechanisms for handling multimedia.

Although WAP's support for MIME types is adequate to handle new media, streaming media is not compatible with WSP/HTTP and requires a different approach. Integration of multimedia capabilities with WAP microbrowsers could be accomplished using a multimedia markup language such as the Synchronized Multimedia Integration Language (SMIL – pronounce "smile"). SMIL (*www.w3.org/audiovideo*) is an XML-based language designed to control presentation of multimedia in a bandwidth-efficient way. An extended SMIL-capable microbrowser could orchestrate audio and video transfer and playback. The Wireless Application Environment architecture is suited for this purpose with a built-in mechanism to support a number of user agents within the same device. A multimedia user agent tailored to process streaming audio and video could easily coexist with microbrowsers and telephony applications.

With the rise in popularity of Internet digital music standards such as MP3 (MPEG Layer-3), it is no surprise that music downloads are a topic of interest in the WAP Forum. Devices that are a combination of a traditional radio receiver and cellular handset are already in production, and it is a logical step to integrate an MP3 player with such devices to create a dynamic personal entertainment center. The ability to download music files from any location is compelling, but you have to wonder how quickly such multimedia applications will swamp the advances in bandwidth promised by 3G networks!

WAP's limited monochrome bitmap standard has been criticized as insufficient, particularly for devices such as palmtops that are capable of rendering greyscale or color graphics. Support for color graphics has been announced by Phone.com; the Portable Network Graphics standard, an 8-bit color standard, is supported in the UP.Browser version implemented in the Hitachi C309H. Color graphics will be included in WAP version 2 but it is likely that these will coexist with the WBMP standard because most handsets do not support color or even greyscale display.

Currently, WAP animation is possible, using timers and bitmaps, but is hardly inspiring in this form. Formal support for animation will increase the entertainment value of WAP, and the impetus for this is probably a result of competition from I-Mode.

End-to-End Security

For highly secure applications, WAP's current security model assumes a strong relationship between the WAP gateway owner and the content provider. This is required because of the transition from WTLS used over the mobile network and TLS run over the Internet. Information that is encrypted for the WTLS link must be decrypted at the gateway and then reencrypted for TLS. At this point, the information is no longer secure. A scheme that removes the need for decryption and reencryption at the WAP gateway has been proposed by the WAP Forum (the WAP Transport Layer E2E Security specification). This is illustrated in the scenario shown in Figure 13-1. The user requests information from a protected origin server (Fort Knox). The default WAP gateway directs this request to an origin server (redirector) that returns an HTTP status 300 response message containing an XML navigation document. The mobile device uses the navigation document to establish a direct secure connection with a WAP-capable subordinate proxy. The subordinate proxy provides direct access to a secure origin server and securely handles further communications with the mobile device. When the user has completed the secure transaction, the protocol switches back to the regular WAP gateway.

Full Public Key Infrastructure

Before the full gamut of mobile commerce applications is possible, a complete public key infrastructure (PKI) must be in place. This requires mobile devices capable of securely storing digital certificates for use in digital signatures and strong authentication (as specified by the wireless identity module, or WIM, specification). This also requires a server-side infrastructure that enables WAP services to verify a client's credentials

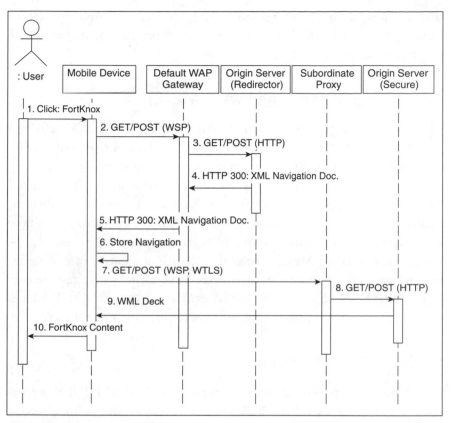

FIGURE 13-1. End-to-End Security Scenario

through a mutually agreed on certificate authority (e.g., Verisign or Entrust). Certificate authorities can include governments, post offices, banks, and corporations, and the infrastructure for this is already in place in some countries. However, truly global mobile commerce requires a worldwide chain of certificate authorities enabling cross certification between corporations and nations. The fact that no such framework has been established within the existing Internet indicates that legal, business, political, and cultural barriers must be overcome before this can happen. Smaller scale PKI is possible, and the widespread availability of personal secure devices should do much to foster this. Visa is a member of the WAP Forum and has proposed secure payment methods for WAP that are similar to the PKI-based Secure Electronic Transaction (SET) initiative. These methods may prove to be more successful than their wired Internet predecessors.

Integration of Java and WAP (MExE)

The Mobile Station Application Execution Environment (MExE) is a Java-based suite of protocols that allow mobile devices to execute applications. It is designed to execute thick client applications on a Java virtual machine within a mobile handset environment. The MExE standards define a system of classmarks (basically levels of capability) to define the abilities of the host device. This allows applications to take advantage of features and prevents them from attempting to use unsupported functionality. MExE incorporates WAP standards, providing an environment in which potentially competitive technologies can coexist. It is likely that MExE will be useful primarily on higher end devices due to the processing demands of the Java application environment.

Push Becomes Common

The WAP push specifications were complete as of WAP 1.2. These standards require new or enhanced WAP gateways that are push capable as well as push-enabled mobile devices (and, of course, push applications). Push technology can work over existing networks, but will benefit from the always-on nature and faster response times of the newer packet-switched networks. There are still security and access issues to resolve. The technology on which WAP push is based (Phone.com's 'alerts') was primarily a closed system, used by gateway operators, and third party (push application) access was not an issue. The success of SMS applications in Europe we hope will serve as a model for the evolution of WAP push.

Location Support

The WAP Forum is currently working on support for location-aware applications in collaboration with other industry bodies such as the W3C. Describing and transporting location data is surprisingly com-

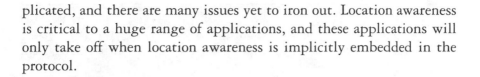

plicated, and there are many issues yet to iron out. Location awareness is critical to a huge range of applications, and these applications will only take off when location awareness is implicitly embedded in the protocol.

Beyond WML

HTML and XML have recently come together in the Extensible Hypertext Markup Language (XHTML) specifications. A subset of XHTML called XHTML Basic has been selected as a common industry standard for limited devices (such as mobile handsets) by the W3C (see the sidebar "XHTML"). The WAP Forum has stated that WML will complete a migration to XHTML by the time the next major version of WAP is released (mid-2001). This migration is positive because it removes one of the major complaints against WAP – the use of a non-HTML-based markup language. When WAP adopts XHTML this may pressure others (e.g., Palm and I-Mode) to migrate their own HTML-based languages to this W3C industry standard. This evolution is a good reason for ensuring that your WAP solutions employ a clear separation of view and data! Fortunately, because both markup languages are based on XML, it should be fairly simple to convert existing WML applications to XHTML. In addition, if you are familiar with WML, you will already have overcome most of the hurdles that those comfortable with HTML will experience when moving to XHTML (e.g., closing all element tags and quoting attribute values).

XHTML

XHTML is a reformulation of HTML 4 as an application of XML. XHTML documents use the same elements as those found in HTML 4, but within the more constrained syntax of an XML-compliant language. This has an advantage in the mobile device world because well-formed XML markup is easier for parsers to process than HTML (WML also has this advantage). That means that WAP gateways will be able to encode and decode XHTML in much the same way as

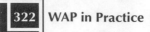

they currently process WML. Translation between XHTML and WML should also be simple, especially when moving from WML to XHTML. With the exception of WML's event-handling model, most of WML's tags are a subset of XHTML Basic (discussed later).

One large change from HTML is the modular approach taken by XHTML (as of version 1.1). The XHTML markup definition has been broken up into many modules, each dealing with a distinct aspect of presentation. XHTML Basic is a subset of these modules selected for processing by simple devices (e.g., wireless handsets). XHTML Basic modules include:

> Structure (e.g., `html`, `head`, `body`, and `title`)
> Text (e.g., headers such as `h1`, paragraphs such as `p`, and emphasis such as `em`)
> Hypertext (the anchor element, `a`)
> List (e.g., `dl`, `li`)
> Basic Forms (e.g., `form`, `input`, `select`, and `option`)
> Tables (e.g., `table`, `td`, `th`, and `tr`)
> Image (`img`)

The modular approach has also been adopted for cascading style sheet (CSS) definition, and it is envisaged that modules will allow negotiation of content and style in a format that is appropriate for a given device. Prior to receiving content, a device will negotiate those modules it understands, and a document will be made available containing only those modules that can be handled. XHTML is extensible, and new modules can provide additional capabilities (an example of this is Forms Markup Language, or FML, that provides a more powerful mechanism for creating Web forms than available in traditional HTML). ◾

FUTURE COMPLEMENTARY TECHNOLOGY

Complementary technology includes Bluetooth, improved networks, interfaces, and location services.

Local Area RF Networks

Bluetooth and wearable computers rival WAP as hot topics in the mobile computing space. Bluetooth is an industry standard for short-range radio communication among mobile devices that support device discovery, authentication, and encryption. Although Bluetooth has a myriad of uses, we examine one immediate benefit that it brings to the wireless Web.

Bluetooth allows the components of a wireless Web client to be distributed in space. The separation of cellular modem from handheld computer and computer from visual or voice interface creates a highly localized network dubbed the personal area network, or PAN (to keep things consistent with wide and local area networks). This PAN solves the problem of creating the perfect all-in-one mobile client, and device engineers are freed from the design challenge (or nightmare!) of combining a quality user interface, processor, and RF modem in one physical package. One can imagine a wearable computing solution consisting of a miniature color monitor embedded in your glasses with an ear bud/microphone for voice communications all talking to separate belt-mounted devices to handle the computing and RF transceiver functions.

Improved Visual and Voice Interfaces

The multimedia and virtual reality research of the last two decades has a natural outlet in the unwired body networks just discussed. Is it far fetched to imagine an application-supplied reality superimposed on our current one, courtesy of special glasses and a wireless Web interface? Imagine standing on a street corner in Paris and seeing history reenacted before your eyes by a location-aware application. Wouldn't architecture and history come to life if you could turn toward the Eiffel Tower and watch its construction or view the storming of a virtual Bastille from rue Saint-Antoine? Voice recognition and synthesis technologies are also making their way out of the lab and promise to supplement more traditional Web interfaces.

2.5G and 3G Networks

Because WAP was designed to be as independent of underlying networks as possible, WAP applications will run over the enhanced second-generation (2.5G) and third-generation (3G) networks to be deployed over the next few years. In fact, these packet-switched digital networks (e.g., General Packet Radio Service and Wideband Code Division Multiple Access) are superior to the current digital circuit switched networks, not only in terms of speed, but by virtue of their

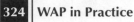

always-on nature. Higher speeds and virtually instant connections open up the wireless Web to more demanding applications such as bandwidth intensive multimedia. The initial predictions for throughput on 3G networks have been lowered by recent real-world testing, but it is still realistic to expect bandwidth that equals or exceeds today's dial-up desktop Internet.

So why do we still need the WAP network protocols? Bandwidth still costs money and consumes device power, so efficient use of available bandwidth will remain a concern to reduce network usage fees and extend a device's time between battery charges. In addition, new applications will consume increasing bandwidth (e.g., color displays, increased use of still images, and video). At the same time, the number of users will rise dramatically (if industry analysts are even vaguely close to the mark). This increased load will rapidly reduce the effective throughput of packet-switched networks because this is a function of concurrent active users. Also, the intermittent coverage experienced by users on the move will remain an issue with the new networks.

Location-Aware Networks and Devices

Location awareness promises to be a key technology. This means that integrated GPS/cellular devices and land-based location systems will become a normal part of the wireless Web in the next few years. Who owns the location information, how it will be packaged and transmitted, and the issue of subscriber privacy all need to be resolved. However, the value of knowing a user's location is too great to prevent this from becoming a standard element of WAP.

FUTURE COMPETING TECHNOLOGY

A variety of technologies have been proposed as alternatives to WAP. On the application side, there is Sun's J2ME lightweight Java specification, and NTT DoCoMo's I-Mode has recently surfaced as a possible thin client competitor to WAP. On the network side, proponents of

Internet standards would like to replace WAP's network protocols with ones closer to the IP-based protocol stack including TCP/IP and HTTP. Existing technologies such as SMS and the Subscriber Identity Module (SIM) Toolkit will also compete with WAP in the wireless application space. SMS was discussed in Chapter 2, and its popularity will no doubt continue in Europe until WAP and suitable store-and-forward WAP applications can match its capabilities. The SIM Toolkit is a Global System for Mobile Communications (GSM) standard technology that defines standards for applications deployed on smart cards. Applications developed on this technology will be popular in the short term in Europe and Asia. However, it is not clear whether these SIM Toolkit applications will migrate to networks other than GSM or will survive the transition to 3G network standards.

J2ME

Various lightweight forms of Java have been proposed for mobile phones and handheld computers. The MExE environment is one such environment that promises to complement rather than compete head on with WAP. The Java 2 Micro Edition is Sun's name for a lightweight version of Java, specifically designed for devices such as handheld computers. Java was originally designed to be embedded in devices and is an ideal language for this due to its device-independent bytecode interpreter and excellent support for networking. The J2ME run-time environment is supplied by the stripped-down Kilobyte Virtual Machine (KVM) that is finding its way into hand-helds such as the Palm and Symbian devices as well as the more powerful handsets (e.g., Motorola's iDEN products – see *www.motorola.com/LMPS/iDEN*).

When they first appeared, it was predicted that Java applets would dominate the Web, supplanting HTML-based applications by virtue of a superior user interface and procedural logic. Although this has not happened, you could argue that mobile devices are better suited than the desktop computer for an applet model of computing. This is especially true if these applications remain resident once downloaded and can be used repeatedly without further download delays. Downloaded, locally hosted applications can carry out the majority of processing locally, consuming costly network bandwidth only when absolutely necessary. In theory, these applications can also make use of a device's unique capabilities. However, there are a few problems with the heavier client approach to the wireless Web. First, the applet must be downloaded, consuming considerable bandwidth in the process. Second, unless custom applets are to be written for each device, the applet must somehow use a device's input and output mechanisms without knowing the exact nature of the device. The current J2ME specifications do not specify device-independent interface libraries, although Sun has proposed a device-independent user interface called 'Truffle'. This is a cut-down version of Java's Abstract Windowing Toolkit (AWT) and allows for features like touch screen input (rather than assuming a keyboard and mouse). More information can be found at *java.sun.com/products/personaljava*.

Other problems with the heavier client application model include database access over the wireless network (JDBC connections), although thin JDBC clients and JDBC proxy servers or local databases can alleviate this. Java applications will no doubt play an important role in the future wireless Web, but alongside WAP solutions, hopefully in an integrated MExE environment.

I-Mode

NTT DoCoMo, the purveyors of the I-Mode service, are members of the WAP Forum and have adamantly denied that their wireless Web solution competes with WAP. Despite this, you can compare the success of I-Mode in Japan to WAP's slower uptake in Europe and America and conclude that I-Mode must have something that WAP is lacking. Why not simply drop WAP and go with a proven success story like I-Mode? This ignores two fundamental factors in I-Mode's success – the cultural context and the technical solution. NTT DoCoMo is the second largest ISP in the world. With origins in a state-controlled monopoly, it has a virtual stranglehold over Japan's wireless Web. The users of I-Mode have been very quick to take to the services it offers despite the fact that these closely resemble the current choice of WAP applications (e.g., banking, horoscopes, news, and messaging). It has been suggested that Japan's relatively low desktop Internet use has actually helped this happen and that Japanese I-Mode subscribers have embraced the wireless Web because they do not carry the preconceived notion that Web access should be a rich and colorful experience. On the technical side, I-Mode runs over a Japanese-specific network and uses a proprietary proxy gateway to carry out similar functions to a WAP gateway. This means that I-Mode has not had to cope with the complexity and cost of supporting multiple networks, bearers, and third party devices. The same factors that contributed to I-Mode's success in Japan may make it difficult to extend (at least in its current form) to other networks and countries.

Some of the planned upgrades to the WAP standard are probably a result of competition from I-Mode. The migration to XHTML and support for color graphics and animation are examples of this reaction.

IP over Mobile Networks

Most future mobile networks assume an Internet Protocol (IP) basis for data communications. This allows TCP/IP and HTTP to run directly over these networks without translation to a foreign bearer. It is likely that tweaked versions of TCP/IP and HTTP will be developed to deal with the same issues addressed by the WAP protocols (e.g., push capabilities and long-lived sessions could be added to HTTP). The WAP Forum has stated that direct support for TCP will be part of WAP version 2. Whether this means that, in the case of mobile networks that can support TCP/IP, the WAP gateway will disappear, is not public knowledge at this point.

FUTURE APPLICATIONS

Applications will be popular if they improve the quality of a user's life — reducing stress, simplifying tasks, entertaining, and connecting. Many new applications are possible even with today's capabilities, but the range will expand radically as the technologies we discussed here mature. For example, instant messaging applications are not possible without pervasive support for push technology. Interactive multimedia-based entertainment is not realistic over 9600 baud connections. Location awareness may even be the key to the missing killer wireless app.

Entertainment

According to Kevin Bradshaw of Digital Bridges, Internet usage shows that the two most popular services on today's wired Web are chatting and playing (as reported in the WAP Congress 2000 Notes 3, May 2000, Cannes France – *www.the-arc-group.com*). There are already a variety of WAP game portals offering single and multiplayer games. Small single-player games (e.g., Tic Tac Toe) can be contained in a single WML deck with associated WMLScript file. This allows a game to be cached locally providing an economical way to fill time while waiting for a bus or plane. New games can be accessed when you lose interest in the old, providing an advantage over traditional games that require installation or come prebundled with a device. Mobile gaming comes into its own, however, when multiple players can interact in near real time. Packet-switched networks and push protocols are needed before this will become widely popular, but the personal nature of the device and an always-on connection open up some interesting possibilities. Fantasy adventure games and other role-playing entertainment is one area that could benefit from this technology. Adding location awareness and high-quality mapping displays would make these games even more compelling. Demographics say that today's teenagers will be the most influential users of the wireless Web. Entertainment applications may be the drawing card that leads to widespread acceptance.

Location Aware

Devices that integrate GPS or land-based positioning with Internet access enable a new class of location-aware applications. Current GPS devices used by navigators, travelers, and surveyors rely on stored information for geographic and civil information such as land maps and location of roads and services. Opening up access to the Web will improve the accuracy of this information and allow data gathered in the field to update central repositories in near real time. In-car navigation systems would be far more valuable with integrated up-to-the minute information on local services such as gas stations, entertainment facilities, and restaurants. The usefulness of a location-based service was brought home the other day when a driver stopped me and asked for directions. He had been driving around the neighborhood for over an hour after being given misleading directions to a nearby street on two separate occasions. Had the driver had access to an online locator service, he would have been spared a great deal of frustration. Other possible applications of location-aware services include fleet management and asset tracking that currently must use more expensive satellite-based or proprietary solutions.

Push

If the success of SMS is any indication, push-based applications including mobile instant messaging and paging will play a major role in WAP's success. It is likely that transmission of time-sensitive information such as stock alerts and schedule changes will be integrated with wireless portals. Push also adds an element of excitement to auctions services and will probably become an accepted component of Internet auctions as they move onto the wireless Web. Any activity that can be done more efficiently in an asynchronous interrupt-driven (as opposed to polling) fashion is a natural application for push technology.

M-Commerce

Mobile commerce applications are enabled by a combination of public key infrastructure and personal devices with built-in security mechanisms. Durlacher Research predicts that targeted advertising, financial services, and online shopping (e.g., retail, ticketing, and reservations) will be the primary sources of m-commerce revenue as the market matures (*www.durlacher.com*) with business applications, telemetry, customer care, and entertainment playing an important

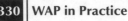

part as well. Mobile commerce applications benefit from both push and location technology, and we can expect to see innovative applications that take advantage of these factors as well as the mobility of the user.

Mobile Middleware

Mobile middleware is a somewhat nebulous term describing a broad class of programs that indirectly enable mobile applications. Some examples of mobile middleware are personalization and targeted advertising services, device tailoring, payment and billing, and HTML filters. These are often better bought than built because their construction requires specialized knowledge (and maintaining them to a best-of-breed level will be time consuming!).

As we discussed in Chapter 9, personalization of the mobile user interface can be critical to an application's success. Middleware that helps a company "own" its clients by building a profile and tailoring the interface to their needs is becoming very popular in the Web world. It promises to be even more popular in mobile commerce applications where mobile device limitations mandate a user-tailored interface. Targeted advertising can be integrated with other mobile services, just as on the Web, banner ads currently fund commercial Web sites. Targeted advertising relies on personalization and can also take advantage of location and push, if available. One area receiving a lot of attention is the subscription model where users sign up to receive electronic coupon offers or pushed notifications tailored to their interests. This approach has the potential advantage over banner ads of being less obtrusive and better focused on users' needs.

There is a lot of concern among developers over having to tailor the user interface for a proliferation of client devices. A service that translates general-purpose WML into device-tailored markup relieves developers of this burden. Such middleware would use a combination of HTTP headers and user agent profiles (as they become available) to adjust content and could coexist with the WAP application or be deployed as a separate proxy application between the client and the application server.

Billing and payment middleware provides an interface from an m-commerce application to online payments services, accounting systems, and the financial infrastructure. Such applications are little different from their Web siblings, but can take advantage of two components not usually available in the desktop Web – client digital certificates (the wireless identity module, or WIM) and the mobile operator's established relationship with the client. Client-side certificates and digital signatures open up the possibility of truly secure payments where each purchase is "signed for," protecting both the client and vendor from abuses. The relationship between a client and mobile operator can also be used with the mobile operator's account providing a central payment clearinghouse for small value transactions.

Transcoding middleware promises a painless migration from the wired to the wireless Web. It is a common misconception that HTML content can be automatically filtered to produce effective wireless applications. Vendors of transcoding middleware have done little to dispel this myth, and the quest for a quick and inexpensive path to the wireless Web will create a significant market for Web to WAP translation. For a more detailed discussion of this class of software, refer to Chapter 9.

CONCLUSION

That concludes our look at the Wireless Application Protocol. WAP is ready for use now. Dozens of mobile handsets and handheld computers support WAP, commercial gateways are proliferating, and the first wave of WAP services has crested. We are at the very beginning of the wireless Web, and this is a dynamic and interesting place to be! Changes we can expect in the next few years include the following:

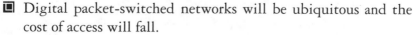 Push applications and location-based services will become the norm.

■ Digital packet-switched networks will be ubiquitous and the cost of access will fall.

- The user experience will be improved by better interfaces and intuitive applications. Multimedia and voice/data integration will make today's wireless interfaces seem quaint.

- Today's security issues will be resolved and open access to the wireless Web will replace walled gardens.

The wireless Web will change the way we live and work. WAP holds the key to this potential!

 # WML 1.3 Reference

Note: Most elements and attributes have been available since WML version 1.1. Elements and attributes added in 1.2 and 1.3 are noted (a list of these changes appears at the start of Chapter 5). Refer to the Wireless Markup Language Version 1.3 specification available at the WAP Forum site (*www.wapforum.org*) and document-type definition (*www.wapforum.org/DTD/*) for the definitive reference to WML.

All elements described here contain the following attributes.

id	A unique identifier for the tag within the deck.
class	A name of a class or classes of which the tag is a member.

<a>

Description:	Defines a hyperlink. The destination of this link is specified as a URI, which is usually the address or ID of another tag either in the same deck or within a new deck. The 'a' tag is a shorter form of the 'anchor' tag.
Contains:	*Text*, , <img>
Is Contained By:	<fieldset>, <td>, <em>, <strong>, <b>, <i>, <u>, <big>, <small>, <p>, <pre>
ATTRIBUTE (*=REQUIRED)	**DESCRIPTION**
*href**	The destination URI.
title	A brief string identifying the link.
accesskey	**New in WML 1.2.** A keyboard shortcut equivalent to selecting this link.
xml:lang	The natural or formal language of the tag or its attributes.

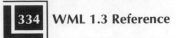

\<access>

Description:	Specifies access control information for the deck. A deck may contain only one access element. When access control is not specified, cards in any deck can access this deck; otherwise the 'domain' and 'path' attributes specify which other decks may access it.
Contains:	
Is Contained By:	\<head>
ATTRIBUTE	**DESCRIPTION**
domain	The domain suffix of allowed referring pages.
path	The path prefix of allowed referring pages.

\<anchor>

Description:	Defines a hyperlink. The destination of this link is specified as a URI, which is usually the address or ID of another tag either in the same deck or within a new deck. The 'a' tag is a shorter form of this tag and should be used for simple navigation due to its more compact encoding.
Contains:	*Text*, \ , \<img>, \<go>, \<prev>, \<refresh>
Is Contained By:	\<fieldset>, \<td>, \<em>, \<strong>, \<b>, \<i>, \<u>, \<big>, \<small>, \<p>, \<pre>
ATTRIBUTE	**DESCRIPTION**
title	Specifies a brief text string identifying the link.
accesskey	**New in WML 1.2.** A keyboard shortcut equivalent to selecting this link.
xml:lang	The natural or formal language of the tag or its attributes.

\<b>

Description:	Indicates that the text within the tags should be rendered with bold formatting.
Contains:	*Text*, \<em>, \<strong>, \<b>, \<i>, \<u>, \<big>, \<small>, \ , \<img>, \<anchor>, \<a>, \<table>
Is Contained By:	\<fieldset>, \<td>, \<em>, \<strong>, \<b>, \<i>, \<u>, \<big>, \<small>, \<p>, \<pre>
ATTRIBUTE	**DESCRIPTION**
xml:lang	The natural or formal language of the tag or its attributes.

\<big\>

Description:	Indicates that the text within the tags should be rendered with a large font.
Contains:	*Text*, \<em\>, \<strong\>, \<b\>, \<i\>, \<u\>, \<big\>, \<small\>, \<br\>, \<img\>, \<anchor\>, \<a\>, \<table\>
Is Contained By:	\<fieldset\>, \<td\>, \<em\>, \<strong\>, \<b\>, \<i\>, \<u\>, \<big\>, \<small\>, \<p\>
ATTRIBUTE	**DESCRIPTION**
xml:lang	The natural or formal language of the tag or its attributes.

\<br\>

Description:	Ends the current line and starts a new line.
Contains:	
Is Contained By:	\<fieldset\>, \<anchor\>, \<a\>, \<td\>, \<em\>, \<strong\>, \<b\>, \<i\>, \<u\>, \<big\>, \<small\>, \<p\>, \<pre\>

\<card\>

Description:	A container of layout, navigation, input, and other fields. A card may form a single unit of user interaction (i.e., one physical screen) or may be divided into multiple physical screens by the WML browser.
Contains:	\<onevent\>, \<timer\>, \<do\>, \<p\>, \<pre\>
Is Contained By:	\<wml\>
ATTRIBUTE	**DESCRIPTION**
title	Brief description that may be used by the browser to label this object.
newcontext	If "true" the current browser context will be reset upon entry to this card.
ordered	Describes the organization of content within the card. When "false" the WML browser may choose to reorder content to better suit its capabilities.
xml:lang	The natural or formal language of the tag or its attributes.
onenterforward	The URI that is loaded when the user enters the card using a 'go' task.
onenterbackward	The URI that is loaded when the user returns to the card from a programmable soft key (using a 'prev' task) or via a Back button.
ontimer	The URI that is loaded when a timer expires.

<do>

Description:	Provides a general mechanism for a user to interact with a card. The visual presentation of the do tag depends on the device but is always mapped to a user accessible 'widget,' such as a button.
Contains:	<go>, <prev>, <noop>, <refresh>
Is Contained By:	<card>, <template>, <fieldset>, <p>, <pre>
ATTRIBUTE (*=REQUIRED)	**DESCRIPTION**
*type**	Provides a hint to the browser about the intended use of this event handler and hence how it should be displayed. The following types are defined, although others may be used by vendors: 'accept' (positive acknowledgment); 'prev' (backward history navigation); 'help' (request for help); 'reset' (clearing or resetting state); 'options' (request for options or additional operations); 'delete' (delete item or choice); 'unknown' (a generic do element).
label	A string suitable for labeling the 'do' widget. Should be six characters or less.
name	The name of the do event binding.
optional	If true, the browser may ignore this element.
xml:lang	The natural or formal language of the tag or its attributes.

<em>

Description:	Indicates that the text within the tags should be rendered with some form of emphasis.
Contains:	*Text*, <em>, <strong>, <b>, <i>, <u>, <big>, <small>, , <img>, <anchor>, <a>, <table>
Is Contained By:	<fieldset>, <td>, <em>, <strong>, <b>, <i>, <u>, <big>, <small>, <p>, <pre>
ATTRIBUTE	**DESCRIPTION**
xml:lang	The natural or formal language of the tag or its attributes.

\<fieldset\>

Description:	Groups related fields and text providing additional control over layout and navigation. Fieldset elements may be nested.
Contains:	Text, \<em\>, \<strong\>, \<b\>, \<i\>, \<u\>, \<big\>, \<small\>, \<br\>, \<img\>, \<anchor\>, \<a\>, \<table\>, \<input\>, \<select\>, \<fieldset\>, \<do\>
Is Contained By:	\<fieldset\>, \<p\>
ATTRIBUTE	**DESCRIPTION**
title	A title that may be used in the presentation of this object.
xml:lang	The natural or formal language of the tag or its attributes.

\<go\>

Description:	Declares a 'go' task, indicating navigation to a new URI. If the URI names a WML card or deck, the execution of the task will cause that item to be displayed.
Contains:	\<postfield\>, \<setvar\>
Is Contained By:	\<do\>, \<onevent\>, \<anchor\>
ATTRIBUTE (*=REQUIRED)	**DESCRIPTION**
*href**	The destination URI.
sendreferer	If "true," a request for a new URI will contain the URI of the deck containing this task – this can then be used for server-based access control.
method	The HTTP submission method. Possible values are 'POST' (submission data included in request) or 'GET' (submission data appended as a query to the URI requested).
enctype	**New in WML 1.2.** The type of content encoding that will be used for this submission. The default is "application/x-www-form-urlencoded," and this is the only value allowed for a GET. POST submissions may also be encoded as "multipart/form-data" (recommended for form fields that are expressed in a character set other than US-ASCII).
cache-control	**New in WML 1.3.** If set to "no-cache," the WML browser will reload the URL from the origin server and the HTTP "cache-control" header (set to "no-cache") will be sent with the request.
accept-charset	The list of character encodings for data that the origin server must accept when processing input. The value of this attribute is a comma- or space-separated list of character-encoding names.
id	A unique identifier for the tag within the deck.
class	A name of a class or classes of which the tag is a member.

`<head>`

Description:	Contains information about the deck including metadata and access control.
Contains:	`<access>`, `<meta>`
Is Contained By:	`<wml>`
ATTRIBUTE	**DESCRIPTION**
id	A unique identifier for the tag within the deck.

`<i>`

Description:	Indicates that the text within the tags should be rendered with italic formatting. Authors should attempt to use the strong and em tags in place of the b, I, and u tags, except where explicit control over text presentation is required.
Contains:	*Text*, `<em>`, `<strong>`, `<b>`, `<i>`, `<u>`, `<big>`, `<small>`, ` `, `<img>`, `<anchor>`, `<a>`, `<table>`
Is Contained By:	`<fieldset>`, `<td>`, `<em>`, `<strong>`, `<b>`, `<i>`, `<u>`, `<big>`, `<small>`, `<p>`, `<pre>`
ATTRIBUTE	**DESCRIPTION**
xml:lang	The natural or formal language of the tag or its attributes.

`<img>`

Description:	Declares an image to be included in the text flow.
Contains:	
Is Contained By:	`<fieldset>`, `<anchor>`, `<a>`, `<td>`, `<em>`, `<strong>`, `<b>`, `<i>`, `<u>`, `<big>`, `<small>`, `<p>`
ATTRIBUTE (*=REQUIRED)	**DESCRIPTION**
alt*	Text to substitute for the image if it cannot be displayed.
src*	The URI of the image to be shown.
localsrc	An alternative source for the image. If this image exists, it takes precedence over an image specified in the 'src' parameter.

vspace	The amount of white space to be inserted above and below the image. If specified as a percentage, the resulting space is based on the available vertical space, not the size of the image.
hspace	The amount of white space to be inserted to the left and right of the image. If specified as a percentage, the resulting space is based on the available horizontal space, not the size of the image.
align	Image alignment with respect to the baseline of the text. It has three possible values: "bottom," "middle," or "top."
height	The height of the image. If specified as a percentage, the resulting size is based on the available vertical space, not on the size of the image.
width	The width of the image. If specified as a percentage, the resulting size is based on the available horizontal space, not on the size of the image.
xml:lang	The natural or formal language of the tag or its attributes.

<input>

Description:	A text entry object with user input constrained by the optional format attribute.
Contains:	
Is Contained By:	<fieldset>, <p>, <pre>
ATTRIBUTE (*=REQUIRED)	DESCRIPTION
name*	The name of the variable to set with the result of the user's text input. The variable's value is used to preload the text entry object.
type	The type of text-input area (values allowed are "text" (text entry control) or "password" (text entry control entered characters are not directly displayed).
value	The default value of the variable named in the name attribute. When the variable named in the 'name' attribute is not set to a value, it will be assigned this value.
format	An input mask controlling user entry. The string consists of formatting characters and static text that will be displayed in the input area. Refer to Table 5-2, which defines formatting characters.
emptyok	Indicates that this input element accepts empty input when a non-empty format string has been specified.
size	The width, in characters, of the text-input area.
maxlength	The maximum number of characters that can be entered by the user.

Tabindex	The tabbing position of the current element. Used to determine the relative order in which elements are traversed when tabbing within a card.
Title	A title for this element that may be used in the presentation of this object.
accesskey	**New in WML 1.2.** A keyboard shortcut equivalent to selecting this field.
xml:lang	The natural or formal language of the tag or its attributes.

\<meta\>

Description:	The meta element contains generic meta-information relating to the WML deck. Meta-information is specified with property names and values.
Contains:	
Is Contained By:	\<head\>
ATTRIBUTE (*=REQUIRED)	**DESCRIPTION**
http-equiv	May be used in place of name and indicates that the property should be interpreted as an HTTP header. Used when you want to send an HTTP header to the WML browser and/or WAP gateway from an origin server.
name	Specifies the property name. The browser will ignore any metadata named with this attribute, so use 'http-equiv' when specifying metadata in an origin server application.
forua	When set to "true," specifies that the property should be passed through to the browser.
*content**	Specifies the property value.
scheme	Specifies a form or structure that may be used to interpret the property value.

\<noop\>

Description:	Specifies that nothing should be done (i.e., "no operation"). This can be used within a card to override a task that has been specified in a template.
Contains:	
Is Contained By:	\<do\>, \<onevent\>

\<onevent\>

Description:	Binds a task to an intrinsic event for the immediately enclosing element (e.g., an 'onevent' element inside a card element associates an intrinsic event binding with that card element).
Contains:	\<go\>, \<prev\>, \<noop\>, \<refresh\>
Is Contained By:	\<card\>, \<template\>, \<option\>
ATTRIBUTE (*=REQUIRED)	DESCRIPTION
type*	The name of the intrinsic event (e.g., "onenterbackward").

\<optgroup\>

Description:	Groups related option elements into a hierarchy. The browser may use this hierarchy to facilitate layout and presentation.
Contains:	\<optgroup\>, \<option\> Note that \<optgroup\> must contain at least one of these nested elements.
Is Contained By:	\<select\>, \<optgroup\>
ATTRIBUTE	DESCRIPTION
title	A title for this element that may be used in the presentation of this object.
xml:lang	The natural or formal language of the tag or its attributes.

\<option\>

Description:	Specifies a single choice in a select element. Each option may have one line of formatted text. Option elements may be arranged in hierarchical groups using the 'optgroup' element.
Contains:	Text, \<onevent\>
Is Contained By:	\<select\>, \<optgroup\>
ATTRIBUTE	DESCRIPTION
value	The value to be used when setting the name variable. This attribute may contain variable references, which are evaluated before the name variable is set.
title	A title for this element that may be used in the presentation of this object.
onpick	The URI that is loaded when the user selects or deselects this option.
xml:lang	The natural or formal language of the tag or its attributes.

<p>

Description:	Defines a paragraph that may specify line wrap and alignment. If the text alignment is not specified, it defaults to left. If the line-wrap mode is not specified, it is identical to the line-wrap mode of the previous paragraph in the current card.
Contains:	*Text*, <em>, <strong>, <b>, <i>, <u>, <big>, <small>, , <img>, <anchor>, <a>, <table>, <input>, <select>, <fieldset>, <do>
Is Contained By:	<card>
ATTRIBUTE	**DESCRIPTION**
align	The text alignment mode for the paragraph (default is "left"). Can be "left," "center," or "right."
mode	The line-wrap mode for the paragraph. The default is "wrap," which specifies breaking text; "nowrap" specifies nonbreaking text.
xml:lang	The natural or formal language of the tag or its attributes.

<postfield>

Description:	Specifies a field name and value for transmission to an origin server in a URL request.
Contains:	
Is Contained By:	<go>
ATTRIBUTE (*=REQUIRED)	**DESCRIPTION**
*name**	Parameter field name.
*value**	Parameter field value.

<pre>

Description:	**New in WML 1.2.** Provides a preformatted block of WML that will usually be literally interpreted (line breaks and other layout retained) by supporting WML browsers.
Contains:	*Text*, <a>, <anchor>, <do>, <u>, , <i>, <b>, <em>, <strong>, <input>, <select> **Note that <anchor>, <do>, and <u> were added to this list in WML 1.3.**
Is Contained By:	<card>

ATTRIBUTE	DESCRIPTION
xml:space	Set to a fixed value of "preserve" as an instruction to XML processors.

<prev>

Description:	The prev tag declares a 'prev' task, indicating navigation to the previous URL on the history stack.
Contains:	<setvar>
Is Contained By:	<do>, <onevent>, <anchor>

<refresh>

Description:	Declares a refresh task to update the screen and device context (e.g., as specified by the contained 'setvar' tags).
Contains:	<setvar>
Is Contained By:	<do>, <onevent>, <anchor>

<select>

Description:	Provides a list of options from which a user may select.
Contains:	<optgroup>, <option> Note that <select> must contain at least one of these nested elements.
Is Contained By:	<fieldset>, <p>, <pre>
ATTRIBUTE	**DESCRIPTION**
title	A title for this element that may be used in the presentation of this object.
name	The name of the variable to set with the result of the selection.
value	The default value of the variable named in the 'name' attribute.
iname	The name of the variable to be set to the index of the selection (the currently selected option in the select list).
ivalue	The default selection index value.
multiple	If set to "true," the select list should accept multiple selections.
tabindex	Specifies the tab position of the current element.
xml:lang	The natural or formal language of the tag or its attributes.

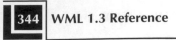

\<setvar\>

Description:	Specifies the variable to set in the current browser context as a side effect of executing a task.
Contains:	
Is Contained By:	\<go\>, \<prev\>, \<refresh\>
ATTRIBUTE (*=REQUIRED)	**DESCRIPTION**
*name**	Variable name.
*value**	Value to be assigned the variable.

\<small\>

Description:	Indicates that the text within the tags should be rendered with a small font.
Contains:	*Text*, \<em\>, \<strong\>, \<b\>, \<i\>, \<u\>, \<big\>, \<small\>, \<br\>, \<img\>, \<anchor\>, \<a\>, \<table\>
Is Contained By:	\<fieldset\>, \<td\>, \<em\>, \<strong\>, \<b\>, \<i\>, \<u\>, \<big\>, \<small\>, \<p\>
ATTRIBUTE	**DESCRIPTION**
xml:lang	The natural or formal language of the tag or its attributes.

\<strong\>

Description:	Indicates that the text within the tags should be rendered with some form of strong emphasis.
Contains:	*Text*, \<em\>, \<strong\>, \<b\>, \<i\>, \<u\>, \<big\>, \<small\>, \<br\>, \<img\>, \<anchor\>, \<a\>, \<table\>
Is Contained By:	\<fieldset\>, \<td\>, \<em\>, \<strong\>, \<b\>, \<i\>, \<u\>, \<big\>, \<small\>, \<p\>, \<pre\>
ATTRIBUTE	**DESCRIPTION**
xml:lang	The natural or formal language of the tag or its attributes.

\<table\>

Description:	Used with the 'tr' and 'td' tags to create aligned columns of text and images.
Contains:	\<tr\>
Is Contained By:	\<fieldset\>, \<em\>, \<strong\>, \<b\>, \<i\>, \<u\>, \<big\>, \<small\>, \<p\>
ATTRIBUTE (*=REQUIRED)	**DESCRIPTION**
title	A string that identifies the table.
align	Defines the column layout via a list of alignment designations – one for each column. "C" is center, "L" is left, and "R" is right aligned.
*columns**	The number of columns in the table (must be greater than zero).
xml:lang	The natural or formal language of the tag or its attributes.

\<td\>

Description:	Holds a single table cell of data within a table row (may be empty).
Contains:	*Text*, \<em\>, \<strong\>, \<b\>, \<i\>, \<u\>, \<big\>, \<small\>, \<br\>, \<img\>, \<anchor\>, \<a\>
Is Contained By:	\<tr\>
ATTRIBUTE	**DESCRIPTION**
xml:lang	The natural or formal language of the tag or its attributes.

\<template\>

Description:	Declares an event bindings (e.g., 'do' or 'onevent') that apply to all cards in the deck.
Contains:	\<do\>, \<onevent\>
Is Contained By:	\<wml\>
ATTRIBUTE	**DESCRIPTION**
onenterforward	The URI that is loaded when the user navigates into a card using a go task.
onenterbackward	The URI that is loaded when the user returns to the card from a programmable soft key (using a 'prev' task) or via a Back button.
ontimer	The URI that is loaded when the timer expires.

`<timer>`

Description:	Exposes a way to process idle time. The timer is started at card entry and stopped when the card is exited.
Contains:	
Is Contained By:	`<card>`
ATTRIBUTE (*=REQUIRED)	**DESCRIPTION**
name	The name of the variable to be set with the value of the timer.
*value**	The default value of the timer.

`<tr>`

Description:	A single table row.
Contains:	`<td>`
Is Contained By:	`<table>`

`<u>`

Description:	Indicates that the text within the tags should be rendered with under-line formatting.
Contains:	*Text*, `<em>`, `<strong>`, `<b>`, `<i>`, `<u>`, `<big>`, `<small>`, ` `, `<img>`, `<anchor>`, `<a>`, `<table>`
Is Contained By:	`<fieldset>`, `<td>`, `<em>`, `<strong>`, `<b>`, `<i>`, `<u>`, `<big>`, `<small>`, `<p>`, `<pre>`
ATTRIBUTE	**DESCRIPTION**
xml:lang	The natural or formal language of the tag or its attributes.

`<wml>`

Description:	Defines a WML deck, containing one or more cards.
Contains:	`<head>`, `<template>`, `<card>`
Is Contained By:	
ATTRIBUTE	**DESCRIPTION**
xml:lang	The natural or formal language of the tag or its attributes.

 **Source Code**

This appendix contains source code for the health inspection system examples from Chapters 5, 6, and 7 as well as the development case study found in Chapter 12. The source code in this appendix is available on the Web at *www.wirelessweb-books.com.*

HEALTH INSPECTION EXAMPLE

The health inspection system examples consist of:

- health.wml – main health inspection deck
- premises.wml – premises inspection deck
- food.wml – main food inspection deck
- food2.wml – food inspection details deck
- kitchen.wml – kitchen inspection deck
- kitcalc.wmls – kitchen calculations WMLScript compilation unit

health.wml

```
<?xml version="1.0"?>
<!DOCTYPE wml PUBLIC "-//WAPFORUM//DTD WML 1.1//EN"
          "http://www.wapforum.org/DTD/wml_1_1.dtd">
<!-- Health inspection system demo -->
<wml>
```

```
<!--First card is splash screen-->
<card id="Splash" ontimer="#MainCategories">

  <!--Set notice variable-->
  <onevent type="onenterforward">
    <refresh>
      <setvar name="notice"
              value="The annual charity bake sale will
                     be held next Friday at noon."/>
    </refresh>
  </onevent>

  <timer name="splashTimer" value="50"/>

  <do type="accept" label="Categories">
    <go href="#MainCategories"/>
  </do>
  <p align="center">
    <strong>Health Inspection</strong><br/>
    <em>*Notices*</em><br/>
    <i>The annual charity bake sale will
       be held next Friday at noon.
    </i>
  </p>
</card>

<!--Main health inspection categories-->
<card id="MainCategories" title="Categories">
  <do type="previous" label="Home">
    <go href="#Splash"/>
  </do>

  <p mode="nowrap">
    <strong>Categories</strong><br/>
    <a href="#Staff">Staff</a>
    <a href="food.wml">Food</a>
    <a href="premises.wml">Premises</a>
    <a href="#Animals">Animals</a>
  </p>
</card>

<!--Place holder for staff inspections-->
<card id="Staff" title="Staff">
  <do type="previous" label="Categories">
      <prev/>
  </do>
  <p>Staff inspection subcategories will go here...</p>
</card>

<!--Place holder for animal inspections-->
<card id="Animals" title="Animals">
  <do type="previous" label="Categories">
```

```
      <prev/>
    </do>
    <p>Animals and Pests subcategories will go here...</p>
  </card>
</wml>
```

premises.wml

```
<?xml version="1.0"?>
<!DOCTYPE wml PUBLIC "-//WAPFORUM//DTD WML 1.1//EN"
              "http://www.wapforum.org/DTD/wml_1_1.dtd">
<!-- Premises inspection -->
<wml>
  <template>
    <do type="accept" label="Premises" name="home">
      <go href="#PremisesHome"/>
    </do>
  </template>

  <card id="PremisesHome" title="Premises">
    <do type="accept" name="home">
      <noop/>
    </do>
    <do type="previous" label="Categories" name="prev">
      <go href="health.wml#MainCategories"/>
    </do>
    <p>
      <strong>Select Area</strong><br/>
      <a href="kitchen.wml">Kitchen</a>
      <a href="#Bar">Bar</a>
      <a href="#Dining">Dining Room</a>
    </p>
  </card>

  <!-- Placeholder -->
  <card id="Bar" title="Bar">
    <p>
      <strong>Bar Inspection</strong><br/>
      Bar inspection details will go here...
    </p>
  </card>

  <!-- Placeholder -->
  <card id="Dining" title="Dining">
    <p>
      <strong>Dining Room Inspection</strong><br/>
      Dining room inspection details will go here...
    </p>
  </card>

</wml>
```

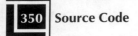

food.wml

```
<?xml version="1.0"?>
<!DOCTYPE wml PUBLIC "-//WAPFORUM//DTD WML 1.1//EN"
                "http://www.wapforum.org/DTD/wml_1_1.dtd">
<!-- Food inspection main deck -->
<wml>
  <template>
    <do type="previous" label="Food" name="home">
      <go href="#FoodHome"/>
    </do>
  </template>

  <card id="FoodHome" title="Food">
    <do type="previous" label="Categories" name="home">
      <go href="health.wml#MainCategories"/>
    </do>
    <p>
      <strong>Food Inspection</strong><br/>
      <a href="#MeatSelect">Meat</a>
      <a href="#DairySelect">Dairy Products</a>
      <a href="#FruitVegSelect">Fruit and Veg.</a>
    </p>
  </card>

  <card id="MeatSelect" title="Select">
    <do type="accept" label="Inspect" name="inspect">
      <go href="food2.wml#MeatInspect"/>
    </do>
    <p>
      <strong>Select Meat</strong>
      <select name="meatType" value="Beef">
        <option value="Beef">Beef</option>
        <option value="Pork">Pork</option>
        <option value="Poultry">Poultry</option>
        <option value="Other Meat">Other</option>
      </select>
    </p>
  </card>

  <card id="DairySelect" title="Select">
    <do type="accept" label="Inspect" name="inspect">
      <go href="food2.wml#DairyInspect"/>
    </do>
    <p>
      <strong>Select Dairy</strong>
      <select name="dairyType" value="Butter">
        <option value="Butter">Butter</option>
        <option value="Cheese">Cheese</option>
        <option value="Milk">Milk</option>
      </select>
```

```wml
      </p>
  </card>

  <card id="FruitVegSelect" title="Select">
    <do type="accept" label="Inspect" name="inspect">
      <go href="food2.wml#FruitVegInspect"/>
    </do>
    <p>
      <strong>Select Fruit or Veg.</strong>
      <select name="fruitVegType" value="Apple">
        <option value="Apple">Apple</option>
        <option value="Cucumber">Cucumber</option>
        <option value="Lettuce">Lettuce</option>
        <option value="Tomatoe">Tomatoes</option>
      </select>
    </p>
  </card>
</wml>
```

food2.wml

```wml
<?xml version="1.0"?>
<!DOCTYPE wml PUBLIC "-//WAPFORUM//DTD WML 1.1//EN"
              "http://www.wapforum.org/DTD/wml_1_1.dtd">
<!-- Food inspection details deck -->
<wml>
  <template>
    <do type="previous" label="Food" name="home">
      <go href="food.wml#FoodHome"/>
    </do>
  </template>

  <card id="MeatInspect" title="Meat">
    <do type="accept" label="Submit" name="submit">
      <go href="food.wml#MeatSelect"/>
    </do>
    <p>
      <strong>$meatType Inspection</strong><br/>
      <fieldset title="packaging">Packaging<br/>
        Material OK?
        <select name="material" value="true">
          <option value="true">Yes</option>
          <option value="false">No</option>
        </select>
        Sealed?
        <select name="seal" value="true">
          <option value="true">Yes</option>
          <option value="false">No</option>
        </select>
      </fieldset>
```

```
      <fieldset title="Preparation Area">Preparation<br/>
        Machinery Clean?
        <select name="machinery" value="true">
          <option value="true">Yes</option>
          <option value="false">No</option>
        </select>
        Air Temp? <input name="temperature" format="N*N"/>
      </fieldset>
    </p>
  </card>

  <card id="DairyInspect" title="Dairy">
    <do type="accept" label="Submit" name="submit">
      <go href="food.wml#DairySelect"/>
    </do>
    <p>
      <strong>$dairyType Inspection</strong><br/>
      <!--demonstrates use of named character entities-->
      Cream content in homogenized milk must be &gt;= 3%.
      Temperatures of cheese &amp; milk should be &lt; 5 degrees.
    </p>
  </card>

  <card id="FruitVegInspect" title="Fruit+Veg">
    <do type="accept" label="Submit" name="submit">
      <go href="food.wml#FruitVegSelect"/>
    </do>
    <p>
      <strong>$fruitVegType Inspection</strong><br/>
      Inspection details will go here...
    </p>
  </card>
</wml>
```

kitchen.wml

```
<?xml version="1.0"?>
<!DOCTYPE wml PUBLIC "-//WAPFORUM//DTD WML 1.1//EN" "http://
  www.wapforum.org/DTD/wml_1_1.dtd">
<!--Kitchen Inspection-->
<wml>
  <card id="Kitchen" title="Kitchen">
    <do type="accept" label="Submit">
      <go href="kitcalc.wmls#area($length, $width)"/>
    </do>
    <p>
      <a href="premises.wml#PremisesHome">Back</a><br/>
      <strong>Enter Kitchen Size</strong><br/>
```

```
     Length (m): <input name="length" format="N*N"/>
     Width (m): <input name="width" format="N*N"/>
  </p>
 </card>

 <!-- Area results + inspection details -->
 <card id="Results" title="Details">
   <!-- Note that fuels will also be retrieved by validate() -->
   <do type="accept" label="Validate">
     <go href="kitcalc.wmls#validate($area, $light, $fans)"/>
   </do>
   <p>
     <strong>Kitchen Details</strong><br/>
     Area is: $area sq.meters<br/>
     ------------<br/>
     Light (lux): <input name="light" format="N*N"/>
     Number of Fans: <input name="fans" value = "0" format="N*N"/>
     Cooking Fuel
     <select name="fuel" value="gas" multiple="true">
       <option value="gas">Natural Gas</option>
       <option value="electric">Electric</option>
       <option value="propane">Propane</option>
       <option value="wood">Wood</option>
     </select>
  </p>
 </card>

 <card id="OKResults" title="OK">
   <do type="accept" label="Another">
     <go href="#Kitchen"/>
   </do>
   <p>
     <strong>No Violations</strong><br/>
     Light: $(light), >= $validLight<br/>
     Fans: $(fans), >= $validFans<br/>
     Fuels: $fuel OK
  </p>
 </card>

 <card id="Warnings" title="Warnings">
   <do type="accept" label="Another">
     <go href="#Kitchen"/>
   </do>
   <p>
     <strong>Warnings</strong><br/>
     $warning
  </p>
 </card>
</wml>
```

kitcalc.wmls

```
/* Health Inspection Application
   Kitchen calculations WMLScript
*/

// Calculate the area of a rectangle and go to
// the results card
extern function area(length, width) {
  var area = length * width;
  WMLBrowser.setVar("area", area);
  WMLBrowser.go("#Results");
};

/* Validate light and fans for the specified area
   Light minimum is measured at counter level
   for preparation area (550 LUX)
   Assume fan averages 500 cubic meters/hour,
   kitchen ceiling is 2.5 meters high, and we need
   8 complete air changes per hour:
     # of fans = (room volume * 8) / 500  or
                 (room area / 25)
*/
extern function validate(area, light, fans) {
  // valid values
  var validLight = 550; // LUX measured at counter height
  var validFans = Float.ceil(area / 25); // see above
  var warning = "";

  // use getVar to get fuels list
  var fuel = WMLBrowser.getVar("fuel");
  var VALID = "VALID";  // assume fuel OK
  var validFuel = validateFuel(fuel, VALID);

  // build warning message if required
  if (light < validLight)
    warning = String.format("Light is less than %d lux. ", validLight);
  if (fans < validFans)
    warning += "Should have at least " + validFans + " fans. ";
  if (validFuel != VALID)
    warning += validFuel;

  // return to the appropriate card in the calling deck
  if (warning == "") { // no problems
    WMLBrowser.setVar("validLight", validLight);
    WMLBrowser.setVar("validFans", validFans);
    WMLBrowser.go("#OKResults");
  }
  else {
    // Explicit navigation
```

```
//      WMLBrowser.setVar("warning", warning);
//      WMLBrowser.go("#Warnings");

    // Use dialogs to get user preference
    if (Dialogs.confirm(warning, "New Test", "Redo" ))
      WMLBrowser.go("#Kitchen");
    else
      WMLBrowser.go("#Results");
  };
};


// Validate fuel combinations returning a warning
// string if invalid or VALID if OK
function validateFuel(fuel, VALID) {
  var SEPARATOR = ";";
  var GASES="gas,propane";
  var gasesSelected = false;
  var WOOD="wood";
  var woodSelected = false;
  var WARNING = "Illegal to mix gas fuels and wood!";

  var nFuels = String.elements(fuel, SEPARATOR);
  for (var i=0; i<nFuels; i++) {
    var thisFuel = String.elementAt(fuel, i, SEPARATOR);
    if (String.find(GASES, thisFuel) >= 0)
      gasesSelected = true;
    if (thisFuel == WOOD)
      woodSelected = true;
    if (gasesSelected && woodSelected)
      break;
  };

  if (woodSelected && gasesSelected)
    return WARNING;

  return VALID;
};
```

ALCOHOL INSPECTION CASE STUDY

The alcohol inspection system examples consist of:

- ▣ WML decks and fragments.

- ▣ Java source code.

- ▣ SQL scripts to set up and populate the database.

WML Decks and Fragments

The following WML decks are used in the alcohol inspection application:

- login.wml, which displays the initial login card.

- unauthorized.wml, which is displayed when user authorization fails.

- inspectionentryp1.wml, which displays the first portion of an inspection entry form.

- inspectionentryp2.wml, which displays the closing portion of an inspection entry form.

- previousschedule.wml, which is displayed after an inspection has been completed.

- scheduleselection.wml, which allows the inspector to query the schedule database by date, location, or next scheduled inspection.

- error.wml, which displays a general error message when a severe system error occurs.

- invalidates.wml, which contains a date entry error message.

The remainder of WML is dynamically generated by the Java code.

login.wml

```
<?xml version="1.0"?>
<!DOCTYPE wml PUBLIC "-//WAPFORUM//DTD WML 1.1//EN"
                     "http://www.wapforum.org/DTD/wml_1_1.dtd">
<wml>
  <card id="Welcome" title="Inspections">

    <onevent type="ontimer">
      <go href="scheduleselection.wml"/>
    </onevent>
    <timer name="splashtimeout" value="300"/>

    <do type="accept" label="Schedule">
      <go href="scheduleselection.wml"/>
```

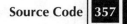

```
    </do>
    <do type="prev" label="Back">
      <prev/>
    </do>

    <p align="center">
      <img alt="Check " src="images/check.wbmp" align="middle"/><br/>
      Inspections
    </p>
  </card>
</wml>
```

unauthorized.wml

```
<?xml version="1.0"?>
<!DOCTYPE wml PUBLIC "-//WAPFORUM//DTD WML 1.1//EN"
                  "http://www.wapforum.org/DTD/wml_1_1.dtd">

<wml>
  <card>
    <do type="prev" label="Back">
      <prev/>
    </do>
    <p>
      Unauthorized access.
    </p>
  </card>
</wml>
```

inspectionentryp1.wml (WML fragment)

```
<?xml version="1.0"?>
<!DOCTYPE wml PUBLIC "-//WAPFORUM//DTD WML 1.1//EN"
                  "http://www.wapforum.org/DTD/wml_1_1.dtd">

<wml>
<card id="ientry" title="Inspection Results">
  <onevent type="onenterforward">
    <refresh>
      <setvar name="checks" value=""/>
      <setvar name="idcount" value=""/>
      <setvar name="status" value=""/>
      <setvar name="comments" value=""/>
    </refresh>
  </onevent>
  <do type="prev" label="Back">
    <prev/>
  </do>
```

```
<p align="center">
  <big>Inspection Results</big>
</p>
<p align="left">
  Checks:
  <select title="Checks" name="checks" multiple="true" value="">
    <option value="10">Tax Stamps</option>
    <option value="02">Stock</option>
    <option value="05">Measures</option>
    <option value="06">Underage</option>
  </select>
  ID's
  <input name ="idcount" format="N*N"/>
  Status:
  <select title="Status" name="status" value="">
    <option value="pass">Pass</option>
    <option value="reinspect">Reinspect</option>
    <option value="fail">Fail</option>
  </select>
  Comments:
  <input title="Comments" name="comments"/>
</p>
<do type="accept" label="Submit">
```

inspectionentryp2.wml (WML fragment)

```
      <postfield name="checks" value="$(checks)"/>
      <postfield name="idcount" value="$(idcount)"/>
      <postfield name="status" value="$(status)"/>
      <postfield name="comments" value="$(comments)"/></go>
    </do>
  </card>
</wml>
```

previousschedule.wml

```
<?xml version="1.0"?>
<!DOCTYPE wml PUBLIC "-//WAPFORUM//DTD WML 1.1//EN"
                    "http://www.wapforum.org/DTD/wml_1_1.dtd">

<wml>
  <card>
    <do type="accept" label="New">
      <go href="scheduleselection.wml"/>
    </do>
    <do type="prev" label="Back">
      <prev/>
    </do>
    <p>
```

```
     You may navigate to the previously displayed schedule by
     using the BACK button or may choose a different schedule query
     by using the New button.
  </p>
 </card>
</wml>
```

scheduleselection.wml

```
<?xml version="1.0"?>
<!DOCTYPE wml PUBLIC "-//WAPFORUM//DTD WML 1.1//EN"
                     "http://www.wapforum.org/DTD/wml_1_1.dtd">
<wml>
<template>
  <do type="prev" label="Back">
    <prev/>
  </do>
</template>

<card id="selection" title="Schedule">
  <do type="help" label="Help">
    <go href="#selecthelp"/>
  </do>
  <p align="center">Schedule</p>
  <p align="left">
    <anchor title="Next Inspection">
      <go method="post" href="servlet/wmlservlet">
        <postfield name="op" value="next"/>
      </go>Next Inspection</anchor><br/>
    <a title="By Date" href="#bydate">Dates</a><br/>
    <a title="By Location" href="#bylocation">Location</a><br/>
  </p>
</card>

<card id="bylocation" title="Location">
  <do type="accept">
    <go method="post" href="servlet/wmlservlet">
      <postfield name="op" value="byloc"/>
      <postfield name="territory" value="$territory"/>
    </go>
  </do>
  <p align="left">
    Territory:
    <select name="territory" value="hal">
      <option title="Halifax" value="hal">Halifax</option>
      <option title="Dartmouth" value="dart">Dartmouth</option>
      <option title="Bedford" value="bed">Bedford</option>
    </select>
  </p>
</card>
```

```
<card id="bydate" title="By Dates">
  <do type="accept" label="Query">
    <go method="post" href="servlet/wmlservlet">
      <postfield name="op" value="bydate"/>
      <postfield name="datestart" value="$startdate"/>
      <postfield name="dateend" value="$enddate"/>
    </go>
  </do>
  <p align="left">
    Start[dd/mm/yyyy]:
    <input name="startdate" title="Start" format="NN/NN/NNNN"/>
    <br/>
    End[dd/mm/yyyy]:
    <input name="enddate" title="End" format="NN/NN/NNNN"/>
  </p>
</card>

<card id="selecthelp">
  <p>
    <strong>Dates:</strong>
    Select inspections scheduled between user entered dates.<br/>
    <strong>Location:</strong>
    Select inspections scheduled for selected areas.<br/>
    <strong>Next:</strong>
    Select the next scheduled inspection.
  </p>
</card>
</wml>
```

error.wml

```
<?xml version="1.0"?>
<!DOCTYPE wml PUBLIC "-//WAPFORUM//DTD WML 1.1//EN"
                     "http://www.wapforum.org/DTD/wml_1_1.dtd">
<wml>
  <card>
    <do type="prev" label="Back">
      <prev/>
    </do>
    <p>
      An error has occurred during processing of the last request.
      Either an internal error has been encountered or the request
      was malformed (unsupported operation?).<br/>
      Please re-try the last operation (though this is
      unlikely to work).
    </p>
  </card>
</wml>
```

invaliddates.wml

```
<?xml version="1.0"?>
<!DOCTYPE wml PUBLIC "-//WAPFORUM//DTD WML 1.1//EN"
                    "http://www.wapforum.org/DTD/wml_1_1.dtd">
<wml>
<card>
  <do type="prev" label="Back">
    <prev/>
  </do>
  <p>
    One or both of the entered dates is invalid.
    Please re-enter.
  </p>
</card>
</wml>
```

Java Source Code

The following Java classes are used in the alcohol inspection application:

- WmlServlet.java, which is the controller for this application.

- InspectionModel.java, which implements the business model for inspections.

- Inspection.java, which encapsulates an inspection.

- Establishment.java, which encapsulates an establishment.

- Operations.java, which contains a set of valid operations that an inspector can perform.

- InspectionDisplay.java, which visualizes inspections, schedules, and establishments.

- PendingInspection_DB.java, which implements SQL operations on the Inspection database.

- DBConnectionManager.java, which provides database connections.

WmlServlet.java

```java
import java.io.*;
import java.text.*;
import java.util.*;
import javax.servlet.*;
import javax.servlet.http.*;

/**
 * WML servlet - processes the inspection operations (see doGet() for
 * supported operations).  This consists primarily of parsing parameters from
 * the requests, constructing a model based on the request, rendering this
 * into WML and passing that to the user agent.
 */
public class WmlServlet extends HttpServlet {

  /* the number of results to display at any one time */
  private final static int MAX_ENTRIES = 4;

  /* the URLBase for static files read/served by the servlet */
  protected static String URLBase = "";

  /**
   * Read the initialization parameters: the database driver class,
   * username and password.
   * These are to be set in the servlet initialization configuration.
   * @throws javax.servlet.ServletException if all initialization parameters
   * could not be read or the DBConnectionManager could not be initialized.
   */
  public void init() throws javax.servlet.ServletException {
    boolean success = false;

    /* the database connection parameters passed to
       DBConnectionManager which will serve connections as needed */
    String jdbcclass = null;
    String dbname = null;
    String dbusername = null;
    String dbpassword = null;
    String maxconnections = null;
    int max;

    URLBase = getInitParameter("URLBase");

    /* read the database connection parameters */
    jdbcclass = getInitParameter("jdbcclass");
    dbname = getInitParameter("dbname");
    dbusername = getInitParameter("dbusername");
    dbpassword = getInitParameter("dbpassword");
    maxconnections = getInitParameter("maxconnections");

    try {
```

```
      max = Integer.parseInt(maxconnections);
    } catch(NumberFormatException nfe) {
      throw new javax.servlet.ServletException("Couldn't read the maximum "
          + "connections parameter.");
    }

    /* validate the parameters; if the DBConnectionManager initializes then
       consider initialization successful */
    success = DBConnectionManager.init(jdbcclass,
        dbname,
        dbusername,
        dbpassword,
        max);
    if (false == success) {
      throw new javax.servlet.ServletException("Couldn't initialize the "
          + "database connection manager.");
    }
}

/**
 * Release all resources held by the servlet, in this case
 * database connections.
 */
public void destroy() {
  DBConnectionManager.release();
}

/**
 * Process POST operations, just a wrapper around doGet
 * @param request the Http request from the user agent
 * @param response where the response is to be written
 * @see #doGet()
 */
public void doPost(HttpServletRequest request,
  HttpServletResponse response) throws IOException, ServletException {
  doGet(request, response);
}

/**
 * Parse out the operation and call the appropriate
 * method.
 * @param request the Http request from the user agent
 * @param response where the response is to be written
 */
public void doGet(HttpServletRequest request,
  HttpServletResponse response) throws IOException, ServletException {
  String operation = null;
  String user = null;

  /* ensure we have an authenticated user */
  user = request.getRemoteUser();
```

```
    if (null == user) {
      /* encode a redirect to the "unauthorized access" deck,
         n.b. this could be caused by the authentication header not
         being passed to us, or incorrect webserver - servlet engine
         integration */
      redirectToDeck(request, response,
        InspectionDisplay.UNAUTHORIZED_DECK);
      return;
    }


  /* extract the requested operation and call the corresponding private
     method for that operation.

     The operation is simply a parameter in the Http GET or POST request.
     Each operation will have corresponding parameters which are parsed
     from the request by the private method which corresponds to the
     operation.  e.g. when op=bydate is found, querybyDate() is called
     to process the operation.  It is responsible for extracting the
     datestart and dateend parameters, querying the database and
     generating a response.
  */
  operation = request.getParameter(Operations.OPERATION);

  /* if an operation was found, trim any whitespace and
     convert it to lowercase to make string comparisons
     simple */
  if (null != operation) {
    operation = operation.trim().toLowerCase();

    if (operation.equals(Operations.OP_INSPECTENTRY)) {
      inspectEntry(request, response, user);
    } else if (operation.equals(Operations.OP_INSPECT)) {
      displayInspectionEntryScreen(request, response, user);
    } else if (operation.equals(Operations.OP_DETAILS)) {
      queryDetails(request, response, user);
    } else if (operation.equals(Operations.OP_QUERYBYDATE)) {
      querybyDate(request, response, user);
    } else if (operation.equals(Operations.OP_QUERYBYLOCATION)) {
      querybyLocation(request, response, user);
    } else if (operation.equals(Operations.OP_QUERYNEXT)) {
      queryNext(request, response, user);
    } else {
      /* unknown operation (this should never happen) */
      redirectToDeck(request, response,
        InspectionDisplay.INTERNALERROR_DECK);
    }
  }
}


/**
 * Redirect the user agent to a static deck via an HTTP redirect.
```

```
 * @param request the Http request from the user agent
 * @param response where the response is to be written
 * @param deck the name of the static WML file
 */
private void redirectToDeck(HttpServletRequest request,
  HttpServletResponse response,
  String deck) {
  try {
    /* some gateways|user agents need the content type
       to be set otherwise they complain about HTML content type being
       passed */
    response.setContentType("text/vnd.wap.wml");
    String encodedURL = response.encodeRedirectURL(request.getContextPath()
      + "/" + deck);
    response.sendRedirect(encodedURL);
  } catch (java.io.IOException io) {
    System.err.println("wmlservlet.redirectToDeck():ioexception encodingURL");
  }
}


/**
 * Send the supplied content to the HTTP response.
 * @param response where the response is to be written
 * @param deck the content
 */
private void writeResponse(HttpServletResponse response,
    String deck) {
  response.setContentType("text/vnd.wap.wml");
   /* tell the user agent to not cache this deck simply
      to ease development.  Caching is a nightmare when
      you are developing and ultimately what is cached and
      not cached is an application dependent decision */
  response.setHeader("Cache-control", "no-cache");

  try {
    PrintWriter out = response.getWriter();
    out.print(deck);
    out.flush();
    out.close();
  } catch (java.io.IOException ioe) {
    /* can't do much about this */
  }
}


/**
 * Process the query next operation.  Output a WML deck with
 * the entries scheduled for the specified inspector ordered by date.
 * @param request the Http request from the user agent
 * @param response where the response is to be written
 * @param inspector the name of the inspector to query for
 */
```

```
private void queryNext(HttpServletRequest request,
    HttpServletResponse response,
    String inspector) {
  /* request parameter related variables */
  String startNdxParam = null;
  int startNdx = 1;

  /*  model and display variables */
  InspectionModel model = null;
  InspectionDisplay view = null;
  StringBuffer deck = null;
  java.util.Vector params = null;
  java.util.Vector values = null;

  /* parse the optional parameters; starting index */
  startNdxParam = request.getParameter(Operations.START_NDX);
  try {
    int x = Integer.parseInt(startNdxParam);
    startNdx = x;
  } catch (Exception e) {
    /* either startNdxParam is null or no int
       could be parsed from it */
    System.err.println("wmlservlet.queryNext():using default startndx");
  }

  model = new InspectionModel();
  if (true == model.queryNext(inspector, startNdx, MAX_ENTRIES)) {
    /* at this point we have a model which may or may not have
       any entries, but we can at least display a deck from it */

    /* here we've made a design tradeoff in favour of simplicity.
       If there are more inspections than can be displayed
       at one time (MAX_ENTRIES), we will use these to add an entry
       to the generated WML deck that executes the same query but
       results in the next MAX_ENTRIES being displayed.
       This is done by building a model which holds
       the number of entries we are willing to display.  The
       start parameter is used to pick the starting query results
       entry from which the model is built.

       N.B. this is fine for a small example application but doesn't
       address scalability issues.  Ideally query results should be
       cached and cached results returned instead of executing
       the same query again.
    */

    params = new java.util.Vector();
    values = new java.util.Vector();
    params.add(Operations.START_NDX);
    values.add(Integer.toString(startNdx + MAX_ENTRIES));
```

```
    /* generate a WML deck containing a single card which will display
       the names of each establishment contained in the model,
       selecting an establishment will result in the establishment
       details being displayed

       by using getContextPath() and getServletPath() we don't need to
       'hard code' our servlet path when we generate href's, we simply
       parse it from the incoming request here and pass it to the routines
       which generate WML

       the operation, parameters and values are supplied so we can
       construct an entry that will display the next set of results
    */
    deck = new StringBuffer();
    view = new InspectionDisplay();
    view.establishmentSelectList(deck,
      model,
      "",
      inspector,
      request.getContextPath() + request.getServletPath(),
      Operations.OP_QUERYNEXT,
      params,
      values);

    /* attempt to add the parameters for this request to the HttpSession
       if it exists.  Other operation processing routines will use this to
       return to this previous operation.

       Once inspection results have been submitted (and accepted) we
       allow the user to return to the list of "query" results by
       executing the latest query operation with the same parameters.

       To accomplish this, we store operation and parameters in the
       user's session and retrieve these once in inspectEntry() which
       processes the inspection results submission.
    */
    HttpSession theSession = request.getSession(true);
    theSession.setAttribute(Operations.OPERATION, Operations.OP_QUERYNEXT);
    writeResponse(response, deck.toString());
  } else {
    redirectToDeck(request, response, InspectionDisplay.INTERNALERROR_DECK);
  }
}


/**
 * Process the query by date operation. Accept a start and end date
 * parameter and output a WML deck with entries scheduled within that
 * range of dates and for the specified inspector.
 * @param request the Http request from the user agent
 * @param response where the response is to be written
```

```java
 * @param inspector the name of the inspector to query for
 */
private void querybyDate(HttpServletRequest request,
    HttpServletResponse response,
    String inspector) {
  /* request parameter related variables */
  String startDateParam = null;
  String endDateParam = null;
  String startNdxParam = null;
  java.util.Date startDate = null;
  java.util.Date endDate = null;
  int startNdx = 1;

  /* model and display variables */
  InspectionModel model = null;
  InspectionDisplay view = null;
  StringBuffer deck = null;
  java.util.Vector params = null;
  java.util.Vector values = null;

  /* extract the start and end dates from the request,
     validate they can be converted to dates */
  startDateParam = request.getParameter(Operations.DATE_START);
  endDateParam = request.getParameter(Operations.DATE_END);

  try {
    startDate  = new java.util.Date(startDateParam);
    endDate  = new java.util.Date(endDateParam);
  } catch (Exception e) {
    /* failed parsing the dates from the request, either the
       parameters did not exist or could not be converted to dates */
    System.err.println("wmlservlet.querybyDate():failed parsing dates");
    redirectToDeck(request, response, InspectionDisplay.INVALIDDATES_DECK);
    return;
  }

  /* parse the optional parameters; starting index */
  startNdxParam = request.getParameter(Operations.START_NDX);
  try {
    int x = Integer.parseInt(startNdxParam);
    startNdx = x;
  } catch (Exception e) {
    /* either startNdxParam is null or no int
       could be parsed from it */
    System.err.println("wmlservlet.querybyDate():using default startndx");
  }

  /* build a model */
  model = new InspectionModel();
  if (true == model.querybyDate(inspector, startDate, endDate,
    startNdx, MAX_ENTRIES)) {
```

```
      /* at this point we have a model which may or may not have
         any entries, but we can at least display a deck from it */
      params = new java.util.Vector();
      values = new java.util.Vector();
      params.add(Operations.DATE_START);
      values.add(startDateParam);
      params.add(Operations.DATE_END);
      values.add(endDateParam);
      /* point to the next group of entries */
      params.add(Operations.START_NDX);
      values.add(Integer.toString(startNdx + MAX_ENTRIES));

    /* generate a WML deck containing a single card which will display
       the names of each establishment contained in the model.
       Selecting an establishment will result in the establishment
       details being displayed */
    deck = new StringBuffer();
    view = new InspectionDisplay();
    view.establishmentSelectList(deck,
      model,
      "",
      inspector,
      request.getContextPath() + request.getServletPath(),
      Operations.OP_QUERYBYDATE,
      params,
      values);

    /* attempt to add the parameters for this request to the HttpSession
       if it exists, other operation processing routines will use this to
       return to this previous operation.

       Once inspection results have been submitted (and accepted) we
       allow the user to return to the list of "query" results by
       executing the latest query operation with the same parameters.

       To accomplish this, we store operation and parameters in the
       user's session and retrieve these once in inspectEntry() which
       processes the inspection results submission.
    */
    HttpSession theSession = request.getSession(true);
    theSession.setAttribute(Operations.OPERATION, Operations.OP_QUERYBYDATE);
    theSession.setAttribute(Operations.DATE_START, startDateParam);
    theSession.setAttribute(Operations.DATE_END, endDateParam);

    writeResponse(response, deck.toString());
  } else {
    /* constructing the model failed */
      redirectToDeck(request, response, InspectionDisplay.INTERNALERROR_DECK);
  }
}
```

```
/**
 * Process the query by location operation. Accept a location parameter,
 * and output a WML deck with entries scheduled within that location and
 * for the specified inspector.
 * @param request the Http request from the user agent
 * @param response where the response is to be written
 * @param inspector the name of the inspector to query for
 */
private void querybyLocation(HttpServletRequest request,
    HttpServletResponse response,
    String inspector) {
  /* request parameter related variables */
  String locationParam = null;
  String startNdxParam = null;
  int startNdx = 1;

  /* model and display variables */
  InspectionModel model = null;
  InspectionDisplay view = null;
  StringBuffer deck = null;
  java.util.Vector params = null;
  java.util.Vector values = null;

  /* extract the location from the request */
  locationParam = request.getParameter(Operations.TERRITORY);

  /* parse the optional parameters; starting index */
  startNdxParam = request.getParameter(Operations.START_NDX);
  try {
    int x = Integer.parseInt(startNdxParam);
    startNdx = x;
  } catch (Exception e) {
    /* either startNdxParam is null or no int
       could be parsed from it */
    System.err.println("wmlservlet.querybyLocation():using default startndx");
  }

  model = new InspectionModel();
  if (true == model.querybyLocation(inspector, locationParam,
    startNdx,
    MAX_ENTRIES)) {

    /* at this point we have a model which may or may not have
       any entries, but we can at least display a deck from it */
    params = new java.util.Vector();
    values = new java.util.Vector();
    params.add(Operations.TERRITORY);
    values.add(locationParam);
    params.add(Operations.START_NDX);
    values.add(Integer.toString(startNdx + MAX_ENTRIES));
```

```
    deck = new StringBuffer();
    view = new InspectionDisplay();
    view.establishmentSelectList(deck,
      model,
      "",
      inspector,
      request.getContextPath() + request.getServletPath(),
      Operations.OP_QUERYBYLOCATION,
      params,
      values);

    /* attempt to add the parameters for this request to the HttpSession
       if it exists, other operation processing routines will use this to
       return to this previous operation */
    HttpSession theSession = request.getSession(true);
    theSession.setAttribute(Operations.OPERATION,
      Operations.OP_QUERYBYLOCATION);
    theSession.setAttribute(Operations.TERRITORY, locationParam);

    writeResponse(response, deck.toString());
  } else {
    /* failed constructing the model */
    redirectToDeck(request, response, InspectionDisplay.INTERNALERROR_DECK);
  }
}

/**
 * Process the details operation.  Output a WML deck with
 * the details of a particular establishment.
 * @param request the Http request from the user agent
 * @param response where the response is to be written
 * @param inspector the name of the inspector asking for
 * details of the establishment
 */
private void queryDetails(HttpServletRequest request,
    HttpServletResponse response,
    String inspector) {
  /* request parameter related variables */
  String establishmentParam = null;
  String scheduledDateParam = null;
  java.util.Date scheduledDate = null;

  /* model and display variables */
  InspectionModel model = null;
  InspectionDisplay view = null;
  StringBuffer deck = null;

  /* parse the establishment id from the request */
  establishmentParam = request.getParameter(Operations.ESTABLISHMENT);

  /* extract the scheduled date from the request, convert to date
```

```
      n.b. this relies on us having written out the date in a format
      that can be parsed by the java.util.Date constructor */
  scheduledDateParam = request.getParameter(Operations.SCHEDULED);
  try {
      scheduledDate = new java.util.Date(scheduledDateParam);
  } catch (Exception e) {
      /* failed parsing the date from the request, either the
         parameter did not exist or could not be converted to a date
         which means we incorrectly built the deck containing
         the request   */
      System.err.println("wmlservlet.queryDetails():failed parsing date");
      redirectToDeck(request, response, InspectionDisplay.INTERNALERROR_DECK);
      return;
  }

  model = new InspectionModel();
  if (model.queryDetails(inspector, establishmentParam, scheduledDate)) {
      /* at this point we have a model which may or may not have
         any entries, but we can at least display a deck from it */
      deck = new StringBuffer();
      view = new InspectionDisplay();
      view.inspectEstablishment(deck,
        model,
        inspector,
        request.getContextPath() + request.getServletPath());

      writeResponse(response, deck.toString());
  } else {
      redirectToDeck(request, response, InspectionDisplay.INTERNALERROR_DECK);
  }
}


/**
 * Process the inspect operation.  Display a WML deck allowing
 * the user to enter inspection details for the specified
 * establishment.
 * @param request the Http request from the user agent
 * @param response where the response is to be written
 * @param inspector the name of the inspector asking for
 * details of the establishment
 */
private void displayInspectionEntryScreen(HttpServletRequest request,
    HttpServletResponse response,
    String inspector) {
  /* request parameter related variables */
  String establishmentParam = null;
  String scheduledDateParam = null;
  java.util.Date scheduledDate = null;
  java.util.Vector params = null;
  java.util.Vector values = null;
```

```
    /* display variables */
    InspectionDisplay view = null;
    StringBuffer deck = null;

    /* parse the establishment id from the request */
    establishmentParam = request.getParameter(Operations.ESTABLISHMENT);

    /* extract the scheduled date from the request, convert to date.
       N.B. this relies on us having written out the date in a format
       that can be parsed by the java.util.Date constructor */
    scheduledDateParam = request.getParameter(Operations.SCHEDULED);
    try {
      scheduledDate = new java.util.Date(scheduledDateParam);
    } catch (Exception e) {
      /* failed parsing the date from the request, either the
         parameter did not exist or could not be converted to a date
         which means we incorrectly built the deck containing the request  */
      System.err.println("wmlservlet.displayInspectionEntryScreen()"
        + ":failed parsing date");
      redirectToDeck(request, response, InspectionDisplay.INTERNALERROR_DECK);
      return;
    }

    /* display the inspection entry deck with the submit operation encoded
       with the parameters we've extracted from this request */
    params = new java.util.Vector();
    values = new java.util.Vector();

    params.add(Operations.OPERATION);
    values.add(Operations.OP_INSPECTENTRY);
    params.add(Operations.SCHEDULED);
    values.add(InspectionDisplay.formatDate(scheduledDate));
    params.add(Operations.ESTABLISHMENT);
    values.add(establishmentParam);
    params.add(Operations.INSPECTOR);
    values.add(inspector);
    deck = new StringBuffer();
    view = new InspectionDisplay();
    view.inspectionEntry(deck,
        URLBase,
        request.getContextPath() + request.getServletPath(),
        params,
        values);

    writeResponse(response, deck.toString());
  }

  /**
   * Accept the inspection data for an establishment scheduled for
   * inspection on a specific date.
```

```
 * @param request the Http request from the user agent
 * @param response where the response is to be written
 * @param inspector the name of the inspector performing
 * the inspection
 */
private void inspectEntry(HttpServletRequest request,
    HttpServletResponse response,
    String inspector) {
  boolean success = false;

  /* request parameter related variables */
  String establishmentParam = null;
  String scheduledDateParam = null;
  java.util.Date scheduledDate = null;
  String checksParam = null;
  String idcountParam = null;
  String comments = null;
  String status = null;

  /* model and display variables */
  InspectionModel model = null;
  InspectionDisplay view = null;
  StringBuffer deck = null;

  /* parse the establishment id from the request */
  establishmentParam = request.getParameter(Operations.ESTABLISHMENT);

  /* extract the scheduled date from the request, convert to date */
  scheduledDateParam = request.getParameter(Operations.SCHEDULED);
  try {
    scheduledDate = new java.util.Date(scheduledDateParam);
  } catch (Exception e) {
    /* failed parsing the date from the request */
    System.err.println("wmlservlet.inspectEntry():failed parsing date");
    redirectToDeck(request, response, InspectionDisplay.INTERNALERROR_DECK);
    return;
  }
  checksParam = request.getParameter(Operations.INSPECTION_CHECKS);
  idcountParam = request.getParameter(Operations.COUNT_OF_IDS);
  status = request.getParameter(Operations.INSPECTION_STATUS);
  comments = request.getParameter(Operations.INSPECTION_COMMENTS);

  model = new InspectionModel();
  success = model.inspectionResults(inspector,
    establishmentParam,
    scheduledDate,
    new java.util.Date(System.currentTimeMillis()),
    parseChecks(checksParam),
    parseInt(idcountParam, 0),
    status,
    comments);
```

```
    /* if there were errors when updating the inspection results
       display the error page */
    if (false == success) {
       redirectToDeck(request, response, InspectionDisplay.INTERNALERROR_DECK);
    } else {
       /* attempt to return to the previously displayed schedule
          by reading the previous operation an parameters from
          the session */
       java.util.Vector opParams = new java.util.Vector();
       java.util.Vector paramValues = new java.util.Vector();
       HttpSession theSession = request.getSession(true);

       if (theSession.isNew()) {
          /* sessions aren't supported in this combination of user
             agents, gateways etc., so display a static deck */
          redirectToDeck(request, response,
            InspectionDisplay.PREVIOUSSCHEDULE_DECK);
       } else {
          /* build a deck which allows the user to return to the previous
             schedule by executing the schedule selection operation they
             chose previously */
          previousOp(theSession, opParams, paramValues);

          view = new InspectionDisplay();
          deck = new StringBuffer();
          view.automatedOperation(deck,
            "Accepted. Select continue to return to previously "
             + "displayed schedule.",
            request.getContextPath() + request.getServletPath(),
            opParams,
            paramValues);
          writeResponse(response, deck.toString());
       }
    }
}

/**
 * Parse an integer from the String or return the default if parsing fails.
 * @param source the string which may 'contain' an int, may be null
 * @param defaultvalue the value to return if an int could not be
 * parsed from source
 * @return the result of parsing an int from source or the defaultvalue
 * if parsing failed
 */
private int parseInt(String source, int defaultvalue) {
  int returnvalue = defaultvalue;

  try {
    returnvalue = Integer.parseInt(source);
  } catch (NumberFormatException nfe) {
    /* ignore; default will be returned */
```

```
    } catch (NullPointerException npe) {
      /* ignore; default will be returned */
    }
    return returnvalue;
}


/**
 * Parse the inspection checks parameter value
 * into an array of Strings.
 * @param checks the inspection checks parameter
 * of the form value;value;value. This may be "" or null.
 * @return an array of Strings containing the inspection checks.
 * May be an empty array.
 */
private String[] parseChecks(String checks) {
    java.util.ArrayList inspectionChecks = new java.util.ArrayList();

    if (null != checks) {
      java.util.StringTokenizer st =
        new java.util.StringTokenizer(checks, ";");
      while(st.hasMoreTokens()) {
        inspectionChecks.add(st.nextToken());
      }
    }

    String[]ret = new String[inspectionChecks.size()];
    for (int i=0; i < inspectionChecks.size(); i++) {
      ret[i] = new String((String)inspectionChecks.get(i));
    }
    return ret;
}


/**
 * Populate the operation parameters and parameter value vectors
 * based on the attributes of the HttpSession. This will be used
 * to direct user agents back to the last "query" operation after
 * completing an inspection.
 * @param theSession the HttpSession object
 * @param opParams the vector holding the operation parameter names
 * @param paramValues the vector holding the operation parameter values
 */
private void previousOp(HttpSession theSession,
    java.util.Vector opParams,
    java.util.Vector paramValues) {
    String operation = (String)theSession.getAttribute(Operations.OPERATION);

    if (null != operation) {
      operation = operation.trim().toLowerCase();
        opParams.add(Operations.OPERATION);
        paramValues.add(operation);
      } else if (operation.equals(Operations.OP_QUERYBYDATE)) {
```

```
            opParams.add(Operations.DATE_START);
            paramValues.add((String)theSession.getAttribute(Operations.DATE_START));
            opParams.add(Operations.DATE_END);
            paramValues.add((String)theSession.getAttribute(Operations.DATE_END));
        } else if (operation.equals(Operations.OP_QUERYBYLOCATION)) {
            opParams.add(Operations.TERRITORY);
            paramValues.add((String)theSession.getAttribute(Operations.TERRITORY));
        } else if (operation.equals(Operations.OP_QUERYNEXT)) {
            /* only need the operation */
        } else {
            /* this isn't an operation that should have been found
               in the session. */
        }
    }
}
```

InspectionModel.java

```
/**
 * Encapsulates the model of Pending Inspections retrieved from the database.
 * Allows for the insertion of inspection results.
 * May provide a partial view on the pending inspections by only instantiating
 * objects for a portion of the database result set.
 */
public class InspectionModel {
  /* holds the list of Inspection instances */
  private java.util.Vector inspectionList = null;

  /* indicates whether there are additional items further on within the
     result set which have not been included in the model, this allows
     the controller to decide to generate views which allow access to
     this data or not */
  private boolean moreEntries = false;

  /** include all retrieved entries in the model when passed as number
      of entries */
   public final static int ALL_ENTRIES = -1;

  /**  start from first retrieved entry when building model */
  public final static int FIRST_ENTRY = 1;

  /**
   * Constructor. The returned model contains no entries.
   * @return an empty model
   */
  public InspectionModel() {
    super();
    inspectionList = new java.util.Vector();
  }
```

```
/**
 * Populate the model with the list of inspections for the
 * specified inspector and scheduled within (and including) the
 * specified date range.
 * @param inspector the name of the inspector to query for
 * @param startDate the start of the date range
 * @param endDate the end of the date range
 * @param startingIndex exclude results prior to this index
 * @param numberOfEntries only include this many entries
 * @return false if unexpected errors were encountered
 */
public boolean querybyDate(String inspector,
  java.util.Date startDate,
  java.util.Date endDate,
  int startingIndex,
  int numberOfEntries) {
  boolean success = true;

  java.sql.Connection connection = null;
  java.sql.ResultSet rs = null;

  connection = DBConnectionManager.getConnection();
  if (null == connection) {
    System.err.println("InspectionModel.querybydate(): "
      + "failed getting connection");
    success = false;
  } else {
    rs = PendingInspection_DB.querybydate(connection,
      inspector,
      startDate,
      endDate);
    if (null == rs) {
      success = false;
    } else {
      populateModel(rs,
        startingIndex,
        numberOfEntries);
    }
    DBConnectionManager.freeConnection(connection);
  }
  return success;
}

/**
 * Populate the model with the list of inspections for the
 * specified inspector and location.
 * @param inspector the name of the inspector to query for
 * @param location the location identifier
 * @param startingIndex exclude results prior to this index
 * @param numberOfEntries only include this many entries
 * @return false if unexpected errors were encountered
```

```
  */
public boolean querybyLocation(String inspector,
  String location,
  int startingIndex,
  int numberOfEntries) {
  boolean success = true;

  java.sql.Connection connection = null;
  java.sql.ResultSet rs = null;

  connection = DBConnectionManager.getConnection();
  if (null == connection) {
    System.err.println("InspectionModel.querybyLocation():failed "
      + "getting connection");
    success = false;
  } else {
    rs = PendingInspection_DB.querybylocation(connection,
      inspector,
      location);
    if (null == rs) {
      success = false;
    } else {
      populateModel(rs, startingIndex, numberOfEntries);
    }
    DBConnectionManager.freeConnection(connection);
  }
  return success;
}

/**
 * Populate the model with the list of inspections for the
 * specified inspector.
 * @param inspector the name of the inspector to query for
 * @param startingIndex exclude results prior to this index
 * @param numberOfEntries only include this many entries
 * @return false if unexpected errors were encountered
 */
public boolean queryNext(String inspector,
  int startingIndex,
  int numberOfEntries) {
  boolean success = true;

  java.sql.Connection connection = null;
  java.sql.ResultSet rs = null;

  connection = DBConnectionManager.getConnection();
  if (null == connection) {
    System.err.println("InspectionModel.queryNext():failed "
      + "getting connection");
    success = false;
  } else {
```

```
    rs = PendingInspection_DB.querynext(connection,
      inspector);
    if (null == rs) {
      success = false;
    } else {
      populateModel(rs, startingIndex, numberOfEntries);
    }
    DBConnectionManager.freeConnection(connection);
  }
  return success;
}


/**
 * Populate the model with the a single inspection entry for the
 * specified inspector, establishment and scheduled date.
 * @param inspector the name of the inspector to query for
 * @param establishment an establishment identifier
 * @param scheduled the date the establishment is scheduled to be
 * inspected
 * @return false if unexpected errors were encountered
 */
public boolean queryDetails(String inspector,
  String establishment,
  java.util.Date scheduled) {
  boolean success = true;

  java.sql.Connection connection = null;
  java.sql.ResultSet rs = null;

  connection = DBConnectionManager.getConnection();
  if (null == connection) {
    System.err.println("InspectionModel.queryDetails():failed"
      + "getting connection");
    success = false;
  } else {
    rs = PendingInspection_DB.queryestablishment(connection,
      establishment,
      scheduled);
    if (null == rs) {
      success = false;
    } else {
      populateModel(rs, FIRST_ENTRY, 1);
    }
    DBConnectionManager.freeConnection(connection);
  }
  return success;
}


/**
 * Populate the model from the supplied result set starting with the
 * startingIndex entry up till and including
```

```
 * startingIndex + numberOfEntries - 1.  It is possible for the model
 * to contain no entries.
 * @param startingIndex start from this point within the result set, assumes
 * 1 = first row
 * @param numberOfEntries the number of entries from the result set to use
 * when builing the model
 */
private synchronized void populateModel(java.sql.ResultSet rs,
    int startingIndex,
    int numberOfEntries) {
  /* temporary variables */
  Inspection inspection = null;

  /* assume the default initial vector size is good enough */
  inspectionList.removeAllElements();

  try {
    /* position the resultset just before the starting index
       n.b. absolute() has been inconsistent, necessitating the
       use of next() */
    for (int i=1; i < startingIndex; i++) {
      rs.next();
    }
  } catch (java.sql.SQLException sqe) {
    /* ignore the exception, it means we've tried to walk off
       one of the ends of the result set */
    System.out.println(sqe.toString());
    sqe.printStackTrace();
  }

  try {
    /* iterate over the result set entries constructing Inspection
       instances and adding them to the model until the specified
       number of Inspection instances is reached or the result set is
       exhausted */
    int ndx = startingIndex - 1;
    final int lastNdx = startingIndex + numberOfEntries - 1;
    while(rs.next() && (ndx < lastNdx)) {
      inspection = new Inspection(new Establishment(rs.getString("id"),
          rs.getString("listitem") /* listitem */,
          rs.getString("name") /* longname */,
          rs.getString("address") /* address */,
          rs.getString("longname") /* city */,
          rs.getString("licensetype") /* license type */,
          rs.getDate("expirydate") /* license expires date */ ),
        rs.getDate("scheduled") /* inspection scheduled date */);
      ndx++;
      inspectionList.add(inspection);
    }
    /* determine if there are more results which could be included */
    if ((false == inspectionList.isEmpty()) && (false == rs.isAfterLast())) {
```

```
      moreEntries = true;
    }
  } catch (java.sql.SQLException sqe) {
    /* this was unexpected */
    sqe.printStackTrace();
  } catch (java.lang.Exception e) {
    /* as was this */
    e.printStackTrace();
  }
}


/**
 * Return true if there are more entries that
 * are not included in this model.
 * @return true if there are more entries in the results that
 * are not included in this model
 */
public boolean moreEntries() {
  return moreEntries;
}


/**
 * Returns an iterator over the list of pending inspections.
 * @return iterator
 */
public java.util.Iterator iterator() {
  return inspectionList.iterator();
}


/**
 * Insert the supplied inspection data for the specified establishment.
 * @param inspector the inspector performing the inspection
 * @param establishment the unique identifer for the establishment
 * @param scheduled the scheduled date of the inspection
 * @param inspected the actual inspection date
 * @param inspectionChecks the inspections performed
 * @param ids the number of ids verified
 * @param status the overall status of the inspection; pass,
 * reinspect, fail
 * @param comments general comments regarding the inspection
 * @return true if the inspection results were accepted and
 * establishment was removed from the list of pending inspections
 * (keyed by establishment, scheduled date)
 */
public boolean inspectionResults(String inspector,
  String establishment,
  java.util.Date scheduled,
  java.util.Date inspected,
  String[] inspectionchecks,
  int ids,
  String status,
```

```
      String comments) {
      boolean success = false;

      java.sql.Connection connection = null;
      connection = DBConnectionManager.getConnection();

      if (null == connection) {
        System.err.println("InspectionModel.inspectionResults():failed getting"
          + " connection");
      } else {
        success = PendingInspection_DB.updateinspectionresults(connection,
          inspector,
          establishment,
          scheduled,
          inspected,
          inspectionchecks,
          ids,
          status,
          comments);
      }
      DBConnectionManager.freeConnection(connection);
      return success;
    }
}
```

Inspection.java

```
/**
 * Encapsulates a pending inspection which includes an establishment,
 * and inspection date.
 */
public class Inspection {
  private Establishment establishment;
  private java.util.Date scheduled;

  /**
   * Constructor for a pending inspection
   * @param establishment the establishment to inspect
   * @param schedule the date the inspection is scheduled
   */
  public Inspection(Establishment establishment,
    java.util.Date scheduled) {
      super();
      this.establishment = establishment;
      this.scheduled = scheduled;
  }

  /**
   * Return the Establishment instance.
   * @return the Establishment to be inspected
```

```
  */
  public Establishment getEstablishment() {
    return establishment;
  }

  /**
   * Return the scheduled inspection date.
   * @return the scheduled date of the inspection
   */
  public java.util.Date getScheduled() {
    return scheduled;
  }
}
```

Establishment.java

```
/**
 * Encapsulates an establishment. Provides methods to instaniate objects,
 * and retrieve attributes.
 * N.B. No database updates of Establishments are supported.
 */
public class Establishment {
  /* see the constructor for an explanation of the attributes */
  private String id;
  private String listitem;
  private String longname;
  private String address;
  private String city;
  private String licensetype;
  private java.util.Date    licenseexpiry;

  /**
   * Constructor.
   * @param id a unique identifier for the establishment
   * @param listitem a string be used when displaying the establishment
   * in lists
   * @param longname the full name of the establishment
   * @param address the street address
   * @param city the name of the city
   * @param licensetype the license type, i.e. the type of establishment.
   * No validation of this value is performed
   * @param licenseexpiry the license expiry date
   */
  public Establishment(String id,
    String listitem,
    String longname,
    String address,
    String city,
    String licensetype,
```

```java
      java.util.Date licenseexpiry) {
         super();
         this.id = id;
         this.listitem = listitem;
         this.longname = longname;
         this.address = address;
         this.city = city;
         this.licensetype = licensetype;
         this.licenseexpiry = licenseexpiry;
   }

   /**
    * Return the id attribute.
    * @return the id attribute
    */
   public String getId() {
      return id;
   }

   /**
    * Return the list item attribute.
    * @return the list item attribute
    */
   public String getListItem() {
      return listitem;
   }

   /**
    * Return the long name attribute.
    * @return the long name attribute
    */
   public String getLongName() {
      return longname;
   }

   /**
    * Return the address attribute.
    * @return the address attribute
    */
   public String getAddress() {
      return address;
   }

   /**
    * Return the city attribute.
    * @return the city attribute
    */
   public String getCity() {
      return city;
   }
```

```
/**
 * Return the license type attribute.
 * @return the license type attribute
 */
public String getLicenseType() {
  return licensetype;
}

/**
 * Return the license expiration date.
 * @return the license expiration date
 */
public java.util.Date getLicenseExpiry() {
  return licenseexpiry;
}
}
```

Operations.java

```
/**
 * The various POST parameters that both must be processed and
 * output in generated WML decks.
 */
public final class Operations {
  /* the operations */
  public final static String OPERATION = "op";
  public final static String OP_INSPECT = "inspect";
  public final static String OP_INSPECTENTRY = "inspectentry";
  public final static String OP_DETAILS = "details";
  public final static String OP_QUERYBYDATE = "bydate";
  public final static String OP_QUERYBYLOCATION = "byloc";
  public final static String OP_QUERYNEXT = "next";

  /* the parameters supplied with the operations */
  public final static String ESTABLISHMENT = "est";
  public final static String INSPECTOR = "insp";
  public final static String SCHEDULED = "sched";
  public final static String DATE_START ="datestart";
  public final static String DATE_END ="dateend";
  public final static String TERRITORY = "territory";
  public final static String START_NDX = "start";
  public final static String NUMBER_OF_ENTRIES = "number";
  public final static String INSPECTION_CHECKS = "checks";
  public final static String COUNT_OF_IDS = "idcount";
  public final static String INSPECTION_STATUS = "status";
  public final static String INSPECTION_COMMENTS = "number";

  /* Declare the constructor private, so no instances can be constructed */
  private Operations() {
  }
}
```

InspectionDisplay.java

```
/**
 * Generate WML output for the various Inspection data models and
 * output needs.  This is generally split into displaying detailed content
 * (e.g. the details of an establishment) and displaying lists of items for
 * action (lists of inspections for user selection).
 *
 * For the sake of simplicity internationalization of the output is
 * not performed.
 */
public class InspectionDisplay {
  /* WML related constant strings
      n.b. use of the 1.3 DTD the simulators being slow to display decks
      (as they attempt to access the DTD while compiling).
      You can use 'local' DTD or reference the WML 1.1 DTD
      which is 'built into' the phones
      WML 1.3 DTD is provided for reference
  */
  final private static String prologue1_3 = "<?xml version=\"1.0\"?>"
              + " <!DOCTYPE wml PUBLIC \"-//WAPFORUM//DTD WML 1.3//EN\""
              + " \"http://www.wapforum.org/DTD/wml13.dtd\">\n";

  final private static String prologue = "<?xml version=\"1.0\"?>"
              + " <!DOCTYPE wml PUBLIC \"-//WAPFORUM//DTD WML 1.1//EN\""
              + " \"http://www.wapforum.org/DTD/wml_1_1.dtd\">\n";

  /* static WML decks for various purposes */
  public final static String UNAUTHORIZED_DECK = "unauthorized.wml";
  public final static String INTERNALERROR_DECK = "error.wml";
  public final static String INVALIDDATES_DECK = "invaliddates.wml";
  public final static String INSPECTIONENTRYP1_DECK = "inspectionentryp1.wml";
  public final static String INSPECTIONENTRYP2_DECK = "inspectionentryp2.wml";
  public final static String PREVIOUSSCHEDULE_DECK = "previousschedule.wml";


  /* initial size of StringBuffers used when constructing cards and decks,
      to offset the overhead of growing them */
  private final static int initialBufferSize = 512;


  /**
   * Format a date into a string such that it can be easily parsed
   * into a date again.
   * @param d the date
   * @return the date in the form "YYYY/MM/DD"
   */
  public static String formatDate(java.util.Date d) {
    int year = d.getYear() + 1900;
    int month = d.getMonth() + 1;
    int day = d.getDate();
```

```
    return new String(Integer.toString(year) + "/"
      + Integer.toString(month) + "/"
      + Integer.toString(day));
}


/**
 * Add a full description of the establishment (suitable for
 * inclusion in a WML card) to the supplied StringBuffer.
 * The caller is responsible for the adding paragraph tags.
 * @param card the StringBuffer to add output to, must not be null
 * @param establishment the establishment instance to display
 */
private void establishmentDetails(StringBuffer deck,
    Establishment establishment) {
  /* simply retrieve each attribute and append to the deck
     with appropriate (minimal) formatting tags */
  deck.append(establishment.getLongName());
  deck.append("<br/>\n");
  deck.append(establishment.getAddress());
  deck.append("<br/>\n");
  deck.append(establishment.getCity());
  deck.append("<br/>\n");
  deck.append(establishment.getLicenseType());
  deck.append("<br/>\n");
  deck.append("Expires: ");
  deck.append(establishment.getLicenseExpiry().toString());
  deck.append("<br/>\n");
}


/**
 * Add a full description of the establishment and the inspection
 * scheduled date to the supplied StringBuffer.
 * The caller is responsible for the adding paragraph tags.
 * @param deck the StringBuffer to add output to, must not be null
 * @param inspection the inspection instance to display
 */
private void inspectionDetails(StringBuffer deck,
    Inspection inspection) {
  establishmentDetails(deck, inspection.getEstablishment());
  deck.append("Sched: " + inspection.getScheduled().toString());
  deck.append("<br/>\n");
}


/**
 * Add an item (link) for the inspection to the supplied StringBuffer.
 * Links are used because current Nokia phones don't work well
 * with select lists.
 * @param deck the StringBuffer to add output to, must not be null
 * @param inspection the inspection instance containing the establishment
 * instance to display
```

```
  * @param encodedURL the URL resulting the display of details for the
  * establishment, must have been encoded in order to be properly
  * processed by servlets
  * @param String inspector the inspector
  */
 private void inspectionListItem(StringBuffer deck,
      Inspection inspection,
      String encodedURL,
      String inspector) {
   Establishment establishment = inspection.getEstablishment();

   deck.append("<anchor title=\"Details\">");
   deck.append(establishment.getListItem());
   deck.append("\n");
   deck.append("<go href=\"" + encodedURL + "\" method=\"post\">\n");
   deck.append("<postfield name=\"" + Operations.OPERATION + "\" value=\""
      + Operations.OP_DETAILS + "\"/>\n");
   deck.append("<postfield name=\"" + Operations.INSPECTOR + "\" value=\""
      + inspector +"\"/>\n");
   deck.append("<postfield name=\"" + Operations.ESTABLISHMENT
      + "\" value=\"" + establishment.getId() + "\"/>\n");
   deck.append("<postfield name=\"" + Operations.SCHEDULED + "\" value=\""
      + formatDate(inspection.getScheduled()) + "\"/>\n");
   deck.append("</go>\n");
   deck.append("</anchor><br/>\n");
 }


 /**
  * Generate a single card deck with a full description of the supplied
  * inspection along with an accept Inspect action (via a
  * post action and a supplied URL).
  * @param deck the output buffer
  * @param inspectionModel the data model. Assumed to contain
  * a single Inspection
  * @param inspector the inspector
  * @param encodedURL the href which will be bound to the accept action,
  * must have been encoded in order to be properly processed by servlets
  */
 public void inspectEstablishment(StringBuffer deck,
      InspectionModel inspectionModel,
      String inspector,
      String encodedURL) {
   java.util.Iterator iterator = inspectionModel.iterator();

   deck.append(prologue);
   deck.append("<wml>\n");
   deck.append("<card>\n");
   deck.append("<do type=\"prev\" label=\"Back\">\n");
   deck.append("<prev/>\n");
   deck.append("</do>\n");
```

```
    if (iterator.hasNext()) {
      Inspection inspection = (Inspection)iterator.next();
      Establishment establishment = inspection.getEstablishment();

      deck.append("<do type=\"accept\" label=\"Inspect\">\n");
      deck.append("<go href=\"" + encodedURL + "\" method=\"post\">\n");
      deck.append("<postfield name=\"" + Operations.OPERATION + "\" value=\""
        + Operations.OP_INSPECT + "\"/>\n");
      deck.append("<postfield name=\"" + Operations.INSPECTOR + "\" value=\""
        + inspector + "\"/>\n");
      deck.append("<postfield name=\"" + Operations.ESTABLISHMENT
        + "\" value=\"" + establishment.getId() + "\"/>\n");
      deck.append("<postfield name=\"" + Operations.SCHEDULED + "\" value=\""
        + formatDate(inspection.getScheduled()) + "\"/>\n");
      deck.append("</go>\n");
      deck.append("</do>\n");
      deck.append("<p>\n");
      inspectionDetails(deck, inspection);
      deck.append("</p>\n");
    } else {
      deck.append("<p>\n");
      deck.append("Could not retrieve details on selected establishment.");
      deck.append("</p>\n");
    }
    deck.append("</card>\n");
    deck.append("</wml>\n");
  }


  /**
   * Generate a WML deck of a single card containing a list of establishments
   * built from the supplied model. If necessary add an item which
   * will result in more results being returned.
   * N.B. the caller is responsible for supplying all parameters
   * necessary in order to retrieve further results for display and
   * this class makes no assumptions about how that is accomplished
   * (whether the query is reexecuted, or cached results are
   * accessed, etc.)
   * @param deck  the buffer to append the WML text to
   * @param inspectionModel the data model; a list of Inspections
   * @param title the list title, ignored if null or the empty string
   * @param inspector the inspector
   * @param encodedURL the URL for the go element, i.e. the servlet to pass
   * the post request to
   * @param sourceOperation the operation which resulted in this
   * select list being built,
   * e.g. querybydate
   * @param opParams the list of sourceOperation parameters
   * @param paramValues the corresponding values
   */
  public void establishmentSelectList(StringBuffer deck,
      InspectionModel inspectionModel,
```

```
    String title,
    String inspector,
    String encodedURL,
    String sourceOperation,
    java.util.Vector opParams,
    java.util.Vector paramValues) {
  java.util.Iterator iterator = null;
  Inspection inspection = null;
  int ndx = 0;

  iterator = inspectionModel.iterator();

  deck.append(prologue);
  deck.append("<wml>\n");
  deck.append("<card>\n");
  deck.append("<do type=\"prev\" label=\"Back\">\n");
  deck.append("<prev/>\n");
  deck.append("</do>\n");
  deck.append("<p>\n");

  /* do we have entries or should we display a no entries message ? */
  if (false == iterator.hasNext()) {
    deck.append("No entries.");
  } else {
    /* use the title attribute if supplied */
    if ((null != title ) && (false == title.equals(""))) {
      deck.append("<strong>" + title + "</strong><br/>");
    }

    /* iterate through each element of the inspection model */
    while (iterator.hasNext()) {
      ndx++;
      inspection = (Inspection)iterator.next();
      inspectionListItem(deck, inspection, encodedURL, inspector);
    }

    /* determine if we need to add a "More..." entry to
       the list.  Do this by adding an operation request
       consisting of the original source operation and parameters */
    if (inspectionModel.moreEntries()) {
      /* generate a link that retrieves the next numberOfEntries entries */
      deck.append("<anchor title=\"More\">More\n");
      deck.append("<go href=\"" + encodedURL + "\" method=\"post\">\n");
      deck.append("<postfield name=\"" + Operations.OPERATION + "\" value=\""
        + sourceOperation + "\"/>\n");

      /* add each parameter and value */
      java.util.Iterator p = opParams.iterator();
      java.util.Iterator pValue = paramValues.iterator();
      while (p.hasNext()) {
```

```
        deck.append("<postfield name=\"" + (String)p.next() + "\" value=\""
            + (String)pValue.next() + "\"/>\n");
        }
        deck.append("</go>\n");
        deck.append("</anchor><br/>\n");
      }
    }
    deck.append("</p>\n");
    deck.append("</card>\n");
    deck.append("</wml>\n");
}


/**
 * Return a WML deck which allows for inspection results to
 * be input for a particular establishment. The establishment
 * and all other parameters are supplied by the caller in the
 * opParams and paramValues vectors.
 * @param deck the buffer in which the WML text is output
 * @param URLBase the path to the directory from which static deck
 * fragments are to be read (while this could be the real path of the
 * context passing the URLBase explictly gives control over how the
 * context is laid out)
 * @param encodedURL the URL for the go element, i.e. the servlet to pass
 * the post request to
 * @param opParams a list of the request parameters for the encodedURL
 * @param paramValues a list of the parameter values for the encodedURL
 */
public void inspectionEntry(StringBuffer deck,
    String URLBase,
    String encodedURL,
    java.util.Vector opParams,
    java.util.Vector paramValues) {
  /* the static inspection results entry screen is in two parts,
    these are "joined" by the opParams and paramValues output as
    postfields */
  String inspectionEntryPart1 = null;
  String inspectionEntryPart2 = null;
  String inspectionEntryPart3 = null;

  deck.append(readStaticDeck(URLBase + INSPECTIONENTRYP1_DECK));
  deck.append("<go href=\"" + encodedURL + "\" method=\"post\">");

  /* add each parameter and value */
  java.util.Iterator p = opParams.iterator();
  java.util.Iterator pValue = paramValues.iterator();
  while (p.hasNext()) {
      deck.append("<postfield name=\"" + (String)p.next() + "\" value=\""
        + (String)pValue.next() + "\"/>\n");
  }
  deck.append(readStaticDeck(URLBase + INSPECTIONENTRYP2_DECK));
```

```
}

/**
 * Create a wml deck with a single card which will execute an
 * operation automatically such as returning the user
 * to a previous query results deck (e.g. query by date).
 * @param message a message to display in the card, e.g. Returning to
 * previous query results
 * @param encodedURL the URL for the go element, i.e. the servlet to pass
 * the post request to
 * @param opParams a list of the request parameters for the encodedURL
 * @param paramValues a list of the parameter values for the encodedURL
 */
public void automatedOperation(StringBuffer deck,
 String message,
 String encodedURL,
 java.util.Vector opParams,
 java.util.Vector paramValues) {
 deck.append(prologue);
 deck.append("<wml>\n");
 deck.append("<card>\n");
 deck.append("<do type=\"prev\" label=\"Back\">\n");
 deck.append("<prev/>\n");
 deck.append("</do>\n");
 deck.append("<do type=\"accept\" label=\"Continue\">\n");
 deck.append("<go href=\"" + encodedURL + "\" method=\"post\">");

 /* add each parameter and value */
 java.util.Iterator p = opParams.iterator();
 java.util.Iterator pValue = paramValues.iterator();
 while (p.hasNext()) {
     deck.append("<postfield name=\"" + (String)p.next() + "\" value=\""
        + (String)pValue.next() + "\"/>\n");
 }
 deck.append("</go>\n");
 deck.append("</do>\n");
 deck.append("<p>" + message + "</p>\n");
 deck.append("</card>\n");
 deck.append("</wml>\n");
}

/**
 * Read the specified static WML deck and return it's contents as
 * a String.
 * @param deckName the name of the static deck
 * @return contains the contents of the specified static deck,
 * may be empty if an exception occurred when reading the deck
 */
private String readStaticDeck(String deckName) {
  StringBuffer deck = new StringBuffer(initialBufferSize);
  java.io.BufferedReader deckReader = null;
```

```
  try {
    deckReader = new java.io.BufferedReader(new java.io.FileReader(deckName));
    /* read the entire contents of the file via standard priming
       read loop */
    String deckLine = deckReader.readLine();
    while (null != deckLine) {
      deck.append(deckLine);
      deckLine = deckReader.readLine();
    }
    deckReader.close();
  } catch (java.io.IOException ioe) {
    System.out.println("Caught IOException when reading static deck "
      + deckName);
    System.out.println(ioe.toString());
  }
  return deck.toString();
  }
}
```

PendingInspection_DB.java

```
/**
 * Encapsulates the pending inspection database operations;  queries and
 * updates and therefore is coupled to the particular database design.
 *
 * Methods within this class may modify the attributes of database connections
 * (e.g. readOnly and autoCommit), thus the calling code should take steps to
 * save and restore these attributes if needed.
 *
 * Unexpected exceptions result in the stack being dumped,  it is
 * assumed this is directed to a log by the calling code (ultimately the
 * servlet).
 *
 * N.B. relies on the driver being able to do batch updates.
 */
public class PendingInspection_DB {
  /* query pending inspections by date for a particular inspector, return
     them sorted by date scheduled */
  private final static String dateQuery
    = "SELECT * FROM pending_inspections p, establishment e, "
    + "territory t WHERE p.inspector = ? "
    + "AND p.scheduled >= ? AND p.scheduled <= ? "
    + "AND p.establishment = e.id AND e.territory = t.shortname "
    + "ORDER BY p.scheduled;";

  /* query pending inspections by location (city abbreviation) for a
     particular inspector, return them sorted by date scheduled */
  private final static String locationQuery
    = "SELECT * FROM pending_inspections p, establishment e, territory t "
    + "WHERE p.inspector = ? AND e.territory = ? AND p.establishment = e.id "
```

```
      + " AND e.territory = t.shortname ORDER BY p.scheduled;";


   /* query pending inspections for a particular inspector, return them
      sorted by date scheduled */
   private final static String nextInspectionQuery
      = "SELECT * FROM pending_inspections p, establishment e, territory t "
      + "WHERE p.inspector = ? AND p.establishment = e.id  "
      + "AND e.territory = t.shortname ORDER BY p.scheduled;";


   /* query for details of a particular establishment */
   private final static String establishmentQuery
      = "SELECT * FROM establishment e, territory t, pending_inspections p "
      + "WHERE e.id = ? AND e.territory = t.shortname AND p.scheduled = ?;";


   /* inserts the primary inspection record, the individual checks are inserted
      via the following insert query */
   private final static String insertInspectionResult
      = "INSERT INTO inspection_results (inspector, establishment, "
      + "inspectiondate, idcount, status, comments) "
      + "VALUES(?, ?, ?, ?, ?, ?);";


   /* inserts the individual inspection checks */
   private final static String insertInspectionChecks
      = "INSERT INTO inspection_checks (establishment, inspectiondate, item) "
      + " VALUES (?, ?, ?);";


   /* deletes the pending inspection record (once inspection results have
      been inserted */
   private final static String deletePendingInspection
      = "DELETE FROM pending_inspections WHERE inspector = ? AND "
      + " establishment = ? AND scheduled = ?;";



   /**
    * Query the pending inspections by date range.
    * Assumes the inspector and dates are valid (i.e. non-null
    * and not the empty string), and that the start date
    * is <= the end date.
    * It is quite possible for an establishment to be
    * scheduled multiple times within the same period.
    * @param connection the database connection
    * @param inspector the inspector, assumed to be non-null and <> ""
    * @param startdate the starting date,  a valid date <= enddate
    * @param enddate the ending date, a valid date <>= startdate
    * @return a ResultSet containing the query results or null if
    * an exception occurred. n.b. we shouldn't experience any
    * exceptions due to malformed queries, therefore exceptions
    * indicate "database" problems.
    */
   public static java.sql.ResultSet querybydate(java.sql.Connection connection,
     String inspector,
```

```
      java.util.Date startdate,
      java.util.Date enddate) {
      java.sql.ResultSet rs = null;

      try {
        /* this method only performs reads */
        connection.setReadOnly(true);

        java.sql.PreparedStatement bydate
          = connection.prepareStatement(dateQuery);
        bydate.setString(1, inspector);
        bydate.setDate(2, new java.sql.Date(startdate.getTime()));
        bydate.setDate(3, new java.sql.Date(enddate.getTime()));

        rs = bydate.executeQuery();
      } catch (java.sql.SQLException sq) {
        sq.printStackTrace();
        rs = null;
      }
      return rs;
  }


  /**
   * Query the pending inspections by location(territory).
   * Assumes the inspector and dates are valid (i.e. non-null
   * and not the empty string), and that the start date
   * is <= the end date.
   * It is quite possible for an establishment to be
   * scheduled multiple times within the same period.
   * @param connection the database connection
   * @param inspector the inspector, assumed to be non-null and <> ""
   * @param territory the short name for the territory (taken from
   * territory table)
   * @return a ResultSet containing the query results or null if an exception
   * occurred. n.b. we shouldn't experience any exceptions due to malformed
   * queries, therefore exceptions indicate "database" problems.
   */
  public static java.sql.ResultSet querybylocation(
    java.sql.Connection connection,
    String inspector,
    String territory) {
    java.sql.ResultSet rs = null;

    try {
      /* this method only performs reads */
      connection.setReadOnly(true);

      java.sql.PreparedStatement bylocation
        = connection.prepareStatement(locationQuery);
      bylocation.setString(1, inspector);
      bylocation.setString(2, territory);
```

```
      rs = bylocation.executeQuery();
    } catch (java.sql.SQLException sq) {
      sq.printStackTrace();
      rs = null;
    }
    return rs;
}


/**
 * Query the pending inspections by inspector.
 * Assumes the inspector (i.e. non-null and not
 * the empty string).
 * It is quite possible for an establishment to be
 * scheduled multiple times within the same period.
 * @param connection the database connection
 * @param inspector the inspector, assumed to be non-null and <> ""
 * @return a ResultSet containing the query results or null if an exception
 * occurred. n.b. we shouldn't experience any exceptions due to malformed
 * queries, therefore exceptions indicate "database" problems.
 */
public static java.sql.ResultSet querynext(java.sql.Connection connection,
  String inspector) {
  java.sql.ResultSet rs = null;

  try {
    /* this method only performs reads */
    connection.setReadOnly(true);

    java.sql.PreparedStatement byorder
      = connection.prepareStatement(nextInspectionQuery);
    byorder.setString(1, inspector);

    rs = byorder.executeQuery();
  } catch (java.sql.SQLException sq) {
    sq.printStackTrace();
    rs = null;
  }
  return rs;
}


/**
 * Insert inspection results for a pending inspection.
 * Removes the pending inspection record if the insert is is successful.
 * Any exceptions cause the transaction to be rolled back.
 * @param connection the database connection
 * @param inspector the inspector, assumed to be non-null and <> ""
 * @param establishment the shortname for the establishment, assumed to be
 * non-null and <> ""
 * @param scheduledate the date the inspection was scheduled
 * @param inspectiondate the date the inspection occurred
```

```
 * @param inspectionChecks the checks that were performed (from
 * the resultcodes table), can be null if no checks were performed
 * @param idcount the number of id checks observed
 * @param status the overall status of the inspection
 * @param comments misc. comments, can be ""
 * @return true if the update was successful, false otherwise
 */
public static boolean updateinspectionresults(
    java.sql.Connection connection,
    String inspector,
    String establishment,
    java.util.Date scheduleddate,
    java.util.Date inspectiondate,
    String inspectionChecks[],
    int idcount,
    String status,
    String comments) {
  boolean rollbackTransaction = false;
  boolean success = false;
  int updateCount = 0;
  int ndx = 0;

  java.sql.Date inspectionSqlDate =
    new java.sql.Date(inspectiondate.getTime());

  try {
    /* this method only performs updates (inserts and deletes),
       and only as an atomic transaction */
    connection.setReadOnly(false);
    connection.setAutoCommit(false);

    /* first insert the primary inspection results, then each inspection
       check, finally delete the pending inspection record */
    java.sql.PreparedStatement insertResult
      = connection.prepareStatement(insertInspectionResult);
    insertResult.setString(1, inspector);
    insertResult.setString(2, establishment);
    insertResult.setDate(3, inspectionSqlDate);
    insertResult.setInt(4, idcount);
    insertResult.setString(5, status);
    insertResult.setString(6, comments);
    updateCount = insertResult.executeUpdate();

    if (1 != updateCount) {
      rollbackTransaction = true;
    }

    /* insert each inspection check record */
    if ((false == rollbackTransaction)
        && (null != inspectionChecks)) {
      java.sql.PreparedStatement insertChecks
```

```
          = connection.prepareStatement(insertInspectionChecks);
        insertChecks.setString(1, establishment);
        insertChecks.setDate(2, inspectionSqlDate);

        for (ndx=0; ndx < inspectionChecks.length; ndx++) {
          insertChecks.setString(3, inspectionChecks[ndx]);
          updateCount = insertChecks.executeUpdate();
          /* if we fail inserting an inspection check record,
             set the rollback flag and break out of this loop */
          if (1 != updateCount) {
            rollbackTransaction = true;
            break;
          }
        }
      }

      /* if successful to this point, delete the pending inspection record */
      if (false == rollbackTransaction) {
        java.sql.PreparedStatement deletePending
          = connection.prepareStatement(deletePendingInspection);
        deletePending.setString(1, inspector);
        deletePending.setString(2, establishment);
        deletePending.setDate(3, new java.sql.Date(scheduleddate.getTime()));

        updateCount = deletePending.executeUpdate();
        if (1 != updateCount) {
          rollbackTransaction = true;
        }
      }

      /* if everything has inserted/deleted successfully, commit
         the transaction, otherwise roll back any updates we've made */
      if (rollbackTransaction) {
        connection.rollback();
      } else {
        connection.commit();
        success = true;
      }
    } catch (java.sql.SQLException sq) {
      sq.printStackTrace();
    }
    return success;
  }

  /**
   * Query for the specified establishment.
   * @param connection the database connection
   * @param establishmentId the unique key for the establishment, assumed to
   * be non-null and <> ""
   * @param scheduledate the date the inspection was scheduled
   * @return a ResultSet containing the query results or null if an exception
```

```
 * occurred. n.b. we shouldn't experience any exceptions due to malformed
 * queries, therefore exceptions indicate "database" problems.
 */
public static java.sql.ResultSet queryestablishment(
  java.sql.Connection connection,
  String establishmentId,
  java.util.Date scheduleddate) {
  java.sql.ResultSet rs = null;

  java.sql.Date scheduledSqlDate = new java.sql.Date(scheduleddate.getTime());
  try {
    /* this method only performs reads */
    connection.setReadOnly(true);

    java.sql.PreparedStatement establishment
       = connection.prepareStatement(establishmentQuery);
    establishment.setString(1, establishmentId);
    establishment.setDate(2, scheduledSqlDate);

    rs = establishment.executeQuery();
  } catch (java.sql.SQLException sq) {
    sq.printStackTrace();
    rs = null;
  }
  return rs;
 }
}
```

DBConnectionManager.java

```
/**

 * A simplistic JDBC connection manager which will manage connections
 * to a single database for a single username.
 */
public class DBConnectionManager {
  /* the instance attributes */
  private static String databaseDriver = null;
  private static String databaseName = null;
  private static String databaseUser = null;
  private static String databasePassword = null;

  /* the list of free connections */
  private static java.util.Vector connections = new java.util.Vector();

  /* the number of connections in use */
  private static int connectionsInUse = 0;

  /* the maximum of connections to hold */
  private static int maxConnections = 10;
```

```java
/* private so no instances can be created outside of
   this class */
private DBConnectionManager() {
}

/**
 * Initialize the DBConnectionManager.
 * @param jdbcclass the JDBC driver class name for the database being
 * connected to
 * @param dbname the name of the database being connected to
 * @param dbusername the name the database user used to make the connection
 * @param dbpassword the password for the user specified in dbusername
 * @param max the maximum number of connections to have opened at any one
 * time, if this is < 0, a default value is used
 * @return true if initialization was successful, i.e. a connection to the
 * database was opened, false otherwise
 */
public static boolean init(String jdbcclass,
  String dbname,
  String dbusername,
  String dbpassword,
  int max) {
  /* assume failure */
  boolean success = false;

  if (0 < max) {
    maxConnections = max;
  }
  databaseDriver = jdbcclass;
  databaseName = dbname;
  databaseUser = dbusername;
  databasePassword = dbpassword;

  try {
    /* load the jdbcdriver and attempt to create the first connection,
       if we fail an exception will be thrown, caught and logged  */
    java.lang.Class.forName(databaseDriver);
    java.sql.Connection connection = java.sql.DriverManager.getConnection(
        databaseName, databaseUser, databasePassword);
    connections.add(connection);
    success = true;
  } catch (ClassNotFoundException cnf) {
    /* serious problem, can't even load the database driver */
    System.err.println("Can't load db driver class:" + jdbcclass);
  } catch (java.sql.SQLException sq) {
    System.err.println("Couldn't establish connection to db: database:"
      + dbname + " user:" + dbusername + " password:" + dbpassword);
  }
  return success;
}
```

```
/**
 * Return a connection. If one cannot be found  from the list of
 * return a newly created one. The caller is responsible for
 * setting the various attributes of the connection such as autoCommit mode.
 * @return a Connection or null if one can not be found or created
 */
public static synchronized java.sql.Connection getConnection() {
  java.sql.Connection theConnection = null;

  /* if there are free connections, retrieve one, verify it is valid
     and return it */
  if (0 < connections.size()) {
    theConnection = (java.sql.Connection)connections.lastElement();
    connections.removeElementAt(connections.size() - 1);

    try {
      /* if the connection is closed, try again */
      if (theConnection.isClosed())  {
        theConnection = getConnection();
      }
    } catch (java.sql.SQLException sqe) {
      /* database error occurred, the connection (if any)
         is useless */
    }
  }

  /* if we still don't have a valid connection attempt to create one */
  theConnection = createConnection();
  if (null != theConnection) {
    connectionsInUse++;
  }
  return theConnection;
}


/**
 * Add the connection back to the list of free connections.
 * @param connection the connection to add back to the list
 */
public static synchronized void freeConnection(
  java.sql.Connection connection) {
  connections.add(connection);
  connectionsInUse--;
}


/**
 * Return a newly created connection. If the connection cannot be created
 * or the maximum number of connections has already by created return null.
 * @return a newly created connection or null
 */
private static java.sql.Connection createConnection() {
  java.sql.Connection connection = null;
```

```
    if (maxConnections > (connections.size() + connectionsInUse)) {
      try {
        connection = java.sql.DriverManager.getConnection(databaseName,
          databaseUser, databasePassword);
      } catch (java.sql.SQLException sq) {
        System.err.println("Couldn't establish connection to db: database:"
          + databaseName
          + " user:"
          + databaseUser
          + " password:"
          + databasePassword);
      }
    }
    return connection;
}

/**
 * Release all connections if none are in use.
 */
public synchronized static void release() {
  if (0 >= connectionsInUse) {
    java.sql.Connection connection = null;
    java.util.Iterator iterator = connections.iterator();

    while (iterator.hasNext()) {
      connection = (java.sql.Connection)iterator.next();
      try {
        connection.close();
      } catch (java.sql.SQLException sqe) {
        /* can't do much about this now */
        System.err.println("Caught exception when closing connection: "
          + sqe.toString());
      }
    }
    connections.removeAllElements();

    java.util.Enumeration enum = java.sql.DriverManager.getDrivers();
    while (enum.hasMoreElements()) {
      try {
        java.sql.DriverManager.deregisterDriver(
          (java.sql.Driver)enum.nextElement());
      } catch (java.sql.SQLException sqe) {
        /* can't do much about this either */
        System.err.println("Caught exception when deregistering db driver: "
          + sqe.toString());
      }
    }
  }
}
}
```

SQL Scripts

The following SQL Scripts are used in the alcohol inspection application. These are declared in the order in which they should be executed:

- createinspectors.sql, which creates the inspectors table.

- createterritory.sql, which creates the territory table.

- createresultcodes.sql, which creates the resultcodes table.

- createestablishment.sql, which creates the establishment table.

- createinspectionresults.sql, which creates the inspection_status and inspection_results tables.

- createinspectionchecks.sql, which creates the inspection_ checks table.

- creatependinginspections.sql, which creates the pending _ inspections table.

- populateinspectors.sql, which populates the inspectors table.

- populateterritory.sql, which populates the territory table.

- populateresultcodes.sql, which populates the resultcodes table.

- populateestablishment.sql, which populates the establishment.

- populateinspectionstatus.sql, which populates the inspection_ status table.

- populatependinginspections.sql, which populates the pending_ inspections table.

createinspectors.sql

```
CREATE TABLE inspectors (inspector varchar(20) PRIMARY KEY);
```

createterritory.sql

```
CREATE TABLE territory (
shortname varchar(8) NOT NULL PRIMARY KEY CHECK (shortname <> ''),
longname varchar(20) NOT NULL CHECK (longname <> ''));
```

createresultcodes.sql

```
CREATE TABLE resultcodes (
id char(2) NOT NULL PRIMARY KEY,
description varchar(20) NOT NULL);
```

createestablishment.sql

```
CREATE TABLE establishment (
id varchar(20) NOT NULL PRIMARY KEY CHECK (id <> ''),
listitem varchar(20) NOT NULL CHECK (listitem <> ''),
name varchar(60) NOT NULL,
address varchar(200) NOT NULL,
licensetype varchar(10) NOT NULL,
expirydate DATE NOT NULL,
territory varchar(8) NOT NULL REFERENCES territory);
```

createinspectionresults.sql

```
CREATE TABLE inspection_status (
status varchar(12) NOT NULL PRIMARY KEY CHECK (status <> '')
);

CREATE TABLE inspection_results (
establishment varchar(20) REFERENCES establishment(id),
inspectiondate DATE NOT NULL,
inspector varchar(20) REFERENCES inspectors(inspector),
idcount int2,
status varchar(12) REFERENCES inspection_status(status),
comments varchar(50),
PRIMARY KEY(establishment, inspectiondate)
);
```

createinspectionchecks.sql

```
CREATE TABLE inspection_checks (
establishment varchar(20) REFERENCES inspection_results(establishment),
inspectiondate DATE REFERENCES inspection_results(inspectiondate),
item char(2) REFERENCES resultcodes(id),
PRIMARY KEY (establishment, inspectiondate, item));
```

creatependinginspections.sql

```
CREATE TABLE pending_inspections (
inspector varchar(20) REFERENCES inspectors (inspector),
scheduled date NOT NULL,
establishment varchar(20) REFERENCES establishment (id),
PRIMARY KEY (scheduled, establishment));
```

populateinspectors.sql

```
INSERT INTO inspectors VALUES('poirot');
INSERT INTO inspectors VALUES('marple');
```

populateterritory.sql

```
BEGIN;
INSERT INTO territory VALUES ('hal', 'Halifax');
INSERT INTO territory VALUES ('dart', 'Dartmouth');
INSERT INTO territory VALUES ('bedford', 'Bedford');
INSERT INTO territory VALUES ('truro', 'Truro');
INSERT INTO territory VALUES ('other', 'Other');
COMMIT;
```

populateresultcodes.sql

```
BEGIN;
INSERT INTO resultcodes VALUES ('10', 'Tax Stamps');
INSERT INTO resultcodes VALUES ('02', 'Stock');
INSERT INTO resultcodes VALUES ('05', 'Measures');
INSERT INTO resultcodes VALUES ('06', 'Underage');
COMMIT;
```

populateestablishment.sql

```
BEGIN;
DELETE FROM inspection_checks;
DELETE FROM inspection_results;
DELETE FROM pending_inspections;
DELETE FROM establishment;
INSERT INTO establishment
  VALUES('attic', 'Attic', 'The Attic',
         '1741 Grafton St.', 'Cabaret', '31/12/01', 'hal');
INSERT INTO establishment
  VALUES('bearlys', 'Bearly''s', 'Bearly''s House of Blues and Ribs',
         '1269 Graton St.', 'Eat Est', '31/01/03', 'hal');
INSERT INTO establishment
  VALUES('boomers', 'Boomers', 'Boomers Lounge', '1725 Grafton St.',
         'Lounge', '28/02/01', 'hal');
INSERT INTO establishment
  VALUES('cheers', 'Cheer''s', 'Cheer''s Lounge', '1743 Grafton St.',
         'Lounge', '30/09/01', 'hal');
INSERT INTO establishment
  VALUES('copper', 'Copper Penny', 'The Copper Penny',
         '278 Lacewood Dr.', 'Cabaret', '31/12/01', 'hal');
```

```
INSERT INTO establishment
  VALUES('ess', 'Economy Shoe Shop', 'The Economy Shoe Shop',
        '1663 Argyle St.', 'Cabaret', '31/12/01', 'hal');
INSERT INTO establishment
  VALUES('gatsby', 'Gatsby''s', 'Gatsby''s Bar and Eatery Ltd.',
        '5675 Spring Garden Rd.', 'Eat Est', '30/09/00', 'hal');
INSERT INTO establishment
  VALUES('mafia', 'Ma''Fias', 'Ma''Fias Ristorante and Bar',
        '5472 Spring Garden Rd.', 'Eat Est', '31/12/01', 'hal');
INSERT INTO establishment
  VALUES('marquee', 'Marquee', 'The Marquee Club', '2041 Gottingen St.',
        'Cabaret', '31/12/01', 'hal');
INSERT INTO establishment
  VALUES('oasis', 'Oasis', 'Oasis Bar and Grill',
        '5675 Spring Garden Rd.', 'Eat Est', '29/02/00', 'hal');
INSERT INTO establishment
  VALUES('tickle', 'Tickle Trunk', 'The Tickle Trunk',
        '5680 Spring Garden Rd.', 'SOL', '31/12/00', 'hal');
INSERT INTO establishment
  VALUES('volive', 'Velvet Olive', 'Velvet Olive Cocktail Lounge',
        '1770 Market St.', 'Lounge', '31/12/01', 'hal');
COMMIT;
```

populateinspectionstatus.sql

```
INSERT INTO inspection_status VALUES('pass');
INSERT INTO inspection_status VALUES('reinspect');
INSERT INTO inspection_status VALUES('fail');
```

populatependinginspections.sql

```
BEGIN TRANSACTION;
DELETE FROM inspection_checks;
DELETE FROM inspection_results;
DELETE FROM pending_inspections;
INSERT INTO pending_inspections (inspector, scheduled, establishment)
  VALUES ('poirot','13/07/00','ess');
INSERT INTO pending_inspections (inspector, scheduled, establishment)
  VALUES ('marple','25/08/00','attic');
INSERT INTO pending_inspections (inspector, scheduled, establishment)
  VALUES ('poirot','09/01/00','cheers');
INSERT INTO pending_inspections (inspector, scheduled, establishment)
  VALUES ('poirot','12/08/00','marquee');
INSERT INTO pending_inspections (inspector, scheduled, establishment)
  VALUES ('poirot','01/09/00','volive');
INSERT INTO pending_inspections (inspector, scheduled, establishment)
  VALUES ('poirot','13/08/00','gatsby');
```

```
INSERT INTO pending_inspections (inspector, scheduled, establishment)
  VALUES ('marple','09/09/01','attic');
INSERT INTO pending_inspections (inspector, scheduled, establishment)
  VALUES ('poirot','12/01/01','mafia');
INSERT INTO pending_inspections (inspector, scheduled, establishment)
  VALUES ('poirot','12/03/01','tickle');
INSERT INTO pending_inspections (inspector, scheduled, establishment)
  VALUES ('poirot','07/04/01','copper');
INSERT INTO pending_inspections (inspector, scheduled, establishment)
  VALUES ('poirot','12/01/01','bearlys');
INSERT INTO pending_inspections (inspector, scheduled, establishment)
  VALUES ('marple','07/07/01','boomers');
COMMIT;
```

Glossary

2.5G Updated second-generation cellular networks (e.g., GPRS).

3G Third-generation cellular networks provide packet-switched digital data and support rapid transmission of multimedia content (e.g., WCDMA).

Attribute Describes a particular characteristic of a markup element.

Bluetooth A low-power radio frequency technology that allows secure local communications between a variety of Bluetooth-enabled units.

CC/PP Composite Capability/Preference Profiles.

CDMA Code Division Multiple Access is a digital cellular network standard that uses unique code sequences to multiplex user access.

CDPD Cellular Digital Packet Data.

CHTML Compact HTML is a lightweight version of HTML used by I-Mode.

Context An execution space containing variables, state, and content.

Device A network entity (typically either a client or a server) capable of sending and/or receiving information.

DTD Document Type Definition (when applied to XML) is a document that defines the valid syntax and vocabulary for a class of XML documents.

ECMAScript European Computer Manufacturer Association Script is a standard Web client scripting language that extends HTML (often referred to as JavaScript).

EJB Enterprise Java Bean is a component technology from Sun found within the Java 2 Enterprise Edition specifications.

Element An object in a markup language (such as WML) that is delimited by tags and can contain attributes, text, or other elements.

Enterprise When used as a noun, refers to a corporation or organization. When used to refer to a computer system, typically refers to an extensible system capable of handling heavy use.

Extranet An extension of an intranet to selected clients or partners.

GPRS General Packet Radio Service is an IP digital mobile service that runs on top of GSM.

GSM Global System for Mobile communications is a circuit-switched mobile network standard.

Hash A sequence of bytes that is computed from a (usually longer) text block in such a way that it is extremely unlikely an identical hash could be calculated from a different block of text.

HDML Handheld Device Markup Language is a lightweight mobile device markup language based on HTML developed by Unwired Planet (now Phone.com).

HTTP Hypertext Transfer Protocol.

Hybrid A mobile device that combines the organizational capabilities of a palmtop with the communication facilities of a cellular phone.

IDE Integrated Development Environment is an all-in-one editing, compiling, and debugging environment for a particular language or technology (e.g., C++ or EJBs).

IMAP4 Interactive Mail Access Protocol is a popular Internet mail retrieval mechanism.

I-Mode A Mobile Internet technology similar to WAP but proprietary to the Japanese ISP, NTT DoCoMo.

Intranet A closed IP network accessible by an organization's employees.

IP Internet Protocol: IETF standard for transmission of packet data over the Internet.

ISP Internet Service Provider.

J2EE Java 2 Enterprise Edition is a suite of enterprise specifications built around the Java 2 platform.

KVM Kilobyte Virtual Machine is a lightweight Java virtual machine designed for embedded devices.

LDAP   Lightweight Directory Access Protocol is a protocol for accessing and updating directory information such as user profiles and resource data.

Location aware   A service or technology that makes use of a client's location.

M-Commerce   See *mobile commerce.*

Microbrowser   A lightweight wireless Web browser found in mobile devices.

Mobile commerce   Electronic commerce carried out by a mobile client.

Mobile internet   The union of mobile (e.g., cellular) networks and the Internet.

Palmtop   A general term referring to a class of small handheld computers such as the Microsoft Pocket PC-based platforms, Symbian EPOC hand-helds, and the Palm-connected organizers.

PAP   Push Access Protocol is used for conveying content to be pushed to a client between a push initiator (application) and a push proxy/gateway.

PDA   Personal Digital Assistant is a palmtop computer with bundled personal organization applications.

PDC   Personal Digital Cellular is a Japanese cellular network standard.

Personalization   Customizing an application or service to match a user's requirements.

PIM   Personal Information Management is a class of applications that helps a user organize and use personal information such as addresses and calendars.

POP3   Post Office Protocol is the most popular Internet mail retrieval protocol.

Portal   A Web portal is a gateway onto the World Wide Web, a mobile portal is a gateway for mobile users, and a voice portal is a gateway for telephone voice access.

PPP   Point to Point Protocol is used to connect clients such as mobile devices or desktop PCs to an IP network.

PQA   Palm Query Application is a downloaded skeleton application that controls loading of dynamic Web content in a Palm Web Clipping application.

Private key   A secret electronic key that can be used to encode messages and decode encrypted messages in a public key crypto-system. It is paired with a public key.

Public key   A publicly available electronic key that can be used to encode messages and decode encrypted messages in a public key crypto-system. It is paired with a private key.

Push   A technology that allows a server to initiate an application with a client.

Push initiator   The entity that originates push content.

Push OTA   A protocol used for conveying content between a push proxy/gateway and a mobile device.

Push proxy gateway   A gateway that provides push proxy services, uniting a push initiator with mobile devices.

RAS   Remote Access Server enables a point-to-point connection from a client to an IP network.

Schema   When applied to XML, refers to a way of identifying the vocabulary and syntax of a particular class of XML documents.

SDK   Software Development Kit provides a set of development tools for a particular technology.

Servlet   A server-side Java program designed to run within a Web server.

SGML   Standard Generalized Markup Language is the parent language of HTML and XML.

SIM   Subscriber Identity Module is a form of smart card that contains a mobile subscriber's subscription details and personal information such as addresses and digital certificates.

SMS   Short Message Service is a point-to-point messaging service.

SMSC   Short Message Service Center provides store and forward mechanism for delivery of short messages in SMS.

SMTP   Simple Mail Transfer Protocol is the most popular standard for Internet message interchange.

SQL   Structured Query Language is an industry standard language for performing operations on relational databases.

SSL   Secure Socket Layer is a standard security protocol from Netscape that is the basis of TLS.

T9   A word recognition technology that attempts to identify a word keyed into a handset keypad based on probabilities.

TCP Transport Control Protocol is a reliable Internet protocol.

TDMA Time Division Multiple Access is a digital cellular network standard that uses time slots to multiplex user access.

Telemetry Measurement at a distance (i.e., remote measurement, typically using radio transmission to convey measurements).

TLS Transport Layer Security is an Internet for protocol layer security based on Netscape's SSL.

UDP User Datagram Protocol is an unreliable Internet transport protocol.

UML Unified Modeling Language is an industry standard object-oriented modeling language.

UP Unwired Planet.

URI Uniform Resource Identifier identifies exactly one resource.

URL Uniform Resource Locator locates a resource on the Internet that can be retrieved using the appropriate protocol. A URL is a type of URI.

User agent A client application that typically interacts with a server via a network connection and processes markup and/or script.

WAE Wireless Application Environment is a complete architecture for the execution of Web applications in mobile devices.

WAP Wireless Application Protocol.

WAP Forum The industry body responsible for WAP.

WAP gateway A translating proxy that bridges the WAP and Internet worlds.

WBXML WAP Binary XML describes a standard mechanism for encoding documents written in an XML-compliant language.

WDP Wireless Datagram Protocol is the lowest layer in the WAP protocol stack and is analogous to the Internet's UDP .

Web server An HTTP-enabled Internet server.

WML Wireless Markup Language is an XML markup language for wireless devices.

WMLS or WMLScript Wireless Markup Language Script is an ECMAScript-based language that extends WML to provide client-side scripting.

WSP Wireless Session Protocol is the highest layer in the WAP protocol stack and is analogous to the Internet's HTTP.

WTA Wireless Telephony Application.

WTLS Wireless Transport Layer Security is a WAP protocol that implements a lightweight version of TLS suitable for wireless networks and devices.

XML Extensible Markup Language is a World Wide Web Consortium (W3C) recommended standard for Internet markup languages.

Index

Boldface type is used to indicate the Courier typeface used in the text for source code elements, attributes, and terms.